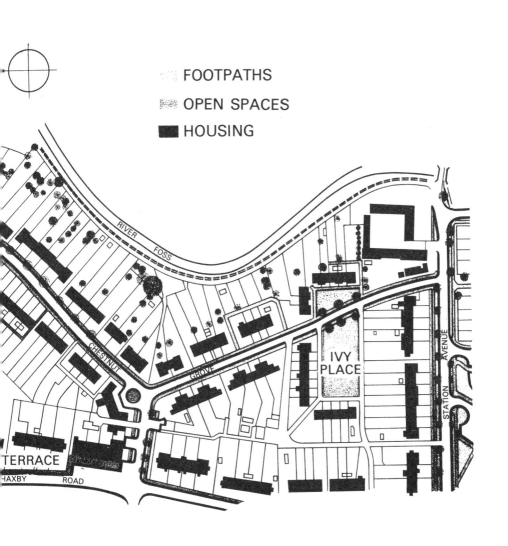

FOOTPATHS

OPEN SPACES

HOUSING

Support of schools, p. xv.

Private Philanthropy and Public Welfare

Private Philanthropy and Public Welfare

The Joseph Rowntree Memorial Trust
1954–1979

LEWIS E. WADDILOVE

London
GEORGE ALLEN & UNWIN
Boston   Sydney

George Allen & Unwin (Publishers) Ltd,
40 Museum Street, London WC1A 1LU, UK

George Allen & Unwin (Publishers) Ltd,
Park Lane, Hemel Hempstead, Herts HP2 4TE, UK

Allen & Unwin Inc.,
9 Winchester Terrace, Winchester, Mass. 01890, USA

George Allen & Unwin Australia Pty Ltd,
8 Napier Street, North Sydney, NSW 2060, Australia

First published in 1983

British Library Cataloguing in Publication Data

Waddilove, Lewis E.
 Private philanthropy and public welfare: the Joseph
Rowntree Memorial Trust, 1954–1979.
1. Joseph Rowntree Memorial Trust—History
I. Title
361.7′632′0941   HV244
ISBN 0-04-902006-4

Library of Congress Cataloging in Publication Data

Waddilove, Lewis E.
 Private philanthropy and public welfare.
Includes index.
1. Joseph Rowntree Memorial Trust—History.
I. Title.
HV245.W25   1983   361.7′632′0941   83–9981
ISBN 0-04-902006-4

Set in 10 on 11 point Bembo by
D. P. Media Limited, Hitchin, Hertfordshire
and printed in Great Britain
by Mackays of Chatham

Contents

List of Plates and Figures

Foreword

by Lord Seebonm

There are four criteria for a successful charitable trust.

First, its objectives must be clearly set down by its Founder and must be of lasting relevance.

Secondly, the Trustees must be both individually and collectively committed to these objectives and personally involved in their implementation. This is important for the Trustees originally appointed, and perhaps even more so for their successors.

Thirdly, it must have an efficient, imaginative and enthusiastic Director.

Finally, it must have adequate resources.

The Joseph Rowntree Memorial Trust has been fortunate in meeting all four of these requirements. The foresight and imagination with which Joseph Rowntree expressed his intentions make the Memorandum he wrote for his Trustees one of the most remarkable documents of its kind – and demonstrates the importance of expressing such concepts in language free from the constraints of legal jargon. The 'concerns' that Joseph Rowntree acquired during his lifetime have been followed by the Trust for the forty-six years since his death. This has involved the Trust in research and action in a wide variety of fields, sometimes successfully and sometimes not. The ability and duty to experiment is an important feature of trusts of this nature and it is almost as important to discover which roads lead to barren tracts of land as it is to find out which lead to exciting vistas of progress and change. Lewis Waddilove has given figures showing the wide spread of activities. The independent report by Austin Heady on the degree of success achieved is reassuring.

While this policy of diversification ensured that there was unlikely to be any serious disaster, the Trust nevertheless took two substantial risks in recent years. First, it accepted the administration of the Family Fund; and secondly it initiated and supported the Centre for Studies in Social Policy (CSSP). The former, apart from teething troubles, has been a resounding success. The future of the latter commitment was, for a period, uncertain, but the merger with Political and Economic Planning (PEP) produced the Policy Studies Institute (PSI), which is turning out to be a robust and influential body. But this is to anticipate what is so well recorded in the following pages and I will end by extending the gratitude of the Trust to Lewis Waddilove, not only for producing a valuable piece of social history, but also for fulfilling our third criterion with great distinction for thirty-three years.

Acknowledgements

This is an account of changes and growth in the constitution and work of the Joseph Rowntree Memorial Trust in all of which the author was directly involved. The members of the Editorial Committee appointed by the Trustees accepted therefore an important and onerous task. There were four members: Lord Seebohm, Sir Charles Carter and Sir Donald Barron, each of whom was, and still is, a Trustee, and Robin Guthrie my successor as Director of the Trust. They read and commented on successive drafts, met to give corporate advice, and thus contributed to the structure of the book and to such objectivity as may have been achieved. My debt to them is great.

Robin Guthrie and his colleagues in the various departments at the Trust office at Beverley House responded generously to every request for the examination of records, and for advice on later developments in some projects which gave a necessary perspective to an account of still evolving work.

In the chapter on the Trust's finance and investment I have made separate reference to the help given by Ralph S. Connelly, the Trust's Finance Officer until 1981.

Modern printing technology has in no way diminished an author's dependence on the patience and accuracy of those who transcribe and copy the dictated and corrected drafts, and finally deliver the completed typescript to the publisher. The greater part of this task has been competently carried to completion by Mrs Linda Lofthouse; I gratefully acknowledge too the help given by Mrs Susan Brown in the early stages.

Lewis E. Waddilove

The Founder's Memorandum

A first draft of a Memorandum on the proposed Trust, marked 'Exceedingly Private', took the form of a paper to Joseph Rowntree's advisers. Some of his intentions were expressed as questions; examples of possible initiatives were given; relations with the Rowntree Company were left uncertain since the form and amount of the property to be appropriated to the Trust had not been settled. But, in essentials, that first paper differed little from the Memorandum written from the Founder's home in St Mary's, York, and dated 29 December 1904, which has remained the principal source of advice and inspiration to the Trustees of the three Trusts which he had decided to establish. This is what Joseph Rowntree wrote:

THE JOSEPH ROWNTREE CHARITABLE TRUST.
THE JOSEPH ROWNTREE SOCIAL SERVICE TRUST, LIMITED.
THE JOSEPH ROWNTREE VILLAGE TRUST.

I desire in the following Memorandum to indicate in general terms the considerations which have induced me to found the above Trusts. I wish it, however, to be distinctly understood that it is of no legal or binding force in any way or direction, and is not intended to restrict or extend the full discretion given to the Trustees and Directors of the legal instruments creating the Trusts, or to affect the interpretation of those instruments. I have thought, however, it might assist those who will be associated with me, and who will succeed me in the direction of these Trusts, to know the thoughts which have influenced me in their creation, and which will guide me in their administration so long as I am spared to take part in it.

It is frequently and truly said that money is generally best spent by persons during their lifetime. I have in the past, according to my power, endeavoured to act in remembrance of this. Considerably larger means have, however, come to me late in life, and the practical question was presented to me: how can this property be applied in the future so as to secure equal results to those which might have been obtained had I had the administration of it over a lengthened period? It is a matter of great satisfaction to me that these Trusts have been established with the cordial assent of my wife and children.

It will be observed that the Joseph Rowntree Charitable Trust and the Joseph Rowntree Social Service Trust, Limited, will come to an end not later than thirty-five years from the date of their formation, while the Joseph Rowntree Village Trust is permanent. The two former Trusts are, in all human probability, likely to be mainly administered by the original Trustees, who are closely in sympathy with my general thoughts and aims, and will, I believe, give to the administration of these Trusts the same thought and direction which I should have given to them myself. The Charitable Trust is established for purposes which are 'charitable' in the legal sense of the word: the Social Service Trust for purposes which, though to my mind at least of equal importance to the well-being of the community, are, as I am advised, mostly outside the limits within which the law at present confines the operations of charitable foundations, and would, if included in the former Trust, impair its legal validity. I hope that in the future those limits may be considerably widened, and that it may be permissible to include among charitable objects those which can only be attained by alterations in the law of the land. If this should be so, the Directors of the Social Service Trust may find themselves able to transfer some of their property to the Charitable Trust. However this may be, my motives in creating the two Trusts are the same. I regard the distinction between them as merely a legal one. In connection with both of these Trusts, there is one general principle that I hope will be kept in mind, namely: that the Trustees and Directors should not, except in very special cases, make grants to existing associations, but should themselves direct and guide the appropriation of the funds. Any appropriation which tended to interfere with donations or subscriptions which others ought to give should in my view be carefully avoided.

The original Trustees and Directors will be familiar with the thought which I now wish to express. I feel that much of current philanthropic effort is directed to remedying the more superficial manifestations of weakness or evil, while little thought or effort is directed to search out their underlying causes. Obvious distress or evil generally evokes so much feeling that the necessary agencies for alleviating it are pretty adequately supported. For example, it is much easier to obtain funds for the famine-stricken people in India than to originate and carry through a searching enquiry into the causes of the recurrence of these famines.* The Soup Kitchen in York never has difficulty in obtaining adequate financial aid, but an enquiry into the extent and causes of poverty would enlist little support. Every Social writer knows the supreme importance of questions connected with the holding and taxation of land, but for one person who attempts to master this question there are probably thousands who devote their time and strength to relieving poverty and its accompanying evils. In my view therefore it is highly undesirable that money should be given by the Trusts to Hospitals, Almshouses, or similar Institutions. The objects of these two Trusts fall under three heads, Religious, Political and Social. I append a few notes as indications of my thoughts in connection with each.

Religious

If the Charitable Trust is to achieve practical results, its income must not be too widely scattered, and doubtless objects connected with the Society of Friends will have first place in the minds of my co-trustees as they have

---

* Whilst taking this illustration from India, I hope that by far the larger portion of this fund will be spent in this country, or in the solution of problems directly connected with it.

in my own. For the reasons stated above, I should not, unless under very special circumstances, think it wise that money should be given towards the erection of Meeting Houses, Adult Schools or Social Clubs, whether in connection with Adult Schools or otherwise. The need for suitable and well-equipped buildings is so obvious, that I think it is almost certain to be supplied. On the other hand, the need for Religious teaching to the Members of the Society of Friends of all ages, especially with a view to the fostering of a powerful Ministry, is a need which is not clearly seen, but upon the right meeting of which the prosperity of the Society will largely depend. I should, therefore, entirely approve of support to the Wood-brooke Settlement, or to kindred efforts. I should, however regret if it were necessary to make grants on account of buildings, but should desire rather to supplement the funds appropriated for the support of a lecturing staff in order that no lack of money should stand in the way of securing the best possible teaching. It would also be in accordance with my views that grants should be made for Scholarships to the Woodbroke or similar Settlement; although an obvious need of this kind is I believe, less likely to require support than the object previously mentioned. I should also approve of expenditure necessary for strengthening the periodical or other literature of the Society. The Historical enquiry in relation to the Society of Friends which my son John Wilhelm is undertaking, with a view to elucidate right principles of Society action, is an object which would rightly come within the scope of the Trust.

In connection with Religious, Political and Social work, it is to be remembered that there may be no better way of advancing the objects one has at heart than to strengthen the hands of those who are effectively doing the work that needs to be done. Not unfrequently one hears of persons doing excellent work whose service is cramped, or who are in danger of breaking down through anxiety about the means of living. It would be quite in accordance with my wish that cases of this kind should be assisted.

Then with regard to our Public Schools, and especially Bootham and the Mount – I doubt whether teachers of the present high calibre will be secured in the future without a considerable advance in salary. Neither the need for these higher salaries nor the supreme importance to the Society as a whole, and to the individual children, of wise Quaker training, appears to be sufficiently seen by Friends, and I do not think that the working of supply and demand will secure an adequate income for the teachers. If therefore, the Trustees saw their way so to give money as to secure highly qualified men and women of moral earnestness as Teachers, without relieving the School Committee of ordinary expenditure, I should quite approve of such education grants being made. And, further, if the prosperity of the Schools demanded a certain number of Scholarships for Members of the Society, I should quite approve of these.

Whilst in favour of an expenditure upon the Schools of the kind indicated above, I should not, for reasons already given, think it wise to expend money upon building alterations.

Political

Perhaps the greatest danger to our national life arises from the power of selfish and unscrupulous wealth which influences public opinion largely through the Press (e.g. the Opium and Drink traffic, and the South African War). If the funds permitted, and the Directors of the Social Service Trust were equal to the task, it would be quite in accordance with my wish that they should control, by purchase or otherwise, a newspaper or newspapers, conducting them not with a primary view to profit but with the object of influencing public thought in right channels.

If, commencing with an experiment near home, the Trustees found they were able, without undue strain, to undertake this work, they might possibly extend it cautiously elsewhere. This should not, however, be done on such a scale as seriously to impoverish either the Religious or Social effort.

I hope those who come after me will do their best to maintain purity of Elections in York. For this end it may occasionally be necessary to prosecute offenders or to lodge petitions against the return of those who have been elected through corrupt means. I should wish the funds of the Social Service Trust to be available for such purposes.

Ordinary subscriptions to political organisations will, I believe, be inexpedient, but occasional crises might arise when the funds of the Trust might rightly be drawn upon. In illustration: It is said that the campaign led by Joseph Arch for the elevation of the Agricultural labourers was on the point of breaking down for want of funds, but was saved by a timely gift from Samuel Morley.

Social

The thought to which expression has already been given of the need to search out the under-lying causes of weakness or evil applies with special force to social questions. If the enormous volume of the philanthropy of the present day were wisely directed it would, I believe, in the course of a few years, change the face of England. Perhaps there is no need more urgent in the present day than for the wise direction of social and philanthropic effort. In a semi-private Memorandum of this kind I may allude to the Temperance work in which I have been engaged as illustrative of what I mean. It was necessary to ascertain once for all the actual facts as to intemperance, its causes – legislative and social – and when these were understood, the remedies that must be applied. I hope this particular work will be carried on as long as the occasion for it lasts.

I have already alluded to the land question. Such aspects of it as the nationalisation of land, or the taxation of land values or the appropriation of the unearned increment – all need a treatment far more thorough than they have yet received.

If one or other of the Directors and Trustees were able to collaborate with competent investigators and workers upon these questions, it would be quite suitable for large sums to be appropriated in this direction.

The same remarks apply to the questions of our Foreign policy and Imperialism.

It will be observed that the amount of money given to the Social Service Trust is larger than the value of the property with which the Charitable Trust has been endowed. This larger appropriation to the Social Service Trust is made in view of the heavy demands which the establishment or support of the newspapers may involve, and also in view of the fact that while the Social Service Trust will have power to make grants towards objects which fall under the Charitable Trust, it will not be within the power of the Charitable Trust to make grants to the objects which fall under the Social Service Trust.

As already stated, the Charitable Trust and the Social Service Trust will come to an end not later than thirty-five years from the date of their formation. Great liberty is, however, given to the Trustees with regard to the manner in which the Trusts shall be wound up. Three separate courses are open to them:

(1) The Trustees have the power, during the continuance of the Trusts, to make use not only of the interest but of the principal, and they might so arrange that the principal was exhausted within the term of 35 years.

(2) If the Trustees were acquainted with men in whose judgment and integrity they had confidence, who would carry out the Trusts, either one or both of them, in accordance with the general aims of the Founder, it would be open to the Trustees, before the end of the thirty-five years, to create new Trusts and to hand over the property to the new Trustees with such conditions regarding the winding up of the new Trusts as they might deem fitting.

(3) The property of the two Trusts can be transferred to the Joseph Rowntree Village Trust.

If the second course is adopted, I hope that in the election of Trustees for the new Trusts the question of their relationship to me or to the then Trustees and Directors will be regarded as altogether subordinate to the paramount consideration of their fitness for the offices they will have to fill.

The question of the creation of a new Trust in connection with the Social Service Trust is one that ought to be maturely considered before the thirty-five years come to an end. This Trust may very possibly acquire Shares giving to it a predominating influence with a portion of the newspaper press, and it will be of great moment that a right influence should be secured for the future of these papers. I hope that they may sound a clear note with regard to the great scourges of humanity, especially with regard to war, slavery, intemperance, the opium traffic, impurity, gambling. The influence of the newspaper should also be on the side of religious liberty, Free Trade and economical government. I feel further that every measure which tends to improve the position of the great mass of the population resident in these islands is of paramount importance. It is difficult so to forecast the industrial and economic development of the country in the next thirty-five years as to speak in other than general terms of what this social policy should be, but if the legislation is influenced by the spirit of human brotherhood and alive to the claims of social justice, the right measures for social advancement will be increasingly seen.

If the Trustees were able so to arrange that after the expiration of the thirty-five years, this newspaper influence should be exercised in the direction indicated above, it would I have no doubt be a source of great satisfaction to themselves and entirely in accordance with my wishes.

I turn now to the Joseph Rowntree Village Trust. As this is of a permanent character, its Trustees will not be burdened with any questions similar to those just discussed. I have sought, in view of the modifications of social conditions which must ensue with the lapse of time, to make the provisions of the Trust as elastic as may be compatible with adherence to the objects of the Trust as defined in the Deed of Foundation. I may be allowed to draw attention to the words in clause 4 of the Deed which say that 'the Founder is specially desirous that nothing may be done under the powers hereby conferred which may prevent the growth of civic interest and the sense of civic responsibility amongst those who may live in any community existing on the property of the Trust'. I should regret if there were anything in the organisation of these village communities that should interfere with the growth of the right spirit of citizenship, or be such that independent and right-minded men and women might resent. I do not want to establish communities bearing the stamp of charity but rather of rightly ordered and self-governing communities – self-governing, that is, within the broad limits laid down by the Trust.

I began this Memorandum by saying that it was not intended to have any legal or binding force. I wish in closing it not only to repeat this disclaimer, but to express the hope that nothing I have written may discourage those who will have the administration of these Trusts, and of any new Trusts which may be created to continue their work; from entering into the fields of social service which I have not indicated and which I cannot at present foresee.

Still more emphatically would I urge that none of the objects which I have enumerated, and which under present social conditions appear to me to be of paramount importance, should be pursued after it has ceased to be vital and pressing in the interests of the community.

I hope that the Institutions to which contributions are made from these trusts may be living bodies, free to adapt themselves to the ever changing necessities of the nation and of the religious Society of which I am a member. The need of seeking to search out the under-lying causes of weakness or evil in the community, rather than of remedying their more superficial manifestations, is a need which I expect will remain throughout the continuance of the Trusts, and some of the principles indicated in this Memorandum, as to the most effective methods with regard to the appropriation of funds, are I think likely to have continued force. At the same time, realising not only that 'new occasions teach new duties', but that 'time makes ancient good uncouth', I have given to the Trustees and Directors of these foundations, very wide powers and very few directions of a mandatory nature as to their exercise.

Joseph Rowntree
  St Mary's, York
  December 29, 1904

The Trustees of the Joseph Rowntree Village Trust 1904–1959 and of The Joseph Rowntree Memorial Trust 1959–1979

The text of the clauses in the Deed of Foundation giving authority for the appointments shown in this table are summarised in Appendix 1.

In this table the word 'retired' is used when a Trustee gave up office at the age of seventy-five in accordance with the voluntary agreement made by the Trustees and recorded in the minutes of their meeting held on 30 March 1962. The word 'resigned' is used when a Trustee gave up office for other personal reasons.

The names used in this list are those appearing in Deeds of Appointment and ordinarily in use within the Trust. Titles, distinctions or degrees held at the time of appointment or conferred subsequently have been omitted.

The Original Trustees, present at the first meeting of the Trust held on 13 December 1904.

Joseph Rowntree	Died 1925
John Wilhelm Rowntree	Died 1905
Benjamin Seebohm Rowntree	Died 1954
Joseph Stephenson Rowntree	Died 1951
Oscar Frederic Rowntree	Resigned 1941
Arnold Stephenson Rowntree	Died 1951

Additional Trustees Appointed by the Founder during his Life Time in Accordance with Clause 7 of the Deed of Foundation

Thomas Henry Appleton	Appointed 13 November 1906	Died 1933
Richard E. Cross	Appointed 17 April 1913	Died 1916

Trustees Appointed by the Continuing Trustees after the Founder's Death, in Accordance with Clause 8 of the Deed of Foundation, whilst not less than Four of the Original Trustees were in Office

Peter Rowntree	Appointed 28 September 1933	Resigned 1948
William Wallace	Appointed 28 September 1933	Retired 1966
Francis D. Stuart	Appointed 31 March 1941	Died 1946

Additional Trustees Appointed after the Founder's Death in Accordance with Clause 8 of the Deed of Foundation, whilst not less than Three Original Trustees were in Office

Jean W. Rowntree	Appointed by Yorkshire Quarterly Meeting 21 July 1943	Resigned 1976

| Henry Clay | Appointed by the Trustees, 23 June 1945 | Resigned 1947 |

Trustees Appointed to Fill 'Subsequent Vacancies' in Accordance with Clause 8 of the Deed of Foundation

NAME	DATE OF APPOINTMENT	BY WHOM APPOINTED	DATE TERMINATED AND CAUSE
William K. Sessions	1 October 1947	The Continuing Trustees	In office on 31 December 1979
Frederic Seebohm	22 January 1949	Yorkshire Quarterly Meeting	In office on 31 December 1979
Thomas F. Green	9 September 1949	The Continuing Trustees	Died 1966
Christopher J. Rowntree	20 October 1951	Yorkshire Quarterly Meeting	In office on 31 December 1979
Lloyd Owen	9 November 1951	The Continuing Trustees	Died 1966
Madge Butterfield	23 July 1955	Yorkshire Quarterly Meeting	Retired 1967
Donald J. Barron	11 March 1966	The Continuing Trustees	Resigned 1973
Charles F. Carter	23 April 1966	Yorkshire Quarterly Meeting	In office on 31 December 1979
Jean Braithwaite Coggan	10 December 1966	The Continuing Trustees	Resigned 1975
Walter B. Birmingham	21 October 1967	Yorkshire General Meeting	Resigned 1972
Peter M. Barclay	5 October 1972	The Continuing Trustees	In office on 31 December 1979
H. Cedric Shaw	2 February 1974	London Yearly Meeting	In office on 31 December 1979
Donald J. Barron	2 October 1975	The Continuing Trustees	In office on 31 December 1979
Erica F. Vere	3 July 1976	London Yearly Meeting	In office on 31 December 1979

Introduction
Looking Backward and Forward

The Joseph Rowntree Memorial Trust was born on 29 July 1959. But it was a reincarnation. On the 4 December 1904 Joseph Rowntree had established the Joseph Rowntree Village Trust – the largest of three trusts, launched as a single enterprise, to which he transferred about one-half of his property. His original intention was to found one trust covering all the main fields of his interest, and competent to sustain over a period of years the work to which he and his family had set their hands. He thought that each generation should provide for its own needs in ways relevant to the conditions of the time. So his Trust was to have a life of thirty-five years, during which he expected that both income and capital would be used to finance a concentrated programme of work.

He failed to achieve this simple purpose. One part of the activities in which he was engaged with his eldest son Seebohm was concerned with housing; property had been acquired and a body was needed to hold and administer it which would be permanent. Therefore a trust was established – the Joseph Rowntree Village Trust – as the vehicle for Joseph and Seebohm's housing interests. Then he was advised that other parts of his work lay outside the boundaries set by the law relating to charity. A non-charitable trust – the Joseph Rowntree Social Service Trust Limited – was set up to sustain and develop these activities. To complete the design, he established a general charitable trust with wide powers – the Joseph Rowntree Charitable Trust. Each of the last two were to come to an end in thirty-five years, when any remaining assets could pass to the Joseph Rowntree Village Trust as the permanent body. Power was, however, given to their Trustees to renew them, if at the time and in the light of experience they decided that this was right. So there were three trusts rather than one, and of the three one was permanent; in time the others became so.

In founding his Trusts, Joseph Rowntree wrote two papers in which he committed himself, his family and the Trustees who would administer his bequests, to some principles about the use of money by those who owned it, by those who might later administer it and by those who might inherit it. The first paper was directly primarily to his Trustees. It gave advice which he was anxious that they should heed, but which, because he made no claim to foresee needs beyond his own time, he did not wish to have any legal force. It has had an influence on the development and policies of all three trusts which it is impossible to overstate; the document has therefore been reproduced in full following the Foreword at the opening of this book. This charge to the Trustees explains the discussions and decisions which Part I of this book records; without it the Trustees' application to Parliament in 1959 for a new charter giving wider powers would almost certainly have been refused.

Joseph Rowntree wrote a second paper three years after he founded the

Trusts which is headed 'Memorandum written for my children upon the opportunities of wealth, and the dangers connected with it'. It is marked in his own handwriting in red ink, 'Private'. The paper was so marked because at least by implication it referred to individuals. The opening paragraphs are in general terms and give a more intimate glimpse of the man who founded the trusts and the reasons why his influence on their development over threequarters of a century has been so profound. He writes:

> The prosperity which has attended the Cocoa Works business in the last few years, following upon a long period of struggle, is likely to place my children in possession of considerable wealth. This wealth, if rightly used, affords the opportunity of widely-extended usefulness; but the observation of a life-time has led to the belief that any considerable amount of wealth more often proves to be a curse than a blessing. In the remembrance of this, and with a wish to make a right use of what has come to me, I have, with I believe the hearty assent of my children, given what I suppose may be about one-half of my property to the establishment of the three Trusts; but, after this gift, my children will, if the business remains moderately profitable, find themselves in possession of large incomes.
>
> Let me, in the first instance, indicate what I believe are the special dangers attendant upon wealth which should be most carefully guarded against. Perhaps the first and most obvious danger is self-indulgence. My father wrote of 'that ease loving and self-considering spirit which makes us dwarfs in all that is great and beautiful'.

His concern in this more personal paper is not so much with the great issues of principle which he discussed in his Memorandum to Trustees, but with the unhappiness which he believed so often befell those who acquired wealth and from which he was anxious to preserve his successors. In a passage developing this theme he writes:

> It would be an act of great unkindness on the part of any parent if, for want of thought and resolution, he (or she) allowed a son or daughter to grow up in self-indulgent habits. This position will be at once accepted, but the thought needs to be continually kept in mind and resolutely acted upon. When the means are forthcoming, it is so easy and so pleasant to give children almost all they ask for. Then, further, it may need a good deal of thought rightly to call out, at the different stages of early life, unselfish thought and effort for others. The duty of the 'simple life' has been much insisted upon of late, but I know how easy it is in the various forms of personal expenditure to acquire, step by step, expensive habits which, so far from increasing the real richness and fullness of life, add to its burden. One of the mischievous ways in which these expensive habits tell, is by increasing the barrier between wealthy people and their fellows. It lessens that realising sense of human brotherhood, which it is of such paramount moment to maintain.

The theme is developed in a later paragraph.

> The best work almost required a mind free from personal worries.
> Yet most men, as their means increase, increase their expenditure also
> and anxiety about meeting current expenditure is quite often as great
> among the rich as among the poor. A simple and most necessary
> sailing order is not to adopt a scale of expenditure which closely
> approximates to your income. If you want to give largely, and really
> by your gifts to achieve any great result, you must have a margin
> upon which to draw. It really is a piece of culpable stupidity on the
> part of those who have ample means, to adopt a scale of expenditure
> which keeps them continually harassed about money matters and
> prevents them from making their mental powers or their wealth
> available for local or national needs.

The passage of years has not reduced the force or relevance of these views
though it may have increased the difficulty of their application.

This is not the place to examine further the thought and action of a
remarkable man writing in his sixty-ninth year. The task has been discharged elsewhere and by others.[1] So much, however, is necessary to an
understanding of the almost total reconstruction after fifty-four years of
the largest of Joseph Rowntree's foundations and the only one designed
from the outset to be permanent.

An account of the work of the Joseph Rowntree Village Trust during its
first fifty years was published in 1954 to commemorate the Trust's jubilee.
It was called *One Man's Vision* (Allen & Unwin, 1954). The book included
in its introductory chapters an account of the origins and development of
the three Trusts and of the relations between them. The present volume
carries the story of the Village Trust from 1954 to the end of the Trust's
seventy-fifth year in 1979. In 1959 the Trust's name was changed as part of
the reconstruction of that year to the Joseph Rowntree Memorial Trust.

During those first fifty years the resources of the Village Trust and the
energies of its Trustees had been directed to raising the standard of design
of houses let at low rents, and the quality of the environment in which
their occupants lived. But this never implied a housing programme
designed for those living on roughly similar incomes. The Trustees saw
their task as the creation of communities in which families and individuals
from all walks of life could find a home and play a part in the corporate life
of their neighbourhood. The definition for legal purposes of those for
whom homes were to be provided concluded with the words 'The working classes (which expression shall, in these presents, include not only
artisans and mechanics but also shop assistants and clerks and all persons
who earn their living, wholly or partially, or earn a small income, by the
work of their hands or their minds, and further include persons having
small incomes derived from invested capital, pensions, or other sources)'.
The definition makes clear the comprehensive housing provision which
the Founder had in mind. Decades later the validity of his work as a

[1] Ann Vernon, *Quaker Business Man* (London: Allen & Unwin, 1958).

charitable purpose was to be called into question, with profound implications for the work of the Trust and for the capacity of a growing voluntary housing movement to contribute significantly to the quality of urban life.

Consistent with the Founder's view of housing provision, the Trust had been given wide powers to contribute to the needs of family and neighbourhood life of which housing is but one component. Joseph himself doubted whether there would be a great and growing demand for houses in the area in which he worked and in a letter commented, 'I think it is just possible that before very long the income of the Trust may be applied elsewhere'. He had also stressed a principle to which he attached great importance, 'Still more emphatically would I urge that none of the objects which I have enumerated and which under present social conditions appear to me to be of paramount importance should be pursued after it has ceased to be vital and pressing in the interests of the community'. So towards the end of the first fifty years the Trustees had begun to turn their attention to wider social questions affecting family and community life. They had seen their consultant architect, Sir Raymond Unwin, appointed as the first Chief Architect to the newly-created Ministry of Health in 1919, and had noted a rising public concern with the national provision for housing and a national and international commitment to the study of housing questions. They had therefore concluded that their own direct involvement in the design and building of houses should be reduced, and Trust resources transferred to the 'new duties' which, as the Founder had reminded them, 'new occasions' would teach.

So the last chapter of *One Man's Vision* introduced the possibility of a new range of activity for the Trust in the opening years of its second half-century and reflected on the problems of adaptation that might be met. The book closed with this paragraph:

> Here, in the not distant future, the Joseph Rowntree Village Trust may meet problems of adaptation to new conditions which are already acute for many older foundations, and to which the Nathan Committee[1] has given consideration. This record is evidence of the value, during fifty years of social change, of a Trust embodying the ideals of its Founder and making available to the service of the community resources for social experiment and demonstration. On experience which has been gained in this way, present-day reforms have been largely based, and there is as yet no evidence that the nation will have less need of such service in the second half of the twentieth century. It should not be beyond the wisdom of the British people to find ways to enable Trustees to adapt their powers to a changing social order, whilst preserving the independence and freedom on which the vigour and variety of such experiments as those described here have been dependent.

The Trustees have not been able fully to resolve the problem of adapting their powers and policies to the needs of a changing social order. The effort

---

[1] *Report of the Committee on the Law and Practice relating to Charitable Trusts.* Cmd 8710. December 1952.

to do so has involved them in promoting a private Act of Parliament, the Joseph Rowntree Memorial Trust Act, 1959; this was the re-incarnation referred to at the beginning of this chapter. It has further involved the separation from the main Trust of all housing activities by the creation in 1961 of a separate Joseph Rowntree Memorial Housing Trust. The obligation to adapt in accordance with the Founder's intention calls still for continuing and – it must be said – frustrating efforts to reconcile the comprehensive approach to housing provision stressed by the Trust's Founder with the current official view that houses built by a charitable body must be limited to those which meet the needs of the 'poor' and disadvantaged.

The first part of this book examines the Trustees' experience in these matters as they began to identify what should be the nature of the 'new duties' which their commission from their Founder required them to undertake; the conclusions they reached required an extension of their powers by legislation. Throughout the twenty-five years the use of Trust resources for housing in accordance with the Founder's intention was beset with legal difficulties which were still unresolved at the end of the period. The Trustees tried to interpret the changes they felt obliged to make to those concerned with them, or affected by them, so that public confidence in the integrity and purpose of the Trustees was retained. They had also to take account of the policies of the other two Rowntree Trusts which, contrary to the Founder's expectation, had continued to operate and to develop new policies relevant after thirty-five years to the Founder's intention as they conceived it.

In the second part of the book an account is given of the development of the Trust's housing policy and practice in conditions very different from those of 1904 when its housing powers were first defined. In the early years of the Trust, a small scale development near York had been used to demonstrate ideas about house design, town planning and community life; that demonstration was an important part of the movement which found expression in the New Towns, and influenced housing policy throughout the western world. The Trustees have continued this policy in the different conditions which the big public commitment to housing has brought. They have undertaken small projects both at home and overseas designed to demonstrate particular principles and, through them, to influence the policy of central and local authorities and of the voluntary housing movement.

There then follows in Part III an account of the wide range of activity made possible by the extension of their powers which has absorbed the greater part of the Trust's resources over the last twenty-five years. For part of this time it was the largest supporter outside government of research and experiment in housing policy, in the personal social services and in the training of social workers. Sometimes the Trustees acted on their own initiative; sometimes they responded to proposals made by others; often new work resulted from the meeting of minds sharing a common concern. Of particular interest is the deliberate attempt made by the Trust to work directly with local and central government, seeking a financial commitment from public bodies, not on financial grounds, but as evidence of serious involvement in the particular study or experiment and to the application to public policy of any relevant results.

With some misgiving, the Trustees accepted responsibility for the deployment of resources provided directly by the government. An account is given, from the point of view of the Trust, of the Family Fund, set up to assist families having the care of a very severely handicapped child. Some have seen in this a new and hopeful approach to the allocation of public funds to groups in particular need.

The Trust has had close relationships throughout its history with the city of York. This has led to special initiatives at York University, to the administration of a fund set up by the Lord Mayor to relieve distress caused by floods, and to support for social activities which would not have been undertaken elsewhere.

The passing of the 1959 Act enabled the Trust to operate overseas. At the request of governments and established voluntary organisations in East, Central and Southern Africa, it financed self-help housing and the co-ordination and strengthening of voluntary social effort in five countries. Part IV tells the story of this unusual partnership with central and local authorities at home and abroad.

In the last two decades there has been increasing public concern both here and in the United States with the affairs of trusts and foundations. Part V therefore describes how the Trust is administered – the appointment and terms of service of Trustees, the recruitment of the staff and the role of advisers in the development of policy.

Of critical importance during this period in the history of the Trust has been its financial policy and the changing relationships with the Rowntree Company, whose shares constituted its original endowment. The Founder established in the Trust Deed in 1904 a unique relationship between the Trustees and the Company which itself produced difficulties for both parties half a century later. How these were resolved and the considerations which led to the decision to diversify the Trust's investments are examined; the consequences for immediate income and longer term expectations are analysed. These are the issues which occupy the concluding chapter.

Part I *The Reconstruction of the Trust*

1 *The Search for New Duties*

The Trust's Deed of Foundation is dated 13 December 1904. Its jubilee was therefore reached in December 1954. Whilst the book written to commemorate that jubilee was going through the press, Seebohm Rowntree died on the 7 October 1954 at the age of eighty-three. He was the last of the original Trustees who joined Joseph Rowntree in founding the Trusts fifty years earlier. When the Trustees met on 8 October 1954, they recorded these facts, and minuted, 'it is in a full sense the end of an era'.

On the 3 December 1954, with advance copies of *One Man's Vision* on the table before them, the Trustees considered a paper headed 'Future activities of the Trust'. The paper was presented by Thomas F. Green, Headmaster of Bootham School, who had been a Trustee since 1949 and at this memorable meeting was appointed Vice-Chairman. It is worth quoting a short extract from the minute which records the views he presented:

> With the termination of the first fifty years of its life and the passing of B.S. Rowntree who was the last of the foundation Trustees, he (Thomas Green) realised that it was the occasion for careful consideration as to what should be their future service to the community. It might be that they would wish to repeat the housing experiment of New Earswick in some other place but he did not feel a concern to do this as he regarded it as the duty of local authorities, whose architects were now initiating much experimental work. There was still some housing to be carried out at New Earswick and this should continue. From time to time appeals for assistance were brought to the notice of the Trustees and help was given for a number of objects but he stressed that the Trustees should not wait for other people to come along with projects but initiative should be exercised within the Trust itself.

Thus began a continuing discussion on what should be the role of the Trust in the next stage of its history. There were three separate strands in this consideration; to explain the character and policy of the Trust as it exists today, each must be separately examined. They can best be presented in the form of questions: Given the clearly expressed intentions of the Founder, how should the Trust's resources be applied in the 'new era' which the Trust was entering? Second, what importance should be attached to the impact of any new departures on the work of the other two Rowntree Trusts which had decided to extend their life beyond the thirty-five years originally prescribed by the Founder and which expired in 1939? Third, what problems arose from the limitations of the powers conferred by the original Deed of Foundation and how might these be overcome?

The questions were not entirely new. Earlier Trustees had started the debate during the second world war. On the 24 May 1943 Seebohm Rowntree had written to his colleagues suggesting that in future the proportion of the Trust income devoted to housing was likely to diminish. He reminded them that their Trust Deed enabled them to spend their resources, 'on any object which is of benefit to the working classes'. There was a danger that the income of the Trust would merely be spent, 'on objects which came to our notice from time to time without thinking whether these constitute the best way in which we can utilise the Trust income'. Seebohm Rowntree referred in his note to the practice of the Carnegie and Pilgrim Trusts which settled a defined programme of work for a period of four or five years ahead. He drew a distinction between a policy of responding to proposals made by persons and institutions seeking grants, and that of initiating from within the Trust the work for which its resources should be used.

The proposals advocated in Seebohm Rowntree's paper carried forward in a logical and imaginative way the work on which the Trust had already been engaged. They did not 'break new ground', to use a phrase much beloved by later Trustees. He argued that wider use should be made of the experience in planning and house design built up at New Earswick as a result of the work of Sir Raymond Unwin and Barry Parker. There was little evidence in local authority housing that the lessons had been applied. New building was needed to give older people a home suited to their needs thus freeing the family houses many of them occupied. Single people of both sexes would, in the postwar world, want a home of their own. The experience of the Village Colleges in Cambridge should be studied to see what implications they might have for educational development in the Trust's estate. He referred to the Peckham Health Centre – a service for the promotion of health which had been interrupted by the war – and thought that its emphasis on family membership accorded with the principles which the Trust had sought to follow. Was enough being done, Seebohm Rowntree asked, to ensure the best use of fuel in low-cost homes, whether for cooking, heating, lighting or refrigeration?

Once the implications of freeing the Trust's income from the need to provide capital for house construction were grasped, many proposals for new types of work were pressed on the Trustees. In those early postwar years, cautious voices were raised questioning whether the powers of the Trust were as wide as had been supposed. The series of consultations with the Charity Commission and with counsel to which these questions led are discussed in a later chapter. Their immediate result was a decision made in September 1946 to defer indefinitely a variety of proposals, broadly in the field of education; and for the next ten years to use the Trust's resources for housing, with Seebohm Rowntree's 1943 letter as the starting point.

So the events of 3 December 1954, with a summary of which this chapter began, might seem to be a re-run of the recorded discussions and initiatives of a decade earlier. But Thomas Green had been right; 1954 was in fact 'the end of an era'. In 1943 there was no corporate view on what the task of the Trust should be. The three surviving Founder Trustees had been in office forty years; newly-appointed Trustees had not yet taken the measure of their task. Not until 1946 was an Executive Officer appointed for the purpose of helping in the formation of corporate views and policies. In contrast the mood and the convictions of the eight Trustees who met on 3 December 1954 made certain that a new era had begun.

By common, if unspoken, consent, the difficult issue of legal powers was left aside until a corporate view had emerged about the purpose for which the Trust's resources should be deployed. The minute of record of this first discussion about a new role for the Trust includes a summary of the views expressed by each of the seven Trustees present and of a letter to the Chairman from the one absent Trustee. There was a shared view that the Trust's interest in housing should not be abandoned; there were limited but important additions to the New Earswick estate which should be made and there might well be particular aspects of housing and neigh-bourhood on which the Trust would want to concentrate part of its resources. The prospect of some initiatives in social research attracted some Trustees; this they thought might suggest an institute of social research in York, to complement the institutes of historical research and architectural studies already established by a group with the ambitious name of the York University Promotion Committee. But the Trust should avoid large scale research with no clearly defined aim, and should seek to combine enquiry with practical experiment. In any new work, the Trustees wished to remain as closely involved as had their predecessors in the housing development of that period. Particular interests were identified; industrial relations, the doubts which some had on the way the welfare state was being developed, youth, and the use of leisure. A short list of names of persons who might be drawn into consultation was agreed. The Trustees then turned their attention to such immediate mat-ters as the appointment of a new colleague to replace Seebohm Rowntree, the affairs of the schools at New Earswick and, for good measure, the proposed expenditure of £257.9s.0d. on four pieces of playground equip-ment for the Homestead gardens!

During the following six months it was left to the Trust's Executive Officer to continue discussions with individual Trustees and prepare a paper which should be the basis of discussion at a first meeting with a group of the consultants named at the meeting in December 1954. The meeting gathered in the evening of 24 June 1955. Four guests had been invited: Professor R.M. Titmuss, of the London School of Economics and Political Science; Dr Michael Young, Director of the Institute of Com-munity Studies; Mr Louis Moss of the government social survey and Dr John Bowlby of the Tavistock Institute of Human Relations. Dr Bowlby had been unable to accept. Trustees were closely questioned about the interests described in the paper which had accompanied the invitation to the meeting. Were they interested primarily in social research or social action, Professor Titmuss wanted to know, thus introducing a stimulating discussion on the relations between research and action. Dr Young was impressed with the contribution of the Trust in housing and related fields; why not continue in them, but extend the research component by examin-ing the results of work elsewhere so that conclusions relevant to policy might be drawn? Did the Trust want to employ people in a research unit of their own or would they be willing to hand over the work to others? If the former, had they considered the difficulties of engaging and retaining staff for work of this kind? Louis Moss referred to those parts of the national provision for social services which were concerned with the needs of the 'generality' of people rather than with 'social failures'. We had, Mr Moss said, no appraisal of housing policy, of how far the houses we provide meet the needs of those who live in them. Of the occupants of hospital beds at any given time, forty per cent were mentally ill. There were opportunities here for enquiry by an independent trust, of a sort which could not be initiated from within the public service. The discussion embraced other changes in society, prominently the increased employment of women, and the resulting implications for children, for the elderly, for relationships within marriage and for the community generally. Trustees asked whether they ought to consider taking an initiative with others in establishing for social research, a council comparable to the Medical Research Council. Interestingly, Professor Titmuss, Dr Michael Young and Mr Louis Moss advised against such a development at that stage; not many years later the Heyworth Committee, of which Charles F. Carter, soon to become a Trustee, was a member, made just such a recommendation which was accepted by the government who appointed Dr Michael Young as its first chairman.

The response to this first encounter with people engaged in those fields of research and development which most appealed to the Trustees was swift and decisive. Three days later on 27 June 1955, the Trust's Executive Officer wrote to the Chairman of the Trust drawing out the lessons to be learnt from the evening discussion and suggesting how the Trust might move to decisions on its role for the immediate future. This letter was sent to all Trustees with a covering note from the Chairman. On 25 July, five Trustees available in York, who had been accustomed to meet as a small executive from time to time mainly to deal with matters concerning the Trust's housing estate, met to consider 'what are the next steps to be taken in connection with the important problem of the future activities of the Trust'.

They were concerned first with the question put to them by Michael Young. Did they propose to set up their own research organisation, bearing in mind the problems identified in the earlier consultation, or were they planning to offer grants to established researchers, whether within universities or research organisations? Then, did they wish to follow Professor Titmuss in his concern for the most disadvantaged groups in the community, or were they to be concerned with raising the quality of life generally, thus influencing relationships and increasing personal satisfaction whether at work – critical to an increase in the national resources, or at home – the key to the individual's success as a member of the community? Some observed that these were not necessarily alternatives. Trustees could find ways of involving themselves in the initiation and implementation of social research and experiment without seeking to found a new research unit. Studies of morbidity and failure were also ways of identifying the factors which led to health, whether in physical, mental or social terms. Some aspects of what had been discussed were related to the activities in which the Trust had traditionally been engaged. They already had some experience of work in housing and community development, and in offering training and support to families in difficulty.

This discussion enabled Trustees to identify the consultants who should be invited to join them at their next evening gathering, and gave a lead to their Executive Officer who was charged with the preparation of a further paper to bring the outcome of the meeting into focus, and serve as a point of departure for the discussions with the next group of consultants. The names that suggested themselves for the next consultation were Dr John Bowlby, who had been unable to attend the first gathering and on whose work the Trust's own support for families was based; Sir Geoffrey King, Chairman of the National Assistance Board; and Dr Ronald Hargreaves, formerly of the Mental Health Division of the World Health Organisation and then Professor of Psychiatry at Leeds University.

The Trustees gathered with their guests on the evening of 25 November 1955. Sir Geoffrey King had been unable to come; Dr Bowlby and Professor Hargreaves were present. The Trustees were told that their guests were distinguished in the field of family and community relationships, and approached these relationships from a study of what was broadly described as mental health. They thought it should be a 'listening' occasion; they would expect to reach conclusions about their future activities at their next meeting. They would then need to move to the implications for their relationships with their sister Trusts and to the problems of legal powers. Some ideas had already been rejected, they were:

To commission an eminent person to undertake a major enquiry into the functioning of present day society, and in particular the source of the dissatisfactions and frustrations which affect human contentment and efficiency.

To commission a number of minor enquiries by young people as a method of selecting both a field of work, and possible people to take part in it.

To support or initiate schemes concerned with the physically or mentally handicapped. This was understood to exclude studies of treatment or daily care, but not an enquiry into the factors which might result in physical or mental handicap. The Executive Officer's paper then recorded:

. . . certain principles of work have emerged from the Trustees' discussions. It is likely to be wise to start with the interests which the Trustees have already formed, and with the resources immediately at their disposal. This is really only to accept the advice given by Professor Titmuss, and confirmed by the correspondence so far with Dr Bowlby, that successful research and experiment really depend upon the personal concern and interest of a group of people; very great difficulties always attend an effort simply to think out a project which seems of importance and then seek around for people able to carry it through.

The Trust has, during most of its history, sought to promote 'the good life' for the majority of families, and has not entered the various fields of specialised activity in the interest of those who may need particular care. This is probably a matter on which further elucidation should be sought in the next discussions. It does, however, again open the whole field of social, moral and religious work; in other words, it is a guiding principle, but still leaves the Trustees with the task of deciding the particular approach to this object with which they themselves should be concerned. How far is it true to say 'that the factors which prevent ordinary people from obtaining satisfaction from their life at home and at work' can best, and perhaps only, be studied through those who have so signally failed to achieve this result that their plight is clear to all?

One approach to the wider problems which the Trustees have discussed, and which is closely related to the Trust's work since 1904, is that of family and community relationships. It was because this point seemed to be reached at the meeting in July that Dr Bowlby in particular, and later Professor Hargreaves, were suggested as appropriate consultants for the next discussion. The Trust is already engaged in a number of projects along these lines, including re-housing and community enquiries in Bristol and Hull, the renewal and preservation of family life at Spofforth Hall, and the building of a local community at New Earswick and assistance with similar projects elsewhere.

In the light of present day knowledge, it is impossible to exclude from studies such as this the subject of mental health on which there is a fund of special knowledge and experience in and around York. There are many unrelated experiments going on at the moment dealing with family life under quite separate codes. For example, at Spofforth Hall there are mothers under the Home Office who have been charged with neglect; under the Ministry of Health, who have simply failed in their home life; and under the welfare authorities, who need re-housing. But there is, in practice, no difference at all between them, though so far nothing has been done to bring the experience in these fields together and to seek from all the available evidence the causes of the problems which are approached in such different ways.

2 The Three Rowntree Trusts: How Far Their Founder's Purpose was Finally Frustrated

The search described in the previous chapter had begun with Thomas Green's paper to the Trustees on 3 December 1954. Following the meeting with the second team of consultants on 25 November 1955, the Trustees were ready to define the fields of work in which to deploy their resources and to identify the first series of projects they should launch. In fact, another year passed before that stage could be reached; on 15 March 1957, the Trustees were able to record a series of decisions committing funds to a group of projects brought together by their Executive Officer.

The year was occupied in consultation with the other two Rowntree Trusts. The non-charitable Joseph Rowntree Social Service Trust and the Joseph Rowntree Charitable Trust had not come to an end after thirty-five years as contemplated by the Founder but had used the powers he had given them to re-establish the Trusts for a further thirty-five years with the future beyond that time still open. The Village Trust's new fields of work were already within the powers and interests of the Charitable Trust. This was a development which the Founder had never contemplated and for which he had offered no guidance.

The Joseph Rowntree Charitable Trust had, in fact, been in the business of initiating and supporting social research for many years. All the internationally recognised research associated with the name of Seebohm Rowntree had been financed by that Trust. Its income was about half that of the Village Trust; the latter had been more substantially endowed because its income was to be the source of the capital to sustain a continuing house building programme. How far could the release by the Village Trust into the sphere of interest of the Charitable Trust of the substantially greater resources available to it, be reconciled with the division of responsibility in the mind of the Founder when the Trusts were established? It was all very well for the Village Trustees to feel a compulsion to respond to 'new occasions' by turning to 'new duties'; for the other Rowntree Trusts, these were duties laid on them from the outset. Thus now that some provisional conclusions had been reached about the field of work into which the Trust should move, the time had come for consultation by Trustees of all three Trusts.

The Village Trustees decided that it was for them to take the initiative and invite the other Trustees to a joint discussion, since whatever problems existed were of the Village Trust's creation. It was concluded too that it would be better for chairmen and vice-chairmen to meet in the first instance, leaving the possibility of a gathering of all Trustees later. The chairmen and vice-chairmen of the Joseph Rowntree Village Trust, the Joseph Rowntree Charitable Trust and the Joseph Rowntree Social Service Trust accordingly met at the York Station Hotel on Saturday 3 March 1956 at the invitation of the Village Trust. An additional Trustee of the Village Trust who was a Director of the Rowntree Company also attended in view of a possibility – which did not in fact materialise – that the Company might establish a Seebohm Rowntree Memorial Foundation. The field of work of such a body would have had to be taken into account in any discussion of the part to be played by the Rowntree Trusts in social research and allied interests. A paper from each chairman about the work of the Trust for which he had responsibility had been circulated and these provided a background to the discussions. The Chairman of the Village Trust reviewed the Trust's work in housing, and gave reasons for the search for a new role on which the Trustees had been engaged and which had led to the joint meeting; he summarised the series of consultations with external advisers, and recorded the decision to move in a substantial way into the field of social research.

The Chairman of the Charitable Trust, however, raised more fundamental questions which were logically prior to any agreement about a division of interests between the Trusts. 'The Trusts ought to consider', the paper suggested, 'their joint responsibility to the Founder's intention of the unity of the three Trusts'. It might be right in new conditions to depart from the views which the Founder had expressed; indeed he had encouraged those who succeeded him to do so. But any such decision should be made deliberately and the reasons for it understood. 'There would be great loss', he commented, 'if this divergence occurred simply because of unrelated personal interests on the part of individual Trustees.'

The principle which the Village Trust had followed in its explorations was accepted. It should proceed, from the basis of its experience in housing work, to concern itself with current social problems which that housing work had revealed. The Charitable Trust had been engaged on a similar exercise; the starting point for that more general Trust had been its traditional work in adult education, in Quaker education and in social research which had been a major activity of the Trust. Now it seemed that all three Trusts might be involved in this field. The Chairman of the Charitable Trust thought that if their total impact on social policy was to be both substantial and effective there should be some kind of 'general staff' which might operate in two ways. There should be, 'if found possible', a greater degree of common membership between the Trusts; in any event a liaison committee representing their interests in relation to social research should be set up, and a person appointed with responsibility for bringing together social research undertaken by any of the Trusts or by subordinate bodies which they might create. The meeting considered, too, the question which had constantly arisen in the Village Trust's discussions; how far in this new field of work could the Trustees follow the Founder's intention that expenditure should be directed by the Trustees themselves; and how far would they need to commission others, whether within or outside universities? The two methods were not seen as incompatible, the Trusts were not concerned only with extending the frontiers of knowledge – the traditional role of the university – but they were morally committed to action following research. They would need to seek the co-operation of the universities and research institutes for specific projects within a wider programme to which they would be committed. There was much discussion about the relationship between aspects of research concerned with the family, the wider community and industry; the issues to be studied, the Chairmen and their deputies agreed, had much in common and those working in these different fields needed to be aware of this even though their approach was necessarily different.

The immediate decision to be made seemed of critical importance to the future of three Trusts launched fifty years before in different social and economic conditions, and with a single group of Trustees responsible for all three of them. All agreed that an officer should be appointed to serve the interests of at least the two charitable trusts in their research activities, and the Village Trust's Executive Officer was identified as this officer. A liaison committee should be appointed by the same two Trusts to give oversight to this work. The two Trusts should as quickly as possible share common accommodation. The different responsibilities of the Joseph Rowntree Social Service Trust, as a non-charitable body, were recognised, and its Trustees were asked to consider how far it could improve communication with the other two Trusts, whether by the use of the joint arrangements now proposed, or perhaps in some other way. There was particular concern that the non-charitable Trust had established a subordinate body with charitable status. This, it seemed, departed from the Founder's clearly expressed view that the distinction between the Charitable and Social Service Trusts had been for legal purposes only; the sole purpose of the non-charitable body had been to ensure that there was an instrument through which the Founder's concerns could be carried forward even though at the time the resulting work was not recognised as charitable in law. The Joseph Rowntree Charitable Trust was the vehicle for charitable work other than housing, and transfers of resources from the non-charitable to the charitable trust had been contemplated if the need for non-charitable activity did not absorb all the resources given to the Joseph Rowntree Social Services Trust. Transfers of this kind had been made regularly for many years. The meeting also agreed that if a Seebohm Rowntree Memorial Foundation were created later, its administration and work might be brought within the structure now approved. Almost in parenthesis, the Village Trust Chairman commented that social research generally should normally remain the responsibility of the Charitable Trust, leaving the Village Trust, 'to concern itself (though not necessarily to the exclusion of other subjects) with the industrial aspect of human relations'.

This was indeed a grand design to emerge from a single morning's discussion. On 11 May 1956 the Village Trustees accepted the recommendations from the inter-Trust meeting. The Chairman and Vice-Chairman were appointed as the Village Trust representatives on the new liaison committee. Preliminary action to provide office accommodation for the Charitable Trust was taken, with further extension in mind if later a

Seebohm Rowntree Memorial Foundation should be brought into being. The Executive Officer raised one point. Had the Trustees accepted the division of responsibility between the two Trusts proposed by the Chairman of the Village Trust? This allocated social research generally to the Charitable Trust, leaving the Village Trust 'to concern itself (though not necessarily to the exclusion of other subjects) with the industrial aspect of human relations'. Did this mean that the records of the Village Trust's consultations with Professor Titmuss and others should now be passed to the Charitable Trust, because they were concerned wholly with issues now regarded as within the Charitable Trust's sphere? This first practical application of the new arrangements proved unacceptable to the Village Trustees; they wished the whole field of social research to be within their sphere. The resulting problems were left to the new liaison committee to resolve!

At the end of May the Village Trust's acceptance of the inter-Trust meeting's proposals was notified to the Charitable Trust, though without reference to the qualification which had been introduced. On 16 June 1956 the matter came before the Charitable Trustees; the Chairman of the Village Trust was invited to attend for the discussion. This meeting also accepted the proposals, but introduced a doubt, not about the allocation of responsibilities between the two Trusts, but about the definition of the responsibilities of the Village Trust's Executive Officer in his capacity as adviser to the new liaison committee. The Charitable Trustees saw possible difficulties. His appointment, and by implication that of the liaison committee, were therefore made subject to 'the working out of mutually acceptable terms of reference'. The Charitable Trustees did not appoint representatives to the proposed liaison committee at that stage. The Village Trustees a month later accepted that some clarification was needed; they suggested that the liaison committee should be set up but that before any staff appointment was made, terms of reference for the committee should be worked out in consultation with the Chairmen of the other two Trusts.

So after five months of inter-Trust discussions – for the most part between the Village and Charitable Trusts – each maintained the position it had defined at the outset. The Charitable Trust had acted within the Founder's intention in deciding to continue beyond the period of thirty-five years and therefore to pursue a programme of social research which had from the outset been an important part of its work. The Village Trust claimed that the extension of its interests beyond housing was implicit in the charge given to all the Trusts in the Founder's Memorandum. The resolution of the difficulty by appointing a liaison committee with its own advisory officer had run into difficulties; the terms of reference of both committee and officer could not be agreed and were left for discussion between the Chairmen of the two Trusts. By January 1957 the Village Trustees were clear that they must make their own decision about their future work and settle their relationships with their sister Trust in the light of that decision, and in March they allocated funds to a first series of projects.

The Trustees were brought to these decisions by the argument in two papers. The first came from the Trust's Executive Officer, it advocated a clear division of work between the Village and Charitable Trusts, which would not limit the former in exploring and developing its chosen field of social research and experiment. He directed the Trustees' attention to a number of specific projects which should be set on foot at once. This action would serve notice to those engaged in social research that the Trust was in the business, and would define in broad terms the area of its interest; the Trustees would also start to gain experience in observing the proposals which others would bring to their notice and in working out criteria by which to assess them. The Executive Officer then questioned the appointment of a liaison committee, consisting of a small number of representatives from each Trust. He stressed the importance of a corporate commitment by the Trustees to any major project undertaken by the Trust. There had been experience in the recent history of the Trust of subordinate bodies, using Trust resources, on which only a small number of Trustees served. 'Discussions on matters of policy', he said, 'had sometimes to be repeated two or three times; even so the Trustees of the parent Trust could not feel personally interested in, or committed to, the work supported from the funds they had allocated'. It would be unfortunate if this procedure were repeated in the new field of social research which might well be the largest enterprise of the Village Trust. As an alternative to a liaison committee served by an officer with imprecise responsibilities, there should be a clear division of interests between the Trusts and then a review of membership in the light of the work they would undertake.

The second paper was prepared by the Trust Chairman. It was concerned with the work the Trust should undertake and brought together the substance of consultation and exchanges of view within and outside the Trust over a period of years.

The Trustees felt compelled to review their decisions about joint working with the other Rowntree Trusts, the appointment of a liaison committee and the role of their Executive Officer. All this now appeared in a different light from that shed by the exchanges at the meeting of the three Trusts nine months earlier. The Chairman was therefore commissioned to write to the Chairman of the Charitable Trust in terms which are recorded in a minute. It read:

> The Village Trust had now decided to devote a major part of its resources to social research and experiment. They would be prepared to receive proposals based on the experience of persons outside the Trust and contemplate giving some publicity to their proposals from time to time in order to put themselves into touch with as wide a range of activity as possible.
>
> They had considered again the effect which this step might have on the work of the Joseph Rowntree Charitable Trust which although its terms of Trust were much wider than those of the Village Trust now devoted certain of its resources to social research.
>
> They had considered in particular the proposal for a liaison committee to which they had formerly given provisional approval. In the

light of the decision which they had now actually made they thought that this suggestion seemed less favourable. It would mean in fact that recommendations affecting the use of most of the resources of the Village Trust would be made by only two or three members and the rest could not take a proper personal responsibility for the work supported.

There did, nonetheless, seem to be a strong case for the Charitable Trust considering whether or not it wished to continue in this field bearing in mind the wide range of its other responsibilities. The Village Trust would naturally consider at any time specific proposals in which the Charitable Trust had an interest.

On 15 March 1957 the Chairman reported to the Trustees the outcome of his correspondence with the Chairman of the Charitable Trust and a meeting held to seek to reach agreement. There was a difference of view and that was not surprising in view of the implications of the final paragraph of the Trust minute. The Charitable Trust Chairman could not accept that social research should be outside that Trust's sphere of interest; it had been one of the Trust's principal commitments. He would also wish to be free to take advice from the Village Trust's Executive Officer even though the proposal for a joint appointment had to be abandoned. Finally, he hoped for a meeting with the Village Trustees for a more extended exchange of views. That meeting took place at Oxford in October. The Village Trustees had met for three days to have direct discussions with those whose work they had begun to support in order to hear about progress, to consider some new proposals which they had themselves initiated and generally to gain experience in the new types of work in which they were becoming involved. The discussions with the Charitable Trust Chairman took place on the Sunday morning 27 October, as the final session of the weekend meetings.

In fact little new was said. The Village Trust had made its decisions and was in process of implementing them. The Charitable Trust was unwilling to bow out of a field which had been one of its main activities; some Trustees had been chosen because of their professional knowlege in that field. It was true that the Charitable Trust had a wide charter; but that was no reason to abandon a field of work central to the interests of the Trust. The Charitable Trust Chairman thought that the Village Trust would approach the new work in a way different from that familiar to the Charitable Trust. The latter kept strictly to the view of the Founder in supporting only projects which were the personal concern of individual Trustees. He understood, and Village Trustees confirmed this, that the Village Trust was willing to consider projects initiated by outside bodies; they relied too in part on the advice of their staff, whose duty it was to report critically and objectively on the different projects in relation to their contribution to the whole field of work of which they were a part. This might be a change which was inevitable after fifty years of Trust history but the Charitable Trust at present felt no need to adopt it.

The value of this meeting lay in the frank recognition for the first time of the different ways in which the two Trusts had developed. They must continue, it was accepted, to go their separate ways; it seemed inevitable that their pathways would diverge in the years ahead. Some formal arrangements for co-operation were established – the use by the Charitable Trust of such expertise on the Village Trust staff as might prove helpful; the readiness of the Village Trust, with its larger resources, to consider within its general policy projects which the Charitable Trust wished to support but which were beyond its resources.

The intentions were good, but the record in this book of the work and development of the Village Trust over the twenty-five years since these agreements were reached will not reveal any significant examples of their application. Was this inevitable?

In 1904 Joseph Rowntree had established three Trusts as a single and coherent plan to devote to a range of his concerns the resources which unexpectedly, and late in life, had come to him. The same Trustees administered all three Trusts thus demonstrating their common purpose. In retrospect it is clear that their increasingly divergent path was inevitable once the death of the Founder had removed the single source of appointment of Trustees. A Trustee once appointed feels, and is indeed required to feel, a personal commitment to the use of the resources for which he or she has become responsible. Time and effort are required to build up within a body of Trustees a corporate view about the work and development of a large Trust. The process virtually excludes the possibility of adjustment to the corporate view developed by two other bodies of Trustees, mostly unknown persons, with whom the only common link is a Founder who made his own principles and purposes clear, but wisely left his successors to interpret these in a changing world. A common purpose guiding three bodies of Trustees, consisting mainly of the same persons, all involved in the enterprise from the outset, with in addition a limited life for all but one Trust: these were the logical components of Joseph Rowntree's original intention. Once the last was surrendered, time eliminated the others.

3 The Trust Programme is Settled

After their second meeting with consultants on 25 November 1955 the Trustees had postponed final decisions about their future work to allow consultations with their sister Trusts. By January 1957 they were ready to make decisions; the outcome of the inter-Trust discussions was already clear. On 18 January 1957 the Trust Chairman read to the Trustees the paper already referred to.

Three propositions summarised the work they should undertake; they are recorded in the Trust minute of that meeting:

> They should no longer see their main field in housing work, such as they have followed for the past fifty years. The position of housing in general should be left to housing authorities and to unofficial and private enterprise.
>
> They should, however, continue to do secondary work in the field of housing where
>
> i) there appears to be room for constructive experiment in particular directions; or
> ii) it is related to other subjects in their field such, for example, as housing for the old people.
>
> For the rest, the Trustees should look to do work of research or social enquiry (and in addition, where necessary, actual field operations calculated to assist their research or to test out in practice the results of that research) in fields within their legal powers and in directions consistent with what they believe to have been the ideas of the Founder; modified (as he would have wished them to be) by changing conditions and requirements.

There were then some principles which would guide the methods they adopted and the particular projects which might be chosen. Here the Chairman referred to the introduction to the eleventh report published by the Nuffield Foundation which gave an account of its work for 1955–6. The Trustees recorded that 'they could almost accept as it stands the approach of the Nuffield Foundation in the rather remarkable introduction of its recent report'. The passage which so commended itself to the Trustees is quoted here with permission of the trustees of the Nuffield Foundation:

> In spite of the vast acreage of reports they publish and the interest the press intermittently shows in their work, foundations are still, to the general public, mysterious and remote organisations. Sometimes

they seem to be shadowy, universal uncles whimsically distributing largesse to the 'lucky Jims'; sometimes they appear to be local Unescos dreaming up utopian schemes for nothing less than the redemption of mankind. Even some of the people who have come into touch with foundations as applicants for grants may not have discovered the principles on which they work; why one scheme is supported after an apparently similar scheme has been turned down; why a foundation suddenly appears to lose interest in a field which once it enthusiastically cultivated. Perhaps its methods will be clearer if we think of a foundation as a kind of private bank which finances projects that may yield dividends not in terms of cash but of public good. It is a risk-taking bank. It is least interested in secure investments which will produce a modest return. It is out for high dividends and can afford to balance its failures against its successes. Its first concern must be the credit-worthiness of the applicant; its second, the originality of his idea; its third, the soundness of his project. With depressing frequency it may find that the number of good projects is greater than the number of good men to carry them out. Sometimes, indeed, it seems necessary to tempt men to acquire new skills and thus fit themselves for important work which would otherwise not be done.

But a foundation does not restrict itself to those who knock at its door. It must go out and seek profitable investment, sternly resisting the temptation to do what is fashionable and immediately popular. It is not the job of a foundation to sustain work which everybody agrees ought to be done; it dare not even continue to support indefinitely its own successful schemes, for if it does it will quickly consume the resources out of which new ones can be attempted and become a mere disburser of doles, an exhausted creature with a fertile past but no creative future. A foundation must ever be turning away from old friends and familiar ways and nerving itself to walk alone, sustained by the hope that some new and private path may lead to a rewarding prospect.

Again, like a private bank, a foundation receives a vast amount of information. Its visitors and advisers include men and women from the universities, the learned societies, the research institutes, the operative philanthropic societies, the hospitals, government departments, and from government itself. They bring ideas as well as information and they are always ready generously to spend time in thought before giving advice. No foundation could function without their counsel and stimulation; indeed it would be foolish and arrogant to make the attempt. The foundation itself possesses no expertness except in the principles and techniques of philanthropy such as they are, although some of its trustees and members of its staff may be the products of a particular scholarly discipline. Nor would it be a wise thing to seek after expertness. A foundation must be free to make rapid changes of emphasis in its interests.

There were four guidelines on which Trustees were in general agreement; they are recorded in these terms:

The Trustees do not want to sustain work 'which everybody agrees ought to be done', though they might assist in starting such work. They do not want 'to support indefinitely their own successful schemes'. They do not want to 'become a mere dispenser of doles, an exhausted creature with a fertile past but no creative future'. They do want to do pioneer work; to do things which badly need doing and which might not be done, or done so well, without help.

They do not want to put resources into bricks and mortar except temporarily or on a limited scale so far as they feel, in a particular case, this might assist the major ends they have in view.

They do feel their greatest contribution may be in the discovery of facts, and in the drawing of the lessons from those facts. In other words, they would look to their main field as being that of social research or social enquiry; though this would not preclude helping to start off practical work which might assist that research or prove experimentally that the conclusions reached were sound.

They do not want to limit their contribution to the disbursing of grants even for the most promising research. At the same time they do not want to limit their kind of work only to the field in which they as Trustees happen to be expert; or to that work for which they as Trustees can personally find time.

At their next meeting on 15 March 1957, the Trustees settled three issues which emerged from the strenuous debates of the past two years. How much could they devote each year to their new field of work? How should they inform the general public, and the particular groups likely to be interested, of the decisions they had made? What were the immediate projects on which they should embark?

The answer to the first question was simple. The Trustees could safely spend between £100,000 and £150,000 a year (at 1957 prices) for the next three years on their new work. In 1957 this was a not insignificant sum to be devoted to a fairly narrowly defined field of interest; it is an indication of the march of inflation and of the enlargement of the Trust's resources that twenty-five years later the Trust was discussing the use of between £1m and £1½m a year.

On the second question, a draft had been circulated of a statement that might be issued to the press, to appropriate journals, and to other trusts and foundations operating in a similar field. It was stressed that regular periodic reports of the Trust's work should be published.

As to the third question, there were five, or perhaps six, projects on which work might begin at once. The Trustees were willing to become involved in a study of the results produced by recently developed social services; in a seminar on group work in community organisations; in the support of Home Advice Groups; in the establishment of senior fellow-ships for experienced case-workers at the Tavistock Institute; and in a study of families in which the parents had become involved in a charge of child neglect. For later consideration, there were details of a possible involvement by the Trust in the development of a comprehensive mental health service in the City of York. The relevance of the Trust's long experience in housing and neighbourhood work, and of the series of consultations over a period of two years, are both apparent here.

The proposal to publish an immediate statement on the Trust's new policies, on which a decision had been postponed, encountered further difficulty. A revised draft had been circulated for the next meeting which was held in July. Again there was failure to agree either on the precise purpose of the statement or on the text; perhaps, said some Trustees, two statements were needed, directed at different audiences. The Chairman, Vice-Chairman and the Executive Officer were asked to settle the terms of a draft.

The impetus behind so much change and reform was, for the moment, spent. In September when the Trustees met again, the group recommended that the publication of a statement of policy should be abandoned and that instead a first report should be published early in 1958. Some consideration was given to the form and content of the report. In fact, the Trustees quickly became absorbed in the third and most critical question raised at the beginning of 'the new era' in 1954 – what problems arose from the limitation of the powers conferred by the original Deed of Foundation and how might these be overcome? Ideas about a published report were submerged in these more urgent and complex issues. It was after the passing of the Joseph Rowntree Memorial Trust Act in July 1959 that the Trust's Executive Officer raised the subject of a published account of Trust policy and activity. Interest revived, the Trustees saw a draft of the first report of the re-named Joseph Rowntree Memorial Trust at their meeting on 30 October 1959; they discussed it at length on 11 December; it was published in June 1960.

4 *Private Legislation is Agreed*

Doubts about the freedom of the Trustees to use their resources for purposes other than housing, and the education and welfare of those whom they housed, had cast a shadow across every prospect of new pioneer ventures which a rising income seemed otherwise to make possible. The difficulty arose from the terms used in the clause of the Trust Deed which defined its objects; it read:

> The object of the said Trust shall be the improvement of the condition of the working classes (which expression shall, in these presents, include not only artisans and mechanics but also shop assistants and clerks and all persons who earn their living, wholly or partially, or earn a small income, by the work of their hands or their minds, and further include persons having small incomes derived from invested capital, pensions, or other sources) in and around the city of York and elsewhere in Great Britain and Ireland, by the provision of improved dwellings with open spaces and, where possible, gardens, to be enjoyed therewith, and the organisation of village communities with such facilities for the enjoyment of full and healthy lives as the Trustees shall consider desirable, and by such other means as the Trustees shall in their uncontrolled discretion think fit.

Three questions were raised at different stages of a long discussion which first earned a reference in the Trust minutes on 23 November 1945. First, how was the word 'condition' in the objects clause to be interpreted; did it embrace physical, mental, moral and even spiritual condition, or must the interpretation be related to the housing purposes which were central to the Trust's objects, and therefore be construed as 'living conditions'? Second, did the words 'by such other means as the Trustees shall in their uncontrolled discretion think fit' give as wide a choice of activity as, at first sight, a layman would conclude and as, from the terms of his Memorandum, the Founder evidently intended? Third, was the provision of houses for those drawn from a wide range of occupations and incomes, as implied by the definition given to the term 'working classes', a valid charitable activity, or must housing assisted by charitable funds be limited to those in 'poverty'. The Trustees throughout their history had conceived their duty to be that of creating healthy and vigorous communities of the kind so vividly described by the Founder in his Memorandum. Did the law require them to build enclaves for the poor, the deprived and the disadvantaged?

These were daunting questions. The last the Trustees chose to ignore; the task laid on them in the matter of housing seemed clear enough and the homes already built over a period of fifty years could not be demolished.

This particular question was not raised again until presented in abrupt form by the Board of Inland Revenue when the Trust's Private Bill was on its way through Parliament. This is part of a later story.

The first exploration of possible new fields of work for the Trust continued from May 1943 – the date of Seebohm Rowntree's letter to his colleagues – until December 1946 when, as already recorded, the Trustees returned to their traditional work in housing and so continued for almost a decade. In these three and a half years the legal problems presented by any extension to their fields of work focussed on the first two questions raised in the opening paragraphs of this chapter. How widely could the word 'condition' be interpreted; how much could be read into the words 'by such other means as the Trustees shall in their uncontrolled discretion think fit'?

On the second of these two questions the Trustees received encouraging advice from their own legal adviser; the words meant what they said. Seebohm Rowntree was doubtful; he pressed the point in a letter to the lawyer so characteristic of his combination of courtesy and directness that it is reproduced here in full.

I have this morning received your ruling to the effect that the Village Trustees may spend their money for the improvement of the condition of the working classes by any means of which the Trustees, in their uncontrolled discretion, think fit.

Although I know that admission of the fact that the Trustees have never realised that they had such wide powers with regard to the expenditure of their funds may point to carelessness on their part in not having thoroughly mastered the terms of the Trust Deed, I must admit that the fact that we have such extremely wide powers gives me a very welcome shock.

I pondered long over the true significance of the words at the conclusion of clause 2 of the Trust Deed and came to the conclusion that the words 'and by such other means as the Trustees shall in their uncontrolled discretion think fit' referred only to the provision of facilities for the enjoyment of full and healthy lives in village communities which had been organised (which presumably means built) by the Trustees.

I came to this conclusion because it seemed to me almost unthinkable that such immensely wide powers should be given to the Trustees, in so casual a manner as would be done if your reading of the clause is correct.

If you are right in your opinion (and naturally as a layman I hesitate even to doubt this for a moment) then supposing the Trustees thought 'in their uncontrolled discretion' that it could be to the advantage of the working classes to provide free whisky for everybody, no one could say them nay.

I cannot think that if JR had really intended to give them such immensely wide powers these would have been given in a line and a half of the Village Trust Deed. JR's wishes with regard to the way in which the funds should be expended would have been indicated in outline at any rate, as in the case of the other Trusts.

Forgive me for writing thus frankly to you. I only do so because I want to be dead certain that we can take your opinion as absolutely final before we embark upon a scheme of work based upon it.

Both questions of interpretation were discussed with the Charity Commissioners on more than one occasion and on their advice were submitted to counsel. The second question, the Trustees were advised, depended on the first. If 'condition' referred only to 'living' or 'physical' condition then clearly the apparent breadth of work implied by the words 'uncontrolled discretion' was at once logically restricted.

In the outcome, the issues were settled not as general principles to be applied to a range of Trust decisions, but as rulings on two or three specific projects. Two Trustees were anxious to embark on projects in education on which there was no corporate Trust view. These were submitted to the Charity Commissioners who had no hesitation in advising that they were outside the purposes for which the Trust had been established. The decision made as a result in December 1946 to return to the Trust's housing interests came as a relief. What was significant for the future from these exchanges was that a proposal tentatively put forward that the Trustees should proceed by way of private legislation was discouraged by the Trust's own legal advisers and by the Charity Commission, whose legal officer 'knew of no precedent for such a course'!

When the Trustees met in Oxford from 25 to 27 October 1957 they had reached the decisions already recorded about their future work and had completed their 'agreement to differ' with the Joseph Rowntree Charitable Trust about the part they should take in social research and experiment. They had deliberately ignored the problem of legal powers until they were clear what were the objects for which those powers were to be exercised. From time to time in the records of their discussions, there are indications that they knew the issue would have to be faced, though its importance and urgency waxed and waned according to the nature of the immediate proposal under consideration.

A particular and immediate need to examine legal powers arose first at the Oxford meeting. Professor Titmuss, one of their first consultants in the search for a new role, had asked whether the Trust would be interested in supporting a study of the history of pensions and their impact on the social and economic life of the country. Trustees were interested, but doubtful about their powers to use Trust resources for such a purpose, and therefore instructed their Executive Officer to make enquiries of the Charity Commissioners on this specific question, though in the context of the wider search for a new field of work on which the Trustees had embarked.

This meeting with the Commission took place on 6 November 1957. Much had happened in the decade that had passed since the Trustees' first series of negotiations with Commissioners in the immediate postwar years. In the course of writing the papers about new fields of work during the consultations on the future of the Trust already described, the Executive Officer had consulted the Commissioners – making clear that he was not acting on the instructions of the Trustees – in order to ensure that what was being considered was not wholly beyond realisation for a Trust operating under a Deed drafted fifty years earlier. The Commissioners were thus already sympathetic to the ideas which were under discussion within the Trust; they had given preliminary consideration to ways in which they might be able to respond if and when specific and formal proposals were received from the Trustees.

On 13 December 1957 the Executive Officer reported the results of the first discussion with the Commissioners arranged on the direct instructions of the Trustees. His report set the scene for a series of steps, taken in close consultation with the Commission, which led – with only one threatened breakdown – to the passing of the Joseph Rowntree Memorial Trust Act. The arguments presented on behalf of the Trustees and the Commission's response to them have, therefore, a wider importance than the historic changes which became possible in the affairs of the Trust. A summary of the report made to the Trustees is therefore published as Appendix II. The immediate course of action suggested to the Trustees was expressed thus:

> In summary it was agreed that it should be suggested to the Trustees that they should seek from the Commissioners a Scheme of Advice or Opinion; their application would cover the following ground:
>
> 1 The changes in the work of the Trust and the growth of its income as I had described them; the fact of accumulated income was of importance as evidence of these changes.
> 2 The desire of the Trustees to engage in certain work which seemed to them to be the logical development in the present situation of the tasks committed to them by the Founder.
> 3 A list of the categories of work in which the Trustees wished to engage, expressed as broadly as possible.
> 4 The period to be covered by the scheme and a suggested limit to the amount of income to be employed for the purposes described.

The Trustees responded enthusiastically to what seemed to be a new and constructive approach to their problems; the drafting of the request for the Scheme of Advice or Opinion was put in hand at once. 'The step', the Trustees minuted, 'provided an important opportunity for the Trustees and the application should seek as much freedom for the Trustees as the Commissioners will permit'.

The way for the presentation of the Trustees formal proposals had been prepared by sending to the Commissioners a copy of *One Man's Vision* giving an account of the Trust's work during its first fifty years. This drew a note of acknowledgement from the Secretary to the Commission in terms which showed the close interest that was being taken in what seemed to be a new departure in the development of a charitable foundation. The note read:

> It was most kind of you to send along the story of the Joseph Rowntree Village Trust which marked its jubilee. It is, indeed, an

impressive performance; and I am grateful for the way in which it is filling out gaps in my knowledge of the Trust's activities and movements in which it has been in the van.

I was glad to learn that our discussions had been helpful; and with my deepening appreciation of the inspiration that has informed the Trust's work, I hope that it will prove possible to assist further in the future.

By 21 February 1958, a memorandum headed 'Application for a Scheme of Advice or Opinion' had been prepared by the Trust Chairman. The Trustees were on uncertain ground; they decided to send the document to the Commissioners in draft form, suggesting some further consultation before committing themselves to a formal application. They took this view because the submission had now taken the form of a comprehensive review of the Trust's powers, rather than a proposal for approval for certain specific projects. The draft memorandum was indeed a comprehensive review; the following summary of its contents shows how fundamental were the issues raised.

First it reviewed the constitution and development of the Trust since its establishment by Joseph Rowntree in 1904. The argument of this part of the paper led to the conclusion that if the Trustees were to attempt to use the greater part of their enlarged resources to finance housing along lines followed during the Trust's first fifty years, it would need to embark on building programmes substantially greater than any so far undertaken. It was part of the Founder's intention that there should be a reasonable return on the capital so employed; the income from this new building would therefore further increase the Trust's resources. 'It would be doubtful', the memorandum concluded, 'if this "snowball" process of provision of housing by the Trust would be practicable, bearing in mind the difficulties of purchasing large areas of land for housing work, virtually in competition with public authorities. He [the Founder] could not foresee the vast changes in the provision of houses which two world wars have brought.' Hence, the paper explained, 'the Trustees over the last decade have found themselves exercising increasingly the powers given to them which are additional to those related to village communities'.

Second, in a couple of pages were set out the Founder's views as they emerged from the Deed of Foundation itself, and more important, from the memorandum which he wrote at the same time.

In the third part, the Chairman embarked on a more controversial topic; it was headed 'Interpretation of the Founder's views'. Here were recorded the views expressed by the Trust's own advisers in the early 1940s, and the guidance received at that time from Counsel and from the Charity Commissioners. 'It is earnestly asked', the Trustees now pleaded, 'that in this more comprehensive review those earlier views might have further consideration. If accepted, this might go far to meet some of the difficulties of the Trustees'. There followed a summary of the position which the Trustees had reached; they believed they should now make an 'effective contribution in the field of social enquiry and research, coupled with, in the right circumstances, initial assistance to new developments in work

designed, broadly, to ameloriate and improve the condition of the working classes, as defined'. The paper gave an account of the series of consultations with eminent advisers, and the ideas on new fields of work that
these had generated. But always they had found difficulty in relating their
powers to particular proposals and 'have been unable to formulate with
the necessary confidence a full forward policy and programme for the
Trust, because of the uncertainty of the limits of their powers once they
depart from the specific activity which is central to the Trust Deed'. 'It is in
these circumstances', the paper explained, 'that the Executive Officer of
the Trust was asked to initiate discussions with the Commissioners which
have led in turn to the present application'.

The fourth and final part of the memorandum referred to a financial
statement for the following five years which accompanied the memorandum showing the resources likely to become available after all continuing
commitments to the Trustees' housing estates had been met, and provision made for administration. A second enclosure set out seven categories
of activity in which the Trustees thought it would be right in the immediate future to engage. 'For these reasons', the paper concluded, 'the Trustees are asking the Commissioners:

1   to advise them as to the interpretation of their powers; and
2   if necessary, possibly to provide a Scheme of Advice or Opinion
    on which they can base their work at any rate for the next few
    years'.

This document was sent to the Commissioners on 25 February 1958
with a letter reminding the Commissioners of the discussions which had
led to it and explaining why so comprehensive an approach had been
adopted. 'It would be a great help to the Trustees', the letter stressed, 'in
what has become a comprehensive review of the scope and powers of the
Trust, if there could be an opportunity to discuss this statement informally
before it is presented for consideration by the Charity Commissioners'.
To give point to this suggestion, four dates were proposed on which such
a meeting might be held. On 4 March came a response from the Secretary
to the Commission offering the opportunity of a discussion and adding the
encouraging note, 'May I say that I see little reason, if any, why the draft
should not go forward in its present form'.

By 19 March, the Trustees had been able to meet and consider the
outcome of the discussion with the Commission's representative on their
draft paper. The Commission's Secretary had explained that the Trustees
were in error in seeking a Scheme of Advice or Opinion. A Scheme is a
formal alteration to a Trust Deed; an Order of Advice or Opinion provides
protection to Trustees doubtful about their powers to undertake a
specific project. In the light of the case presented by the memorandum and
of the subsequent discussion, the Secretary suggested that Trustees should
seek a Scheme or an Order, leaving the choice to the Commissioners.
Since studying the draft memorandum the Secretary had changed his own
view and now felt that an Order of Advice or Opinion would be inadequate to the circumstances; it seemed that a permanent change in the

powers of the Trust might be justified and this called for a Scheme of the Commissioners which would need to be drafted and advertised in case there were objections. Nor would a limit of time seem appropriate in the changed circumstances; if after say five years, experience showed that further extensions to the Trust's powers were needed, an amending Scheme could be prepared. The Secretary to the Commission further expressed the view that the summary in the memorandum of the discussions held in the 1940's was hardly relevant; he saw little point in harking back to 1946. The essential elements in the present situation, as he saw them, were not, as then, the desire of individual Trustees to pursue particular lines of work, but the manifestly reduced usefulness of, and scope for, the building of houses by the Trust, and its greatly enhanced income.

On 19 March two copies of a revised memorandum were sent to the Commission which took account of these helpful suggestions.

Not surprisingly, the Trustees and their advisers found difficulty in containing their impatience to complete the final stage of the plans over which they had agonised for so long. By the end of April, patience ran out. On 2 May 1958 the Executive Officer wrote expressing appreciation for the help the Trust had received and observing that 'this is a large matter which must take its course'. But, he told the Commissioners, the Trustees had a full meeting on 16 May after which there would be a gap until October, when they had planned a weekend meeting 'to review all the activities with which they are at the moment associated'. So if there were questions the Commissioners needed to raise it would be helpful to take advantage of the May meeting.

The reply came on 12 May. But it was from the Chief Charity Commissioner in person. He recognised that the Trustees 'have reached a very important stage in their work and a stage which involves examination *au fond* of their powers before their future practice is committed'. He regretted that the Commissioners were without clear decision just at the moment when the Trustees were meeting and would welcome such guidance as the Charity Commissioners can give. The letter continued:

Prima facie the situation which faces the Trustees is one which might be resolved by an application to the Court though at the time when some few years ago similar problems were posed the Trustees were disinclined to take that step. At that stage a suggestion had been made that an Order of Opinion and Advice might enable the Trustees to devote surplus income for an experimental period to developing new policies, though it now appears that it would be difficult to set a term to such a period or expenditure as there would be a run off period within which such work would be completed but the term of which it is difficult to gauge.

While this might be a proper course even though some elasticity would have to be set to its term, the fundamental question remains whether the Trustees are being guided strictly and solely by the terms of the Trust or are writing more into it, on the basis of a charge laid upon them by the Founder, than canons of instruction and applicable law authorise. This is the kernel of the question.

It was indeed. The Chief Charity Commissioner went on to show that 'canons of instruction and applicable law' in his view precluded any departure from the general concept behind the Trust's powers and that, as then advised, the Commissioners doubted whether the Trustees were justified at law in adopting as a permanent feature of their work a concern with the underlying causes affecting the conditions of living of the working classes. This was an exact description of what precisely the Trustees wished to do; their efforts to achieve that goal seemed to have brought them back to the point of departure.

But the letter was not written in final terms. It bluntly stated the Commissioners' difficulties but offered, and indeed, requested, further discussion with the Trust's Executive Officer. In an effort to give the guidance needed by the time the Trustees met on 16 May, the Chief Commissioner offered to be available for discussion on 15 May.

A note of the meeting with the Chief Commissioner was prepared in time for consideration by the Trustees on the following day. It is in three parts. First, seven short paragraphs, reproduced below, summarise the Chief Commissioner's prepared opening statement. Second there is reviewed the Trust representative's effort to re-establish the integrity of the Trustees, which seemed to have been called in question in the Commissioner's opening statement, and to bring the discussion back to the point it had reached before his intervention. The third and final part of the report shows how possible solutions to the Trustees' problems were examined: private legislation was brought back into consideration as one of those solutions.

The paragraphs recording the Chief Commissioner's opening statement read as follows:

The answer to the Trustees' request for a Scheme would be in the negative.

Other minds within the Charity Commission had been brought to bear on this, and Counsel had been consulted; they were clear that under the Deed the Trustees were limited to housing and that of the working classes as defined.

For many years the Trustees had been departing from their Deed. They were now housing people who could pay quite high rents, and they had no authority to do so. They were engaged in work, such as the provision of the Homestead Gardens, which could not be related to people for whom the Trust was provided and were therefore in the realm of 'the general benefit of the community', which was not within the Trust Deed.

He was doubtful whether the Trust had any claim now to charitable status, and thought it was really his duty to report this situation to the Inland Revenue for consideration in relation to exemption from income tax.

He thought that Trustees had been unduly affected by the Housing Act 1949, which removed the category of working classes from local authority housing. But this had no bearing on the Trust.

He referred to a quotation from *One Man's Vision* which said that the Trust had supported projects in which Trustees had a personal interest. He remarked that this was a common failing of Trusts.

In his view there was still adequate scope for a housing trust for the people defined in the Trust Deed, and he went on at length about the virtues of almshouse trusts which had been revived in recent years. This, he thought, was the kind of work to which the Trustees should apply themselves.

'This', the Executive Officer commented in his report to the Trustees, 'was hardly a promising beginning'. Here the Commissioner was reminded of the story set out in the Chairman's paper which had led to the present discussion. The Commission's own records would show how meticulous the Trustees had been in seeking advice where their powers had in any way been in doubt, they had in fact taken careful advice on the implications of the 1949 Housing Act to which the Commissioner had referred. Ways of embarking on new and substantial housing work had been examined; the Trustees had themselves visited new towns and urban renewal schemes to see if there was scope for a private trust to become a substantial partner in such enterprises. They had received no encouragement. These examples of the Trustees efforts to resolve the very problems now being raised seemed to move the discussion to a more constructive stage.

'Here was a Trust', commented the Commissioner, 'which had greater resources than it could use within its powers and . . . this was a very unusual situation'. This seemed the right point to answer the implied and damaging criticism of the Trustees made at the outset. The Trust's files record:

> At this point I asked him to refer again to his introductory statement in the light of our discussion. I said he must believe me when I told him that this was not a Trust which was anxious to depart from its Trust Deed or follow personal inclinations of Trustees; it felt deeply committed to the task laid upon it by the Founder and was more sensitive than any other group of men I had met to the legal requirements within which it must work. Long hours had been spent on these matters, and his records would show how much detail I, on behalf of the Trustees, had brought to his colleagues. In the light of this I hoped he would agree that his opening statement had not represented the position fairly. The Chief Commissioner said he entirely accepted this and realised that he had been under a wrong impression.

What then were the possible solutions to these difficulties as they had now been defined? The use of accumulated income did not, the Commissioner thought, present a difficulty. The Trustees could use it in any way which in their opinion contributed to the improvement of the condition of the working classes; the Commissioners would not enquire how their decisions were reached. But for future income, the problems were greater. The Commissioner had reached the conclusion that he could not by

Scheme extend to purposes related to the general community a charity which applied to a broad and defined group. Only by legislation could that purpose be achieved. He examined the possibility of a *cy près* scheme which, he thought, would leave the Trustees in a position not much more satisfactory than at present. Proceedings could be taken to secure change by Royal Charter; this he thought introduced technical difficulties which outweighed any advantage. If the Trustees decided to proceed by private legislation, the Commissioners would be consulted by the Attorney General. He was asked if he would give help at a much earlier stage, when the draft of a Private Bill was being considered; he replied that that was the course he would prefer. Warming to the theme, he recommended that the Trustees should try to have their Bill ready by November, in which case it could become law by the following June. He gave advice on procedure and, for good measure, an estimate of the costs the Trustees would incur.

'Nothing', noted the Trust's representative, 'could be more remarkable than the difference between the beginning and the end of this discussion'. The Chief Commissioner concluded by promising to write a letter which would be different from the one he had contemplated, 'though it would not be possible to predict what future changes of view might occur'. The issue which seemed to have been resolved was thus neatly again left wide open. Even so, the Trustees agreed that they should act at once to begin the draft of a Private Bill.

Four days later on 19 May a letter running to twelve hundred words was received over the signature of the Chief Charity Commissioner. It was a remarkable document; its arguments balanced, as it seemed to a lay reader, with Delphic ingenuity. The Trustees were confined, the letter made clear, to their main objects – the provision of improved dwellings and the organisation of village communities and such other means for the improvement of the condition of the working classes as defined in the Deed as the Trustees in their uncontrolled discretion thought fit. But the Commissioners recognised that the Trustees after long and anxious thought had reached the conclusion that the pursuit of these objects by the repetition on a larger scale of their earlier housing work was impracticable, so they were faced with the necessity at law of some related application of their surplus income. But, the Commissioner suggested, there were ample related fields of housing work:

for example, in such a community for elderly folk as is to be found in Whiteley Village, or in many examples of better housing for definite classes who cannot otherwise escape from their environment or afford such amenities, or perhaps in colonies for the housing and rehabilitation of those who from accident or casualty have need of special training and/or facilities to give them renewed abilities to be self-supporting. The Trustees have no doubt much information and can readily obtain more. The Trustees have themselves aided on occasion various projects for the old or needy, although perhaps these grants were not strictly within their *vires*; this need not deter them from fresh examination of positive fields of action rather than research and enquiry in which they might now seek to break new ground.

A hopeful section of the letter began by a recital of the powers to acquire reports in regard to undertakings and schemes having for their objects the amelioration and improvement of the condition of the working classes. But, said the letter, it was plain that these undertakings and schemes must be in existence under the management of others from whom information and reports might be obtained and paid for; the Trustees could not of themselves set in motion the undertakings and schemes, however fruitful might be the bearing upon their own work of the reports and information which might result. All this effectively precluded, in the Commissioner's view, most of the activities listed in the Trustees' application for a Scheme or an Order of Advice or Opinion. Of the Founder's Memorandum, the Commissioner took the view that it was addressed to the circumstances which might confront the Trustees when the two terminable Trusts came to an end, and it was not thus possible to remove from its context the reference to 'such other means as the Trustees think fit' as an enlargement of the charitable purposes in such a way as to give the Trustees as great a choice as if they were the beneficial owners of the income.

The next paragraph was in terms to raise again the hopes of the reforming Trustees. 'The Trustees must therefore,' it said, 'seek from the most appropriate forum a new field of operations. If they chose to go to the courts or to be guided by the Charity Commissioners, any scheme must declare fresh purposes as closely as may be to the original ones, but if they were to seek a new Charter from Parliament itself they are, of course, at liberty in departing from the concepts embodied in the Deed of Trust to make such proposals as they may be advised.'

The final paragraph suggested an entirely different approach and one that the Trustees regarded as wholly inconsistent with their charge from their Founder. It proposed that income should be earmarked and invested for the extraordinary repair and replacement of the Trust's existing estates; in respect of the remainder of the income they might conceive themselves as a 'grant-making body giving assistance to others whose projects, though perhaps directed towards a wider class than that described with some particularity by the Founder, were developing or aiding specialised communities of whose members the working class, or those who had been members of that class but were now incapacitated by injury, disease or age, were the preponderant element'. The Charity Commissioners by scheme might bring this about and, 'if it were desired to examine further into this or any other possibility, I should be very happy to meet a working party of the Trustees and their advisers for further examination of it'.

The letter threw the Trustees into some disarray. Some Trustees, supported by their own solicitor, concluded that the proposal to proceed by way of private legislation was likely to be opposed by the Commissioners. One Trustee was more forthright in his view that the hoped for solution to the Trust's problems might now be beyond their grasp. The Trust's Executive Officer, from his impressions of the interview with the

Chief Commissioner, recorded a more optimistic view. He hoped the Trustees would be 'patient and persistent' in their project.

In the meantime, the Trust Chairman had made preliminary dispositions to fulfil the direction of the Trustees to proceed as quickly as possible with the preparation of a draft of a Private Bill. He had been recommended to a firm of Parliamentary Agents; it was decided to send to them the note of the Executive Officer's interview with the Chief Commissioner and a copy of the latter's letter which had caused such dismay. They were lawyers with wide experience of private legislation and their views might be of help. The Chairman, the Trust's solicitor and the Executive Officer arranged to see them on 4 June 1958. The dispatch of a letter of response to be sent to the Chief Commissioner was delayed until the views of the Agents were known.

The Parliamentary Agents were encouraging. They expressed the view that the interview with the Chief Commissioner had been arranged at only twelve hours notice; he was preparing to write a considered letter to the Trustees, the notes for which had almost certainly already been prepared. Even though in the course of the interview he had become convinced of the necessity for a Private Bill, it was not surprising that the various alternatives in his mind had found expression in his letter. So on 9 June a brief reply was sent to the Chief Charity Commissioner's twelve hundred word letter. Its terms were the outcome of consultations involving three lawyers; the Trust Chairman, himself a solicitor; and the Executive Officer, over whose innocent signature the letter was dispatched. It is worth placing on record:

I had an opportunity to report to the Trustees upon my interview with you, and they were very grateful for the time and thought and attention you had given to their problems. I am sure this will apply now also to your letter of 19 May. They had no hesitation in agreeing that the best of the courses we discussed appeared to be to promote a private Act of Parliament to make suitable variations in their powers. They greatly appreciated your kind offer of advice and help.

In these circumstances you will probably agree that any attempt at detailed discussion of what may be the exact powers of the Trustees in particular directions may be left in abeyance. It is agreed, of course, that these powers are sometimes difficult of interpretation. That is why, as I told you, the Trustees have continued to seek legal advice on particular issues and why they have valued the contact maintained with the Commissioners, in particular over the past two years. It is for this reason, too, they have valued the degree of discretion the Commissioners are willing to exercise in regard to surplus income; and their acceptance of the difficulties in the way of pursuing some of the main original purposes of the Trust in present-day conditions.

The Trustees, following the lines of our discussion, are now taking steps to get the advice of Parliamentary Agents on the question of preparing a suitable Bill for deposit in the next session of Parliament.

In due course I will, if I may, write to you again. The Trustees would welcome discussions with you on the provisions proposed.

The Chairman himself sent a memorandum to his colleagues on the same day bringing the saga up to date; he enclosed a copy of the letter to the Chief Commissioner just quoted, on which he commented: 'The Commissioner's reply to this letter will considerably clarify the position one way or another'.

On the 12 June, came the anxiously awaited reply from the Chief Charity Commissioner to the letter quoted earlier. It said:

> Thank you very much for your letter of 9 June telling me that after consideration of the whole position the Trustees are minded to seek by Bill in Parliament such changes in the Trusts as will re-orient their powers.
>
> I shall be happy to make any comment which occurs to me on the wording of the Bill when it is in draft, or, if that course were adopted, to consider with you draft instructions to counsel to settle the suitable provisions.

The Trust was again on course.

5 *The Joseph Rowntree Memorial Trust Bill in Parliament*

The Trustees assumed from the outset that their Bill would be unopposed. So unusual a venture in private legislation would almost certainly have failed had objections been raised by the departments to which the draft Bill was circulated. Hence the relief within the Trust at the terms of the letter from the Charity Commissioners just quoted.

From the first meeting with Parliamentary Agents on 4 June 1958 there were almost daily exchanges between the Trust and their legal advisers. Because the issues were complex and the daily decisions of such importance to the future of the Trust, the Parliamentary Agents suggested to the Trustees that their instructions should be delivered to Sir Milner Holland QC. Because provisions had to be settled for inclusion in the Bill, instructions were delivered at the same time to Mr J.A. Wolfe in Sir Milner's chambers in Lincoln's Inn.

To the Trustees and their advisers in York it was an exciting year in which exhilaration, anxiety or even despondency might be the mood of the day as telephone, telegram, the mail or hurriedly arranged conference brought news of the latest urgent decision that had to be made. But an account of those exchanges would be of little interest to those concerned primarily with the development of a Trust as part of the story of British foundations. The documents and correspondence are preserved in the Trust library in York and there they are available for students of these legislative processes which, because they are part of the history of the Crown in Parliament, have no parallel in the world.

Critical to the unfolding history of the Trust are the arguments which for good or ill settled the clause defining the objects of the Trust, the definition of its housing powers, and the freedom given in the investment of its endowment.

In the statement which the Trustees prepared for the Parliamentary Agents as the basis for the instructions which the Agents would deliver to Counsel, they referred to the objects clause devised for the more recently established Carnegie United Kingdom Trust. The Carnegie Trustees were to use their resources 'for the improvement of the well-being of the masses of the people of Great Britain and Ireland, by such means as are embraced within the meaning of the word 'charitable' according to Scotch or English law and which the Trustees may from time to time select as best fitted from age to age for securing these purposes'.

Andrew Carnegie had undoubtedly broken new ground in giving his Trustees so wide a discretion. In an address given on the fiftieth anniversary of the establishment of the Carnegie United Kingdom Trust, Sir

Hector Hetherington, its Chairman, had emphasised to his audience the significance of Carnegie's decision. 'In our own Carnegie UK Trust' he said 'Mr Carnegie did something relatively new. He dedicated that Trust not to one specific purpose, but to the broader end of advancing the general welfare of our whole society, and gave his Trustees a wide discretion to choose, and to vary, their immediate objectives in the light of changing needs'. Because the constituency for the Trust was so wide, 'the masses of the people', Sir Hector was able to record: 'By far the greater part of the Trust's concern has been to encourage the devising and development of those instruments and activities which aimed to raise the level of the pursuits, the interests, and the enjoyment of the generality of our people – a concern for the quality of our civilisation rather than for its material means and conditions.' If this broad intention to foster the general benefit of the community were found appropriate for the Village Trust, then a solution might be offered to the problems, in particular for the Trust's housing programme, created by the strictures of the Chief Commissioner delivered in the first interview quoted in the previous chapter.

In a series of informal exchanges between the Trust office and the Parliamentary Agents before the instructions to Counsel were settled, possibilities were discussed which, as it turned out, foreshadowed further action forced on the Trustees almost twenty-five years later. There was little difference, the Trust argued, between members of the community housed, for example, by the New Towns Corporations, and those housed by the Trust. Was not the charitable status of such housing provided by Trusts itself an anomaly? If so, it would be reasonable to separate the Trust's housing activities into a distinct branch of the Trust which would have no endowment. In so far as it accumulated income not required for its housing purposes it could by deed of covenant pass it to the general Trust. The general Trust could not make grants to the housing Trust, save for specific purposes which were charitable; it could be empowered to make loans on terms as to interest and repayment which would be defined.

Without referring to possible solutions along these lines the instructions to Counsel did however deal with the problem of the charitable status of housing in some detail. The relevant passage in the paper for senior and junior Counsel concluded with this sentence:

> The Trustees accept that there may be some doubt as to whether the provision of housing and the development of village communities is a charitable purpose in law and they are concerned that there should be nothing in any Bill they may promote which might worsen their position and possibly lead to difficulties with the Inland Revenue.

Counsel surprised the Trust representative at the first conference held on 16 July by producing a draft clause defining the objects of the Trust. It was based on the assumption, and Counsel stressed its importance, that 'the main thrust of the new objects clause should be clearly in the same direction as that of the Founder's original initiative. In no other way could the Trustees succeed with their Bill'. The hope of a simple Carnegie-type clause was at that point abandoned. The draft clause, described to Trustees at the next meeting as 'a very skilful attempt indeed' to resolve by a single clause the difficulties which had beset the Trust for the past fifteen years, is reproduced in Appendix III.

The draft was presented as 'first thoughts' for the Trustees to consider. Sir Milner Holland drew attention to three points which seemed to him critical. He had defined the scope of the Trust as 'the public or any section of the public in the United Kingdom or elsewhere'. It would be unwise to attempt some new definition of 'the working classes' as in the original Deed of Foundation. 'The wider the community benefited', said Counsel, 'the more certainly is the Trust charitable'. Their wish to engage in social and allied research presented no difficulty, though Counsel warned: 'The Trust may forge any weapons it thinks appropriate, within its objects, but must not use them'. He continued in words relevant to current controversies, 'To advocate a course of action is not a charitable activity; and I so advise. You may collect any reports, you may publish them and bring them to the notice of those concerned with policy; indeed it would be your duty to do so. But to define and promote the policies you believe should be followed, and to use Trust resources for that purpose, is outside the scope of charity'. On the validity of the suggested housing powers counsel were unambiguous. They felt 'absolutely satisfied' that the provision of low cost housing was a charitable purpose in law. Sir Milner referred to elderly people who might have considerable financial resources but needed care and assistance in their living arrangements. 'Help to people who need help, is,' he said, 'in my opinion clearly a charitable purpose in law'.

On closer examination the Trustees found more cause for anxiety in the terms of the proposed objects clause. In the past the Trust's difficulties seemed to have arisen because the wide purposes defined by the Founder were later held to be restricted by reference to the narrower objects added by way of illustration; the saving introductory clause 'without prejudice to the generality of the foregoing', used now in Counsel's draft, did not seem to have been effective in the 1904 deed. Could the Trustees be sure that the examples given in later clauses did not in fact limit the interpretation of the general clause? Then the use of the term 'living condition' had been a fruitful source of dispute over the previous fifteen years. Did the addition of the words 'mode of life' overcome the problem. The Trustees were doubtful. They were troubled too by the use of the term 'housing trust' in defining their housing powers. A housing trust was already defined by statute; its powers were very limited and its application to the Trust might prove restrictive rather than helpful. The power to undertake research was related to the purpose of securing the best use of the Trust's resources – this was already in the original deed – and also those of 'other authorities and bodies having similar or cognate objects'. Would this enable the Trust to provide material relevant to the formation of policy or to conduct or initiate experimental work as they had in housing which might lead to more imaginative public provision?

All this was conveyed to the Parliamentary Agents on 21 July and, in a second set of instructions, to Counsel four days later. By 31 July came a joint Opinion dealing paragraph by paragraph with the points raised by the Trustees and with it a revised objects clause.

In the meantime the Chief Charity Commissioner had set aside time in his diary to discuss the clause with the Trustees, before his annual leave. He offered a number of suggestions for consideration by Counsel which he thought would be helpful in going still further to meet the wishes of the Trustees.

Whilst these discussions went forward on the objects clause, two other matters had to be considered. The name of the new Trust had to be settled. Senior Counsel at the first conference had advised a change; 'Village' no longer seemed appropriate to a Trust with such wide powers. His own view was that The Rowntree Foundation might be acceptable; curiously enough the Chief Charity Commissioner made the same point and came up with a suggested name: The Joseph Rowntree Foundation. This commended itself to the Trustees, who recognised, however, that the other Rowntree Trusts would need to be consulted.

The choice of name in fact raised two separate issues each made more difficult by consideration of the other. The advice to the Trustees from Counsel and from the Commissioners was that a name should be chosen which was unrelated to any particular field of work the Trust might explore. Thus 'Village' Trust was no longer appropriate. Members of the other Rowntree Trusts offered 'Housing and Research' as an acceptable alternative. Counsel advised strongly against this. One of the important objects in promoting private legislation was to broaden the work of the Trust; some emphasis had been given to housing in order to demonstrate continuity with the Founder's original purpose, but great care had been taken to ensure that this emphasis did not restrict the general powers of the Trust. If in the future the interpretation of the objects clause was again called into question, then the reference to housing in the name of the Trust, together with the emphasis given to it in the objects clause, might well prove embarrassing to the Trustees. A neutral title, along lines followed by most modern foundations, seemed important.

The second difficulty was that the most suitable neutral title – The Joseph Rowntree Charitable Trust – had already been appropriated at the outset by the second Rowntree Trust with charitable status, whose work had included research. The Chairman of that Trust expressed his opposition to a name such as The Joseph Rowntree Foundation but added: 'I say this with a due sense of appreciation that it is easy for us to sit pretty with the only really suitable name!'

The Trustees had met early in October in London for a weekend to review the development of their programme and to settle finally outstanding matters on their Bill which the Parliamentary Agents would then put in order for printing, and then deposit in the Public Bills Office of both Houses of Parliament. The name of the Trust had to be chosen. They sat at their final session after dinner in the lounge of the Cobourg Hotel in the Bayswater Road. A dozen possible names were discussed all of which raised objections mainly from the arguments advanced by counsel for a neutral title or from the susceptibilities of the sister Trusts. The Trustees had, a few years earlier, joined with others in establishing a Trust to aid mothers charged with the neglect of their children; the Trust was called the Elizabeth Fry Memorial Trust. The Trustees remembered the project; the Joseph Rowntree Memorial Trust was the name accepted by all.

The Trust's investment powers raised issues of public policy and were also of critical importance to the Trustees as holders of a substantial proportion of the ordinary shares in the Rowntree Company. A clause was drafted which followed precedents from Court decisions in stipulating the proportion of the Trust's investments to be held in 'wider' and 'narrower' range securities, but isolated the large Rowntree investment as a separate category.

Final instructions on these and other less important matters were delivered to Counsel at the end of the long vacation. On the last day allowed by Parliamentary procedure, 27 November, the Bill had been reprinted and deposited.

Three Departments of State intervened as the Bill began its progress through Parliament. The first was at the Trustees' initiative; they had undertaken to send to the Chief Charity Commissioner a copy of the Bill as deposited in Parliament. This they did, explaining in detail the action taken on the amendments he had suggested to the objects clause. Three days later he wrote expressing pleasure at the name the Trust had chosen; he had been very glad to be of assistance in the enterprise; he could find nothing in the Bill on which to comment; he would 'give every support within my province when the Bill is officially sent to us for comment'. It was the end of two years' continuous discussion with the Commissioners; sometimes Trustees and Commission had been deeply divided. If the outcome reflected a certain persistence on the part of the Trustees, it demonstrated much more the remarkably prompt and wholly constructive approach of the Commissioners to proposals which were not only novel but must have been unwelcome in the difficult issues of law and policy that they raised.

The second official intervention came from the Treasury Solicitor on 22 December. His Department raised three questions on the draft Bill. First, the objects clause had extended the geographical limits of the Trust's operations from the United Kingdom, as in the original Trust Deed, to the United Kingdom or elsewhere. It was a considerable extension! The Treasury Solicitor suggested that the word 'or elsewhere' might have to be removed as a condition which Parliament might impose for granting the further powers which the Trustees were seeking. If this were done, similar reference to the wider geographical area might without objection be added to the later part of the objects clause which was concerned with investigation and research, rather than with operational functions. Second, the Treasury Solicitor pointed out that the courts had worked out a practice for extending the investment powers of Trustees and 'usually authorise one-third of the funds to be invested in trustee securities and two-thirds in a wider range. In no case has the court sanctioned powers as wide as those proposed in the Bill'. Third, it was suggested that provision should be made in accordance with what was usual in investment schemes for the funds to be under continual review by experts. A copy of an investment scheme recently approved by the court was sent 'in case it may be of some assistance'. All three questions raised issues on which the Trustees believed their duty to the Trust and its Founder required them to seek powers and responsibilities different from those which experience and precedent ordinarily sanctioned. Members of the Treasury Solicitor's office, the Trust's Parliamentary Agent and representatives of the Trustees met on 21 January 1959, the latter very conscious that their convictions and their integrity were all they could deploy; a Bill opposed would be a Bill lost.

It was a remarkable meeting of minds. On the geographical limits for the Trust's operational work, all parties agreed that it would be reasonable in the light of the original intentions of the Founder to extend the Trust's operations from the United Kingdom to the Commonwealth, defined as 'all other territories within the Commonwealth and Empire or otherwise under the Queen's protection'. The power to undertake investigations without geographical limit remained.

On the supervision of investments, too, a solution was readily agreed. The Treasury accepted that the expertise available within the Trust was likely to be at least as great as that of a 'local stockbroker' which would have satisfied official requirements. A new clause in the Bill requiring the Trustees to appoint an Investment Committee met the views of both parties.

It was on the freedom of the Trustees to choose the way in which they would invest their assets that problems arose. The Parliamentary Agents, responding to the Trustees' instructions, had drafted a clause virtually giving full freedom of investment, without limit on the proportion of non-Trustee securities. This the Treasury Solicitor found unacceptable for a charitable trust.

The issue, therefore, was the way in which the proportion of non-Trustee securities should be calculated. It was common ground between the parties that the Trust's existing investment in Rowntree shares should not be affected. Was it, however, to be required that no further investment in Rowntree shares or any other equity should be made until the Trust had a holding in Trustee securities equal to not less than half the total equity investment, including the Rowntree holding? That would in practice preclude any further investment in Rowntree shares, or indeed in any other non-Trustee security. The Treasury Solicitor was understanding of the views on this matter expressed by the Founder that the Rowntree investment was of a special character; he agreed that the clause should make clear that any holding in Rowntree shares, whether original, present or future, should be excluded from any calculation as to the proportion of investments to be held in non-Trustee securities. The principle which each of the two parties felt had to be accepted was thus observed. The Trustees secured immediate powers to invest, if they so wished, in equity shares, including additional Rowntree shares; on the other hand the new clause met the Treasury Solicitor's reasonable view that if there were any encashment of Rowntree shares, then the investment of the resulting funds should be subject to the same limits on the proportion of non-Trustee securities as the courts and Parliament ordinarily required. Amendments to the Bill were drafted to meet these new requirements.

On 16 March the Secretaries' Office of the Board of Inland Revenue delivered a letter to the Parliamentary Agents. In the view of the Board the objects as defined in the Bill would not be charitable; the letter gave three reasons for their decision. 'I have therefore to advise you', the Inland

The main entrance
Red Lodge from
ich the windows of
flats look across the
atral green.

(b) The dining room and
lounge – this is so designed
as to project over the
central green and
children's playground, the
library and the swimming
pool.

The entrance to one
he self-contained flats
wing how the
rance corridor has
n designed and
ished.

PLATE 2
(a) Flats for single
people designed by
Swedish architects.
balcony on the first f
and the correspondi
terrace below are
designed to give priv
and are large enougl
be a useful extensio
the living area.

(b) The door from the
entrance hall is on the left;
the stair leads to the raised
bedroom above the
kitchen and bathroom.

(c) Here the door f
the entrance hall is or
right, the raised
bedroom with its
window is seen abov
sliding door to the
kitchen; on the left i
double-glazed door
the balcony.

In 1900 Poplar
ve was designed to
le residents and their
ors to reach the
ses on foot. Perhaps
ccasional horse and
used the village road.

(b)   By the 1930s a
pavement was found
necessary for the safety of
pedestrians and the road
was widened and made
suitable for motor traffic.
Pedestrians were thus
brought nearer to the
houses so that hedges for
privacy made their
appearance.

By 1970 the road
become inadequate
the volume of traffic
vas made to bear.
win's original design
s largely restored. A
v road for traffic was
lt at the rear of the
ses.

PLATE 4 (a) and (b) In Chestnut Grove changes similar to those in Poplar Grove were made.

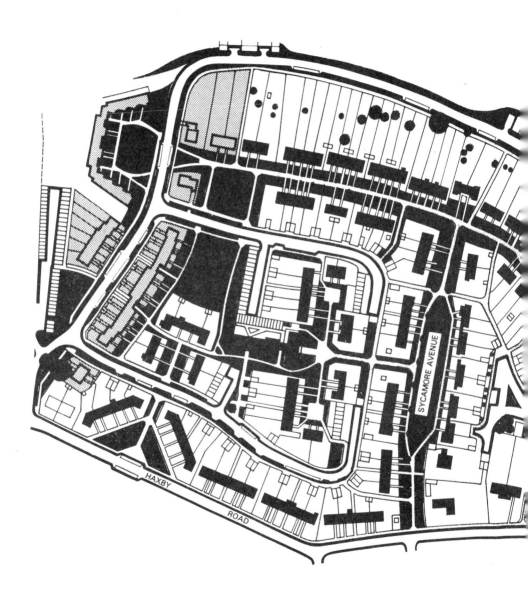

DATE DUE

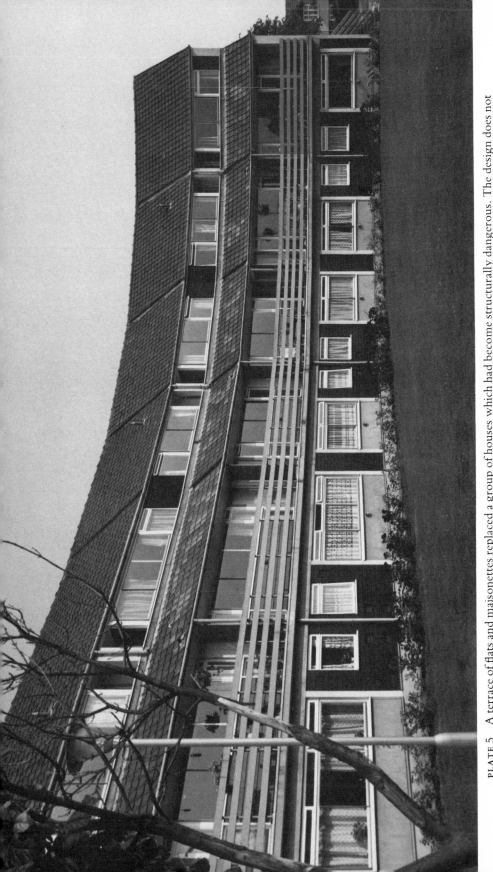

PLATE 5   A terrace of flats and maisonettes replaced a group of houses which had become structurally dangerous. The design does not repeat Unwin's elevations but is in harmony with them.

PLATE 6 (a) and (b)   The old timber roofed hall was built in 1907; with its small stage it remained virtually unchanged until 1968. It is now an entrance hall and a comfortable meeting place and coffee bar for all using the Folk Hall; the internal circular stairway gives access to a gallery, providing pleasant sitting out places, as well as access to other parts of the building.

PLATES 7 and 8 The swimming pool and library, deliberately designed in a modern style, adjoin the Folk Hall and share the facilities which it provides.

PLATE 8

Revenue letter concluded, 'that if the Bill is enacted in its present form it is the Board's view that the exemption from income-tax at present enjoyed by the Trust would have to be withdrawn. This is presumably not the result intended by your clients'. This was surely the under-statement of the Trust's half-century of life. The full text of the letter from the Board of Inland Revenue is printed as Appendix IV

The Board of Inland Revenue first challenged the definition of the Trust's proposed housing powers. 'In the present state of the law' they wrote 'they cannot be regarded as charitable'. Recent cases in the courts made clear, in the Board's view, that an element of 'poverty' was necessary to establish a claim to charitable status for a housing project. Second, the Bill seemed to allow the provision of recreational facilities for a class of persons who might not numerically constitute a sufficient section of the public. The requirement of 'public benefit' for recreational charities is, the Board maintained, specifically retained in the Recreational Charities Act. Third, a clause empowering the Trustees to facilitate the provision of employment for those for whom they provided homes would 'permit the Trustees to engage in non-charitable commercial enterprises for the relief of unemployment among inhabitants of their properties, and its purpose could not therefore be regarded as charitable'.

The Revenue letter forced the Trustees to make difficult and unwelcome decisions which were to distort the housing work of the Trust for the next twenty years and beyond. They compelled a series of further constitutional changes in the structure of the Trust which were continuing at the end of the twenty-five years to which this book relates. What perplexed the Trustees as laymen was that the terms of their Bill did not seem to be in question. The Bill had been introduced into the House of Lords as a Charity Bill, and had survived the scrutiny of the Treasury Solicitor, the Attorney General, the Lord Chairman of the Private Bills Committee and the Charity Commissioners, yet the acceptance of its terms by Parliament would not imply that the Trust's charitable status was also accepted. That critical issue would be settled by administrative decision after the legislature had defined the Trust's powers and that decision could be challenged only in the courts.

In discussion Sir Milner Holland confirmed his confidence in the outcome of any appeal to the courts against a ruling by the Board of Inland Revenue that the Trust was not as a result of the legislation established for charitable purposes. 'But', he said, 'when one considers the financial consequences for the Trust of an adverse decision, I must advise you to come to terms with the Inland Revenue'!

A meeting with a senior principal inspector from the Board of Inland Revenue, accompanied by a representative from the Charity (Claims) Department, was held on 28 April. The Trust was represented by the Parliamentary Agent and its Executive Officer. The issues discussed are of great importance to the Voluntary Housing Movement generally and foreshadow problems of policy with which associations were wrestling twenty-five years later. The text of the report made to the Trustees is therefore summarised in Appendix V. The outcome of the interview for the terms of the Trust's Bill is considered here.

Two or three questions affecting what the Trustees regarded as peripheral powers were easily disposed of by agreed amendments confirming the powers within the scope of charity as the Revenue interpreted it. Housing presented the really difficult problem. At this meeting was ended the hope that a clause could be drafted enabling a charitable Trust to engage in a wide range of housing provision in the interests of the community. Housing, as such, was, in the light of recent court decisions, no longer charitable. Housing, as defined in the objects clause, for people who needed it 'by reason of youth, age, infirmity, or disablement', was unlikely to be charitable. Special accommodation for millionaires with one leg would not be a charitable activity! The element of poverty must be present. The view was pressed that the Trust already had powers wider than those now proposed; it would be a Gilbertian situation to secure a Private Act but to have as a result more restricted powers than those formerly enjoyed. The reply was unequivocal. The Revenue tried to avoid interfering with established trusts. The Trust's present Deed would not be acceptable as establishing a charitable trust if presented at the present time. Many proposals for the establishment of charitable trusts with wide general housing powers were now being received; all were rejected. The Board of Inland Revenue took a broad view of what was ancillary to housing; dwellings for doctors, schoolteachers and others whose work was necessary to the life of a community could come within this provision. But the main purpose of the houses must relate to the relief of poverty.

The very real dilemma in which this would leave the Trustees was explained to the Revenue representatives. They had inherited a housing project which was regarded as charitable when it was developed, and which they still administered as part of their responsibilities. If the new powers were wide enough to embrace this work, the Revenue would withdraw tax exemption not only from the housing activity, for which it was unimportant, but from the whole Trust income. If on the other hand the powers were now limited to what was in law charitable, it must follow that the housing project would be *ultra vires*. The Trust's housing work was no longer, in fact, an object of expenditure of charitable funds (save for specific purposes which were beyond question charitable) but was a contributor to them. Hence the Trustees had no fear of a review of the charitable status of their housing work; but charitable status was essential for the Trust as a whole.

The Revenue wondered if this approach offered a solution to the problem. If the Trust's housing had become a source of income, the Revenue would be concerned with it only in so far as the income derived from it must be spent for a charitable purpose. It became a form of investment. An ideal solution, commented the Trust's Executive Officer, and one that had not escaped the notice of the Trustees. But the Treasury Solicitor would not regard this form of investment as appropriate for charitable funds. The Revenue sadly agreed. They agreed to consider the point and then consult with the Parliamentary Agent about the wording of the clause. It was again stressed that the concern of the Trustees was to establish a valid charitable trust having the wider powers in research to which no objection

had been raised. They would face subsequently, if the necessity arose, that some part of the housing project they had inherited might be held to be outside their powers; the matter had wide implications for housing trusts administering far larger estates than did the Trust. The Revenue representatives indicated their agreement with this view.

The outcome was that the Trust was limited in its housing work to those who needed it by reason of 'poverty, youth, age, infirmity or disablement'. The Revenue commented that if these amendments were made the revised objects clause would 'scrape through' for tax exemption purposes. That the administration and development of the Trust's existing housing estate was now outside their powers as a charitable trust presented a dilemma which would be unique in the housing world. The terms of the clause imposed by the Revenue which finally determined the scope of the Trust's housing powers is included in Appendix III. At once the authorities concerned with the passage of the Bill through Parliament were informed of the amendments and the subsequent stages in the Upper and Lower Houses completed. On 29 July 1959 the Bill received the Royal Assent. The Joseph Rowntree Memorial Trust was born.

The Chief Charity Commissioner, in his most encouraging moment, had said that if the Trustees were disposed to promote private legislation it would be likely to cost £3,500. On 30 September 1959, after all outstanding matters following the passage of the Act had been settled, the Parliamentary Agents sent their account. They had already settled for the professional services provided by senior and junior Counsel and paid the fees required by Parliament. The total account came to £1,469.10.1.

The Trustees met as the Joseph Rowntree Memorial Trust for the first time on 28 August 1959. At their next meeting on 11 December they appointed an investment committee in accordance with Section 6 of the new Act; under its provisions all investments of Trust funds had to be made by, or on the recommendation of, the new Investment Committee.

In 1960 the Charities Act became law. Its provisions followed the recommendations of the Nathan Committee and contained one clause which gave rise to some anxiety and on which representations were made on behalf of the Trust. The clause none the less passed into law without modification. Its effect was to prevent any body of Trustees, notwithstanding the powers given to them in the Trusts within which they operated, from spending money from the Trust resources in preparing a Bill or submitting it to Parliament save with the consent of the court or of the Charity Commissioners. Had this been in force two years earlier, would consent have been given to the Bill which the Trustees had promoted? Was the new clause introduced because of the precedent which the Trustees might be held to have established? The answers may never be known.

6   A Separate Housing Trust

In 1965 the Minister of Housing and Local Government introduced into Parliament a Rent Bill designed to give security of tenure to tenants of rented houses and to introduce a new method of determining a 'fair rent'. It was the Minister's intention to exclude housing associations and trusts from this new control. It had long been accepted that the Joseph Rowntree Village Trust was a housing association within the terms of the Housing Act 1936, and Counsel had so constituted the new Memorial Trust that the status was preserved. The Trust was also accepted as a housing trust in that it had devoted the whole, or substantially the whole, of its funds to housing.

The situation was now changed by the passage of the Joseph Rowntree Memorial Trust Act 1959. This authorised the Trustees to use their greatly enlarged resources not only in the restricted area of housing accepted by the Inland Revenue as charitable, but also in research and in a variety of other ways. For housing purposes the Trust remained a housing association; but because of its wider scope, could no longer claim to be a housing trust as defined by statute. Thus the effect of the new Rent Act, so the Trustees were advised, was to exclude the Trust from the new system of rent regulation in respect of properties which it built with subsidy as a housing association, but to leave it within the rent regulations procedure in respect of all other properties developed under its powers as a housing trust.

The point was brought to the attention of the Ministry of Housing and Local Government when the Bill was first published. The Ministry's enquiries confirmed that the Trust was unique in this respect. Efforts were made to find some way of amending the Rent Bill; this was found impossible save by adding a clause referring specifically to the Trust. The result would have been to produce a hybrid Bill, with procedural complexities which were not acceptable to the government.

This change threatened to add further difficulty to the Trust's housing work. Comparable properties on a single housing estate would be subject to quite different rules and procedures in any future rent revision; the movement of residents within the estate would be hindered, thus frustrating the best use of the available dwellings; the orderly redevelopment of the estate would similarly be more difficult; and the maintenance of a rational structure of rents over the estate as a whole would no longer be within the Trust's control.

Sir Milner Holland, the senior Counsel retained by the Trust when promoting the Private Act, was himself now involved in housing matters. He was Chairman of a Committee on Housing in Greater London, set up by the Minister of Housing and Local Government. The Trust again

sought his advice. He expressed the informal view that the Trustees would need to consider so dividing the Trust that its housing activities would be controlled by a separate Trust Deed which would comply fully with the statutory requirements for a housing trust in that the whole of its resources would be devoted to housing. The Trustees saw a possible further advantage in the separation of their housing interests. They were a charitable body which had inherited a housing project which was no longer a valid charity. The terms of their objects clause in their Private Act had been determined by the need to secure the Trust's charitable status, notwithstanding its extended powers, but this had been achieved at the cost of a highly restrictive clause defining their housing powers. The Finance Act of 1965 in effect now relieved housing associations from the payment of income-tax, profits-tax and corporation-tax. So far as the letting and maintenance of property was concerned, therefore, any financial advantage deriving from charitable status was removed. Did this indicate, the Trustees wondered, that in process of time, legislation might be introduced governing the activities of non–profit making housing associations generally? If such a change came, the Trust could take advantage of it only if its housing activities were separated from the administration of a large endowment used for much wider purposes.

Sir Milner advised that the Trustees should create a new charitable trust in which would be vested the same powers as those of the Memorial Trust in relation to housing. The new Trust would thus qualify as a housing association and a housing trust, and would enjoy the same exemption under the Rent Acts as did the Village Trust prior to 1959. If such a Trust were created, the Memorial Trust could transfer to it, with the consent of the Charity Commission, houses, land, and such other assets as seemed desirable.

He thought that since the passing of the Charities Act of 1960 a different view might be taken of the powers of a charitable housing trust in which case the opportunity could be taken to broaden the restrictive clause which had brought the Trust's housing work virtually to an end. Because of these new possibilities the view of the Charity Commissioners should be sought.

The Charity Commissioners accepted that the Trustees had a duty to restore the status of the Trust as a housing trust and thus repair the damage resulting from new housing legislation. They believed that there were wider grounds for this than the immediate need to seek exemption from rent regulation. Future legislation would be likely to apply only to housing trusts as now defined, so that it was plainly right to restore this lost status as soon as possible. But they were unwilling to consider any extension to the Trust's housing powers as settled by Parliament in 1959.

A Scheme giving effect to these limited proposals came into operation on 1 January 1968. The assets transferred to the new Trust were the real property used for housing purposes, together with a sum of money as working income, equal to the amount of the repairs reserve standing in the accounts of the Memorial Trust. The Trustees of the new Trust were the Trustees for the time being of the parent Trust. The powers of the Trust were those housing powers possessed by the parent Trust under the

Private Act; no further extension was found possible if charitable status was to be preserved. The problems arising from the incompatibility between those powers and the housing project that history had left in the hands of the Trustees remained unresolved.

On 13 October 1967, the Trustees had met representatives of their tenants and explained the change that was being made and the reasons for it. On 1 January 1968, the Joseph Rowntree Memorial Housing Trust began its work. More than sixty years had passed since the Village Trust was set up by Joseph Rowntree in 1904. The burden of his charge to his Trustees had been that they should constantly move to fields of work, relevant to a different time, the demands of which he made no claim to foresee. The Trustees who more than fifty years later came into this inheritance, and had to consider how to discharge the duty laid on them, were surely right, when all other efforts failed, to carry to the bar of Parliament their appeal to be allowed to fulfil their Founder's intentions as they conceived them. Looking at the design of three complementary Trusts, all of which became permanent by using the powers the Founder deliberately gave, it is impossible to deny that other ways of responding to changing needs could have been chosen. The final chapter in this book returns to this theme.

How effectively the Trustees used the powers they had been granted to deploy the growing resources available to them will appear from the account of their work after 1959. The powers for which they fought to extend beyond their original field of housing have proved adequate for all they have wanted to do. The control over their investments for which they secured the agreement of the Treasury Solicitor has been used with skill and success as the account of the Trust's finances will show. The attempt to secure power to implement a rational and progressive housing programme failed; a succession of skilful improvisations has enabled much to be done and has ensured a continuing impact on housing policy and practice. Discussions with the Board of Inland Revenue after the Trust's Bill became law established a workable understanding; the Trust was able to manage and develop competently the considerable estate developed during its first fifty years notwithstanding the decision that it could no longer be regarded as a charitable activity. New projects within the estate which seemed to raise special difficulty were the subject of separate negotiation; in no case were the Trustees proposals rejected. Outside that original project the narrow limits of housing open to the Trust were enforced; by 1979 the problems this presented had become the problems of the voluntary housing movement as a whole; at least the Trust's experience of frustrated effort enabled it to take a leading part in the wider negotiations and litigation that were set on foot. They are now part of a different story.

Part II *A New Direction for the Trust's Housing Work*

7 New Earswick – the Postwar Dilemma

The building of homes and communities was to remain a central part of the Trust's activities. That conclusion is clear from the turbulent and prolonged debate about the Trust's powers to provide homes which had marked the period of constitutional reconstruction just described.

In the second in the series of triennial reports published between 1960 and 1978 the task presented by the New Earswick estate, planned and begun before the turn of the century, is thus described:

> All the houses completed before 1914 have required substantial modernisation and this programme continues. The problem which will soon face the Trust will be the replacement of the earliest houses which, however attractive their elevations, will inevitably fail to satisfy the demands of a new generation with different ideas and standards. The programme of modernisation is being planned as far as possible to give present residents up-to-date facilities, without committing the Trust to expenditure which will prove unremunerative should a general development of the early part of the estate be undertaken within the next few years.[1]

This marked the end of the latest period of development at New Earswick launched in 1946, when proposals for an entirely new role for the Trust were indefinitely postponed. More important, it marked the beginning of a new period of growth and renewal which changed the face of the estate, and equipped it to anticipate without shame the approach of the centenary of its foundation. 1948 could be regarded as the low point in the Trust's housing enterprise. In October of that year, the Trustees considered a paper arguing the case for some new housing initiatives. No building had taken place since 1936. A community planned around a central folk hall had been deprived of further growth, with the centre still at the periphery. The hall itself, remarkable when it was planned in 1907, was ill-fitted for the activities of a postwar community. Houses which had made history in their design and setting, when planned by Raymond Unwin earlier in the century for the low-income family of that period, were now accepted by tenants only as a last resort and because an acute housing shortage left little choice. A bathroom, tolerable heating, and floors on which carpets could be laid, were now essentials and not novelties. Ninety-eight per cent of the houses had three small bedrooms; increasing numbers of these family

[1] Second Report of the Joseph Rowntree Memorial Trust, 1961–3.

homes were occupied by one elderly person. A new programme of building and improvement was essential, the Trustees were advised, unless New Earswick was to become a museum of distinguished work of historical interest rather than the living community of which the Founder of the Trust had written.

The application to the Trust's housing work of the Founder's advice to his Trustees had, in fact, presented them with a dilemma. Even after the building and improvement programme briefly described in *One Man's Vision* had been accepted, Seebohm Rowntree, then nearing his eightieth year, on three occasions – in 1948, 1950 and 1951 – questioned whether his colleagues were right to build new houses when they had no new ideas, whether in planning or house design, to demonstrate. Reluctantly he accepted that whatever the Founder had said about new duties for new occasions, the Trustees had continuing responsibilities to those who had become their tenants; indeed, his colleagues argued that the adaptation of the estate to the needs of a new age might itself provide opportunity for work which would be of use to others faced with comparable problems.

There were other more compelling pressures. Under postwar legislation the Trust was accepted as a housing trust. As such, its Trustees were entitled to government subsidies, and were expected to take their part, as owners of land ripe for development, in meeting the grave housing shortage. They were plainly told that if they did not wish to build on the land they held, then it could be purchased compulsorily by local authorities who needed land for their housing programmes. There could be no doubt about the reality of the conflict facing Trustees now seeking a national role in the field of social research and experiment, but also the inheritors of a distinguished, and in some respects unique, tradition in the planning and design of homes and neighbourhoods.

By 1952 the Trustees and their advisers were increasingly aware that the work they had initiated since 1948 was too limited to be an adequate response to the problems of their estate. They received a second report on every aspect of the New Earswick estate; the population structure, the ill-equipped houses, the provision for community needs and the organisation providing for the representation of those who occupied the houses the Trust had built.

Some new decisions relating to each of these issues were made. More radical changes to the older houses were approved and a timetable agreed for the completion of the programme. Mr Louis de Soissons, RA, the Trustees' consultant architect, discussed these matters with the Trust's Executive Officer. He was blunt. The Trustees, he said, were anxious to do what they called pioneer work. In fact, the new buildings they were now constructing made no contribution to housing progress either in their layout or design. He thought the Trustees were not themselves aware of the new developments taking place in the postwar period. He offered to help in the arrangement of a series of educational visits by the Trustees to places where, in his view, work of unusual merit in housing was in progress. Discussions were set on foot with the tenants' representative council which were to lead to an independent study of the community facilities in New Earswick; this in turn led to constitutional change and to a

reconstruction of the Folk Hall more radical than any of the parties to the discussions contemplated or even wished. New building, modernisation and community provision; these encompassed the structure and life of the New Earswick estate. After the 1952 paper each was subjected to increasingly urgent and radical review as Trustees took the measure of the task they had inherited. A brief review of the story of each will bring the Trust's housing record up-to-date; it will show how the tiny housing project, begun with imagination and foresight before the dawn of the twentieth century, was completed and renewed seventy-five years later to offer homes and an environment comparing favourably with the best practice in the last quarter of that century.

Having become convinced of the scale of their problem, the Trustees set about their own education with thoroughness and enthusiasm. Under the direction of Mr de Soissons, and sometimes in his company, they spent time in the new towns at Harlow and Welwyn, combining the latter with a shorter visit to Hatfield. In the north, they travelled on separate occasions to Peterlee and Newton Aycliffe. They were concerned with site planning, with the design of houses, with provision for the elderly and for single persons, with community facilities and the representative organisations which administered them. Apart from these personal visits, they encouraged their Executive Officer to see comparable housing and community work in Holland, Denmark, Sweden, Norway and the United States. They enquired about innovations in Britain which seemed to have lessons for parts of their work; they sought reports from their advisers on Isleden House, a scheme by the City Parochial Foundation which combined independent living for the elderly with a range of services ordinarily found only in fully residential homes, and on an updated almshouse development in Sturminster Newton. There an imaginative housing manager, anticipating by years the idea of sheltered housing, had persuaded her authority to design and build groups of dwellings in which the support of a warden, and the provision of limited catering, had reduced the need for residential homes for the elderly; the county welfare authority as a result broke new ground by contributing to the housing authority's expenditure on the support services. This period of investigation, the outcome of a certain frustration with their imposed commitment to a housing enterprise, proved fruitful in the Trust's postwar development. It helped to identify the opportunities for progressive work still available in their small estate; it suggested the issues in housing and related social fields in which a Trust with independent resources could initiate or support research directed to the shaping of social policy; it led to new initiatives in housing in the city of York and beyond. A constructive relationship was developed between the Trust's housing work and its research programme which again brought the Trust into the forefront of progress in housing policy and practice.

The first conclusion to which the enquiry led was a negative one. Seebohm Rowntree had been right when he had argued from 1945 onwards that the continued building of new family houses was no longer a proper use of Trust resources. The work should be undertaken only as a necessary part of the management of a housing estate; the houses built

should be examples of good modern practice but there was no reason to suppose that the Trust would discover new principles of design, or novel ways to use new materials, which had not occurred to the research and development teams proliferating in government, in local authorities and in public corporations.

Positively the Trustees set themselves five objectives. Accepting that there would be no material increase in the size of the New Earswick estate, they should progressively move to a better balance of accommodation, so that the different and changing needs of residents could be met within a neighbourhood in which many would wish to remain. Second, and within this general requirement, they should seek to raise the quality of living for the elderly. Third, something better should be offered to the single person seeking a home than the four furnished flats with shared facilities at that time available on the estate. Fourth, in planning new dwellings for these different purposes, the limited life of the earliest part of the estate – though of the greatest historical interest – must be accepted. The quotation from the Trust's second report with which this chapter opened records this decision. Then fifth, the Trustees should accept the implications of their unintended role as the effective public authority in an entire parish. They owned almost all the dwellings, they provided street lighting, repaired the streets, provided and maintained the sewage disposal plant, and continued their predecessors' concern for the well-being of the community. That concern had led earlier Trustees to design and build schools as well as a Folk Hall, and to provide sports fields. Some, but not all, of these responsibilities should now be transferred to public authorities. But the Trustees themselves should look again at the provision for the community that earlier Trustees had made, and be ready to rebuild both physical structures and representative organisations to foster the self-governing communities which it had been the Trust's purpose to create.

A table published in *One Man's Vision* showed the number of dwellings

Table 7.1 *Number of houses of various sizes at New Earswick*

	1946	1948	1951	1954	1980
Bed-sitting rooms	—	—	7(1.3)	7(1.1)	57(7.0)
Furnished flats for single people	4(0.8)	4(0.8)	4(0.7)	4(0.6)	3(0.3)
1 bedroom houses or flats	—	12(2.2)	14(2.6)	32(5.1)	96(11.8)
2 bedroom houses or flats	1(0.1)	1(0.1)	10(1.8)	47(7.5)	197(24.2)
3 bedroom houses	482(93.2)	482(91.2)	482(88.1)	498(79.4)	418(51.3)
4 bedroom houses	20(3.9)	20(3.8)	20(3.7)	30(4.8)	38(4.7)
5 bedroom houses or larger	10(2.0)	10(1.9)	10(1.8)	10(1.5)	6(0.7)
	517(100)	529(100)	547(100)	628(100)	815(100)

Figures in brackets show the number of each type of house expressed as a percentage of all houses in the village.

of each type on the estate, expressed also as a percentage of all houses in the village. The progress towards a more balanced community – the first objective – can be shown by giving this same information for the years 1946, 1948, 1951, 1954, and 1980 (see Table 7.1). Thus can be seen the impact of the new building which has followed the policy decisions taken in 1952, and of the demolitions and reconstructions that have been part of the modernisation of the earlier part of the estate. That process has virtually ended; the table therefore shows the shape of the estate in the final quarter of the Trust's first century.

Homes for the Elderly

The needs of elderly people in New Earswick had been the concern of the Trustees when first considering their postwar policy. In 1945 Seebohm Rowntree had drawn attention to the number of family houses occupied by an elderly person or a couple, simply because nothing more convenient was available. For those needing more support, the local authority home some thirty miles away was often the only choice. So in 1948 twelve bungalows were built; a warden could be called by any of the residents in an emergency. It was the Trust's first postwar housing venture. Later a large house was adapted in which fully residential accommodation was provided, in co-operation with the welfare authority, for four or five people. Then a farmhouse – the Garth – was adapted to provide nine bed-sitting rooms with a common lounge and dining room. This much had been accomplished by the time of the Trust's Jubilee in 1954 and is recorded in *One Man's Vision* published in that year.

Experience in managing the Garth seemed to show that a number of residents there might have continued a more independent life if more help and support had been available to them. There was evidence, too, that the absence of the mental and physical stimulus which responsibility for a personal dwelling provides may contribute to the helplessness which mars the later years of so many. The Trust therefore embarked on a new project using the experience of the group dwellings in Sturminster Newton, and lessons drawn from the design of a comparable scheme in Lidingo, Sweden. What was needed was a group of independent dwellings with enclosed – and warmed – access to a dining room for the residents at the Garth and for those living in the new dwellings who would use it for the main meal of the day. Only a single catering service for the two schemes would enable the Trust, at reasonable cost, to offer the service in a community as small as New Earswick. It was critical, in the view of the Trust at that time, that the cost of this meal, as well as heat and hot water, should be part of the rent, so that residents had no need to make a daily decision whether they could afford to pay for the meal. The 'warmed street' leading to the dining room – and this was an important feature of the Swedish plan which had interested the Trustees – should also be a concourse; residents could meet there and sit together in comfort when they so wished, but withdraw to the privacy of their home at will. A simple system of master and sub-master keys ensured that the same key

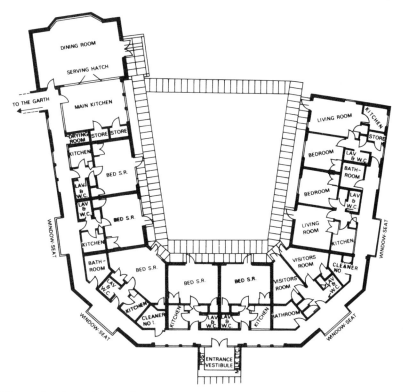

Figure 1 Garth Court – here elderly residents can be sure of timely help when needed, and relief from housework, but are not deprived of the privacy and independence of home.

opened the front door to the concourse but was private to each resident's front door. Figure 1 shows how the requirements were met. For some years this little scheme, known as Garth Court, probably gave more satisfaction than any other amenity provided on the estate. The capital cost was contributed by the Trust, for the scheme did not fall within any public provision for the needs of the elderly. There was a small housing subsidy because the dwellings were self-contained for the purpose of the then current legislation on housing for the elderly. The welfare authority made an annual contribution because the demand for accommodation in its homes was likely to be reduced. The National Assistance Board, later the Supplementary Benefits Commission, anxious to encourage such developments, brought together a variety of allowances so that an elderly person dependent on a retirement pension could meet the charge in the new dwellings and still have a balance of income sufficient for clothing and for the meals the residents provided for themselves.

During the next fifteen years a lot of experience was gained and much research undertaken into ways of meeting the needs of older people. Sheltered housing – independent flats with access to a warden and varying common services – became an essential part of the work of housing

authorities and the exclusive interest of some large and vigorous housing associations. At New Earswick there seemed to be a reduced need for the fully residential accommodation at the Garth, but a growing demand for the flats in Garth Court. The Trustees believed that the provision of the main meal of the day was an important element in the New Earswick scheme; it was unusual elsewhere, and this might perhaps explain in part the problems of later infirmity which troubled those building and managing the more usual types of sheltered housing. Problems of cost were greater now than when the Garth Court was planned. The idea emerged that perhaps the Trust should build a much larger group of self-contained flats, and this time provide catering and other services, not only for the residents, but for elderly people in the neighbourhood coming to a day centre built as part of the complex; the same catering service might also meet the demand for meals on wheels in the area. Red Lodge was the outcome.

There are thirty-two flats, comparable to the sheltered housing being built elsewhere. This time each flat is self-contained. It was thought when Garth Court was planned that bathrooms should be separate so that help could be given to the more infirm. Experience taught that the convenience of a self-contained flat outweighed whatever practical difficulties there might be in providing help with bathing. A central kitchen has the capacity to meet the needs of those residents who choose to take a midday meal, other elderly people in the neighbourhood for whom a luncheon club is a valued convenience, and those who are served by meals on wheels. The neighbourhood benefits also from a launderette which is part of the day centre accessible to the physically handicapped as well as to the elderly.

The finance of the scheme proved no less complicated than that of Garth Court built fifteen years earlier. The thirty-two flats could now be wholly financed by housing association grant under the terms of the 1974 Housing Act. Under its provisions fair rents are assessed by the Rent Officer; that part of the capital cost which cannot be serviced from these rents is met by housing association grant. The cost of the day centre – some £120,000 – fell upon the Trust. The days when the Trust provided capital for building from its income were past; it contributed £25,000, and was grateful to the Hayward Foundation for a grant of £50,000 and to Rowntree Mackintosh Limited, who contributed £35,000. The county welfare authority took responsibility for the day to day cost of staffing the day centre, from which it is able to administer its own services for the elderly and other groups needing support in the area.

The need which such a project met was evident from the demand for the flats and the manifest satisfaction which residents experienced from the combination of security and independence. Plate 1 shows the high standard of decorations and furnishing which the Trustees thought to be essential if full benefit was to be obtained from the large capital investment of public and private funds. Indeed within three years it became clear that the catering and other facilities in the day centre could serve a larger resident population; an extension is therefore under construction which will add thirty-one new flats. In the whole complex, fourteen flats are for couples

and forty-nine for single people. There are three guest rooms and two flats for resident staff. The table of accommodation in New Earswick on page 50 includes in the figures for 1980 the flats in this new extension. The Trustees formed the view, however, that the benefits obtained by expenditure on this scale for sheltered housing and for day centres ought to be more carefully assessed and that the experience of other associations and authorities should also be studied. This was the starting point for the Sheltered Housing Project at the University of Leeds described later.

Flats for Single People

The Trust had been alive to the needs of older people since its first postwar building development in 1948. For the single person in business or professional work only four furnished flats with shared bathrooms and toilets had been available. These were so obviously unsatisfactory that they were demolished to make way for the Red Lodge development described above. The design of Garth Court was heavily influenced by lessons learned in Sweden; the first scheme for single people was not only influenced by Swedish experience but, with the consent of the Trust's consultant architect, was actually designed and equipped by Swedish architects using for the most part fittings from Sweden to which they were accustomed. The features of the building which justified this unusual partnership are shown in Plate 2.

Modernising the Earliest Homes

A new building programme to meet specific needs was the first outcome of the period of intensive investigation and study. The second was the modernisation of the existing dwellings, starting with those built between 1898 and 1913. Typically, the ground floor of these houses consisted of a kitchen-living room with a solid fuel cooking range; a scullery with a copper, and a bath under a hinged table; a large store and, outside the garden door, a w.c. Upstairs were three bedrooms. Thus the kitchen was the only room with a water supply whether for food preparation, domestic use or the family's ablutions. By postwar standards, they were inadequate and inconvenient; their disadvantages were no more easily borne because Unwin had given them an elevation and a setting of quite unusual quality.

   The earliest attempts to provide some minimum additional convenience for residents were unimaginative and damaging to the longer term interests of the estate. A small bedroom was converted to a bathroom. This usually involved no more than fitting a washbasin and a bath; a bedroom was sacrificed to provide a still unsatisfactory bathroom. With the introduction of improvement grants in 1949, the changes became a little more ambitious. The large store on the ground floor was used as the bathroom, though the w.c. remained outside; the scullery, cleared of the copper and bath, became a more useful kitchen; and the range in the living room gave

way to a modern solid fuel cooker and water heater. Still later the store was extended to provide space for the washbasin and bath and also to incorporate the w.c. Various devices then had to be planned to ensure that there was a ventilated lobby adequate to satisfy public health requirements separating the kitchen from the new bathroom. Figure 2 shows the best results which these changes produced.

The changes relieved the most urgent disadvantages under which families living in these houses laboured, but they gave little pleasure either to residents or Trustees. It was little wonder therefore that the Trustees recorded their conviction that the problem which would soon face them would be the replacement of the earliest houses, however attractive their elevations might be. Those living in the forty earliest houses were told that within a few years they must expect that their homes would be demolished and replaced.

There were two anxieties over this decision. First those forty houses were the first demonstration by Raymond Unwin of the ideas about orientation, footpath access and separation of traffic which he later developed at Letchworth and elsewhere. The elevations of the houses were among the finest in Britain for dwellings designed for the needs of the lowest paid workers at the turn of the century. Was there no other choice than demolition, or preservation as part of an architectural museum? If they were to be replaced, what could the Trustees hope to design? They had already accepted the conclusion that it was not within the purpose of the Trust to continue to build when there was nothing of significance which they could contribute to the examples of house design and site planning that they had visited and studied. So Unwin's distinctive terraces would at best be replaced by examples of good current practice.

The Unilever Company at Port Sunlight was facing a similar problem. It was more intractable because the earliest houses there were listed, and demolition was not permitted. An imaginative surveyor had embarked on modernisation of a more radical sort than anything which had been thought possible at New Earswick. After a first exchange of visits, the Port Sunlight surveyor was invited to re-plan a typical New Earswick house that was vacant, and thus demonstrate his conviction that a fully-acceptable modern home could be produced within Unwin's elevations. Residents of the estate were invited to see the modernised house and their views were recorded. The outcome seemed sufficiently encouraging to warrant further experiment. At a meeting of Trustees, the Port Sunlight surveyor carried conviction by his enthusiasm for a project offering a further useful life for the properties under sentence of demolition. Indeed his analysis of the Trust's task was more persuasive than the example offered by the building he had converted. He warned the Trustees that the changes he was advocating would be resisted by the older residents but would be welcomed by the young. That conclusion was confirmed when, later, a systematic survey of opinion on the estate was made by an independent research organisation. His analysis showed that the older houses had an unusually large total area, of which only a part was usable living space. What he called the 'machinery' of the house took up much of the rest. Therein lay the possibility of radical improvement, for modern

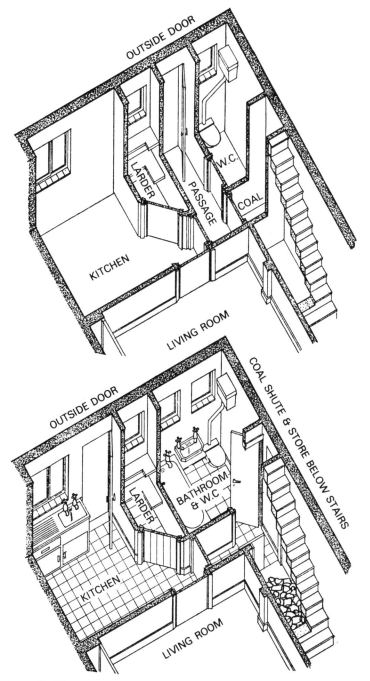

Figure 2 These drawings show one way of giving to an early house the convenience of a bathroom. There is a ventilated passage dividing it from the kitchen.

equipment occupied less space thus liberating more of the house for family use. The living room in the early houses was large; it seemed small because the absence of any entrance hall or lobby meant that part of the room around the front door had to meet that need; then the cooking range with its massive chimney breast further reduced the living area.

With the death of Mr Louis de Soissons in September, 1962 and also of the local architect who had worked with him, the Trustees looked for professional advice to Mr Richard Fraser, the partner in Mr de Soissons firm who had already been responsible for much of the detailed work at the village. He was invited to visit Port Sunlight, to study the whole of Unwin's early development, and to consider the practicability of the thorough modernisation of the individual houses and the adaptation of their environment to meet present day traffic needs.

His report is one of the Trust's historic documents. It established three facts about the estate that Unwin built between 1898 and 1913. First, a home conforming in every respect to the standards the Trust would be required to observe in a new dwelling could be built within the existing elevations, if a sufficiently radical re-arrangement was made. Second, within each house, more usable space would be available to the family than there was in the original design. Third, a reduction in the size of some of the very large gardens would allow a new traffic route to be built; the existing tree-lined roads would become attractive pedestrian ways; a garage could be provided for each home within a few yards of its boundary; adequate spaces would be left for parking by visitors or tradesmen.

Once again a vacant house was converted to show the possibilities of the architect's ideas. It was furnished, and opened at weekends for inspection. The views of visitors were noted. Within a few months the decision to demolish the area had been revoked; the modernisation of both homes and environment was to proceed without delay. Figures 3 and 4 show the new site plan, compared with the old, and the re-planned interior of a typical house is shown in Figures 5 and 6. Plates 3 and 4 show the effect of the new site plan on two of the earliest roads.

For this relatively small area, it was possible to hold meetings of the residents at which the implications could be explained and individual preferences decided. The Trust was able to offer a transfer to another house which would be a new permanent home, or a temporary move, with the right to re-occupy the previous home after the changes were completed.

Deliberately, discussion about the application of similar plans to the entire area built before 1914 was delayed until the first project was largely completed and residents could form a view of the result. Confidence in the architect's work was strengthened when in 1973 a national award for good design in housing was received for the environmental aspects of the first stage in the re-development of the estate. By 1970 a first plan showing a new pattern of streets for the rest of the pre-1914 estate was completed. New traffic routes, pedestrian access to houses and accessible garage space for each house were achieved. The same standards of space and convenience were applied in the re-planning of individual homes. This time the process of consultation was more difficult and more prolonged. A newly

constituted village association provided a channel of communication and ensured that replies intelligible to a layman were given to suggestions made by residents. But there were also public meetings, plans were on permanent display, pressure groups emerged to advance a particular view or to oppose a particular part of the plan. For one small area, four different site plans were drawn to meet the views expressed; it is beyond question that the final plan was in important respects improved from the original proposals as a result of this vigorous consultation and debate.

But the quality of the different contributions to such a debate is not necessarily measured by the insistence or force with which they are presented. Not all residents were able to attend public meetings and some who attended did not have the confidence to catch the chairman's eye and claim the attention of the meeting. So before final decisions were made, the Trustees thought that every adult person living on the estate should have an opportunity to express a view. The village association agreed to co-operate in the venture, provided that the results were made freely available without comment or interpretation by Trustees or their advisers. British Market Research Bureau were commissioned towards the end of 1970 to prepare a questionnaire which was itself discussed by both Trustees and association. The interview at which the questionnaire was completed lasted about an hour; almost every adult resident, apart from a small number who were ill or away from home, took part; ninety per cent of those affected by the proposals gave their help in the enquiry. The report was sent to the Trustees and to the village association; copies were available for any who wished to read it, and a summary of the essential points was published in the bulletin sent to each home. The report was critical of the method used by the Trustees to assess the views of residents. They had relied too much, the investigators argued, on public meetings which were attended for the most part by those committed to a particular view; more time should have been spent in discussion with separate households if the problems which were concerning individuals were to be identified and understood.

It was clear beyond doubt that almost everybody liked the modernised houses – the strongest support came from those who were living in them. But there were detailed changes suggested which were helpful to future plans.

The need to protect the environment from the intrusion of cars was rarely questioned. But residents were divided on the methods which were being adopted, and indeed, on whether the object could be achieved. Here younger people welcomed radical change more than did the older; many were apprehensive that the village they had known would lose the qualities they most valued.

For many the immediate practical problems loomed large. How could the disruption of moving house – and the expense – be overcome? Would the changes in the gardens, which were the price to be paid for new traffic access and pedestrian ways, leave enough choice for those who wanted larger or smaller gardens – and what would be the effect on privacy?

Some of these doubts were resolved as the plans unfolded. Some could be answered only when the modernisation was complete and would

benefit future planners rather than present residents. When that stage was approaching in 1980, Mr Keiji Makino from Japan launched a new study as part of a review of the work of Unwin and Parker, undertaken in the first place as a diploma thesis for the Institute of Advanced Architectural Studies of the University of York (*Research for Conservation*, Joseph Rowntree Memorial Trust, 1980). His reports, with that of the British Market Research Bureau prepared ten years earlier (*The Modernisation of New Earswick*, Joseph Rowntree Memorial Trust, 1971), will provide a virtually unique before and after study of the re-building of a community.

Immediately, the result of the British Market Research Bureau study was that the modernisation scheme, involving a move from home by every family, changes in the size and arrangement of gardens, and a quite new pattern of streets and pedestrian ways, could now go forward without serious controversy. Moreover planners and administrators knew that when the time came for personal arrangements to be discussed with families affected by the next phase of modernisation, no new arguments needed to be deployed; attention could be concentrated on reducing the inconvenience which such changes bring. The scale of those changes can be seen from the plan of the area, printed on the end papers at the beginning and end of this book, showing streets, pathways and gardens before and after the reconstruction.

The physical impact of the modernisation of New Earswick has been so great that it is not easy to bring into perspective its social and philosophical implications. The Founder's emphatic disapproval of the pursuit of any activity 'after it has ceased to be vital and pressing in the interests of the community' seemed to apply to houses already built, as it did to enterprises of other kinds. Once convinced of their inadequacy to meet present day needs, the Trustees' decision to demolish them seemed right and inevitable. When a similar situation was faced at an out-dated Folk Hall, one Trustee wrote, 'What the Founder would have done would have been to demolish it and begin again in a way appropriate to a different age'. But injunctions followed without discrimination can themselves be irrelevant in a different age. It was the almost chance discovery of work in progress at Port Sunlight that averted the demolition of Unwin's pioneer work and enabled the Trust to create from the first neighbourhood he designed in 1896, dwellings and environment adequate for the needs of the 1980s.

The long and thorough consultations with residents affected by the proposals brought results more fruitful than any of those concerned thought possible. It is no light matter to ask a family to leave their home for six months; to reconstruct it; to change the size and shape of its garden, to deprive it of familiar road access; and to offer only the moving expenses as compensation. Yet despite the highly orchestrated opposition of a few, ninety per cent of the residents gave serious thought to the longer term issues, discussed them with independent investigators and gave their full co-operation in carrying the proposals out. Would the same result have been achieved without all the debate and expensive consultation? The plans were certainly improved. Personal interests were more effectively respected whilst public interests did not suffer. In retrospect, the actual changes in the architect's proposals were small: was it the time and trouble

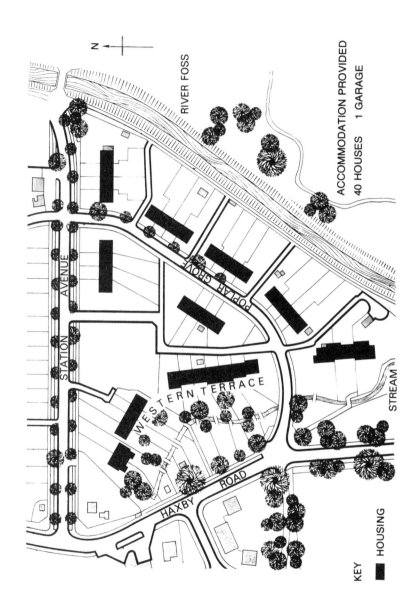

N

RIVER FOSS

STATION AVENUE

POPLAR GROVE

WESTERN TERRACE

HAXBY ROAD

STREAM

ACCOMMODATION PROVIDED
40 HOUSES   1 GARAGE

KEY

■ HOUSING

N

RIVER FOSS

STATION AVENUE

WESTERN TERRACE

HAXBY ROAD

STREAM

14 15 16

FINAL DEVELOPMENT

TO CLOSE POPLAR GROVE AND
LANDSCAPE THE AREA

ACCOMMODATION PROVIDED

40 HOUSES 12 FLATS 52 GARAGES
23 PARKING SPACES 49 DRYING LINES
48 TENANTS' STORES

(CLOTHES DRYING AND TENANTS'
STORES FOR 14, 15, 16
WESTERN TERRACE ARE WITH HOUSES)

KEY

■ HOUSING (2 STOREY) S TENANTS' STORES
■ 3 STOREY FLATS

G GARAGES S TENANTS' STORES
P OFF STREET PARKING
D CLOTHES DRYING LINES

Figures 3 and 4   Original and present day site plans of the Poplar Grove area built before 1900.

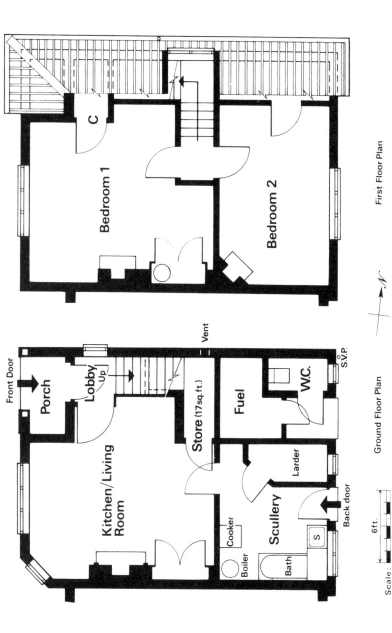

Figure 5 Plan ot house as built – the use of space in the 1902 plan was related to the pattern of living of a wage earning family at that time. Usable space was also restricted by the methods then available for heating.

Within the image:

- Front Door
- Porch
- Lobby — Up
- Kitchen/Living Room
- Store (17 sq. ft.)
- Vent
- Cooker
- Boiler
- Scullery
- Bath
- S
- Larder
- Fuel
- W.C.
- S.V.P.
- Back door

Ground Floor Plan

- C
- Bedroom 1
- Bedroom 2

First Floor Plan

Scale: 6 ft.

N

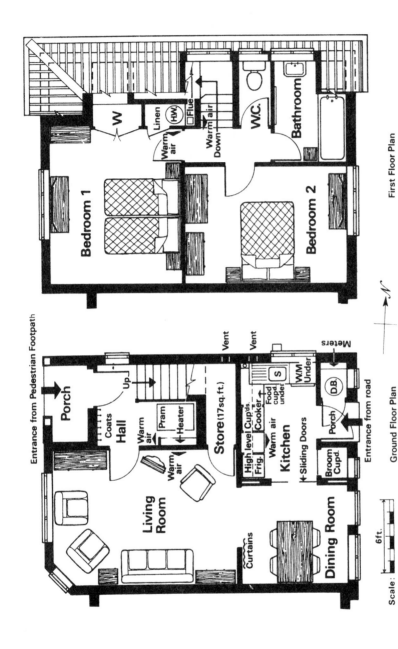

Figure 6 Plan of modernised house – within the same elevation the usable living area has been increased to take the fittings and furniture appropriate to a changed style of living. The new plan complied in every respect with the requirements of the Parker-Morris Report.

First Floor Plan

Ground Floor Plan

Entrance from Pedestrian Footpath

Porch

Coats

Hall

Warm air

Warm air

Living Room

Curtains

Store (17 sq. ft.)

Vent

Vent

High level Cupds.

Frig.

Cooker

Food cupd. under

Warm air

Kitchen

Sliding Doors

Broom Cupd.

Porch

S

WM Under

D.B.

Meters

Entrance from road

Dining Room

Scale: | 6ft. |

Up.

Pram

Heater

Bedroom 1

W

Linen

HW

Flue

Warm air

Warm air Down

W.C.

Bathroom

Bedroom 2

N

put into the consultation by Trustees and their advisers that made change acceptable, rather than any practical outcome of the consultation? The habits of thought of those involved in this very local, but not insignificant, upheaval were almost certainly changed; the indirect consequences cannot be measured and may be considerable. Immediately, all the parties to the discussion were better prepared for other physical and constitutional changes that were soon to follow. As an episode in public affairs it has passed into history, but it is worth a record.

The completion of modernisation of the earlier part of the estate exposed sites for development in what had been regarded as its least attractive part. This was largely because for fifty years the Trust maintained in that area its own private sewage disposal scheme. With the transfer of this responsibility to a public authority, the sewage was pumped to a larger and more distant works so that the already well-planted site could be restored. The area offered the opportunity to introduce into a rented estate a different form of tenure. The heavy subsidies needed for new rented houses, the evident desire of families to own their homes, and the problems for many of entering the property market, prompted the development of half-way schemes. The 'owner' secured a mortgage for the value of one-half the market price of the dwelling and paid a fair rent amounting to only half of that otherwise required. The capital grant needed from the government was thus greatly reduced; the 'owner' on the other hand had acquired an interest in the equity of his house which could be expected to increase in value and thus ease his path to later full ownership of a house of his choice if he so wished.

Another quite new building was designed to replace one of the earliest terraces on the estate demolished because of subsidence. The results can be judged from Plate 5.

Modernisation led to the demolition of one group of homes judged to have reached the end of its useful life. They were an experimental flat-roofed terrace, designed after the First World War and built largely with concrete in an attempt to achieve very low costs. They had presented an insoluble maintenance problem for years. The removal of this block of dwellings gave the opportunity to build on a site in the centre of the estate a second group of flats and maisonettes; those on the ground floor were designed to meet the needs of residents compelled to spend much of their lives in wheelchairs. The demand for such accommodation has not always justified the provision made; the problem for management is to ensure that such a dwelling is vacant at the time it is required.

8   The Organisation of a Community

Community facilities and organisation were identified as the third component of their housing work which called for some new initiative by the Trustees. In deciding how to proceed they took the action which had served them well in their examination of the modernisation proposals and which, as already described, made practicable the reconstruction of the estate they had inherited. To adjust to the needs and aspirations of the postwar world required a study of the physical and constitutional structures which had proved their value elsewhere; the guidelines available from the Trust's own early experience were no longer in themselves adequate. The design of new buildings for community purposes must follow study and consultation about the nature of those purposes, not precede it. And as with the modernisation proposals, the ideas of professional advisers were likely to be adapted and improved from exposure to public debate. The experience which the Trustees gained in this work led to their involvement in research on a national scale; their commitment to a small and local community prompted the use of their independent resources for the study of comparable problems at a national level. Research supported by the Trust in this field will be described later with other projects having their origin in the Trust's own housing programme.

At first sight, to provide the buildings, grounds and equipment for the New Earswick community and to promote a representative organisation to administer them was simple enough. The history can be briefly summarised. Once the estate reached a size when it was no longer possible for all the residents to meet the Trustees, a village council was formed. Nominations were invited through public announcement; on election day all adult residents were asked to call at the Folk Hall and register as many votes as there were places to be filled. Community buildings – the Folk Hall – were provided as soon as a house set aside for the purpose proved inadequate to the numbers wanting to use it. The Trustees built and maintained the hall; the representative village council used it, gaining a revenue from lettings and from the functions which it arranged; this money was used for its own administrative expenses and to pay for cleaning, lighting, heating and similar tenant's expenditure. It had all worked well for fifty years.

Evidence that all was not well now accumulated. Only a small minority of residents thought it worthwhile registering their votes and it was difficult to find men and women willing to stand for election. Disenchantment with local, and even national, representative bodies was not unusual; the problem was discussed at the annual joint meeting of Trustees and village council but no special action was thought to be necessary. Then deficits, increasing in size and frequency, became a feature of the council's

annual accounts. Costs of cleaning, heating, lighting, printing and sports field maintenance rose, whilst the income from the use of the facilities provided did not respond. Mindful of the Founder's strictures about communities 'bearing the stamp of charity' and his wish to encourage 'vigorous and self-governing communities' the Trustees felt uneasy at the increasingly frequent grants they had to make to keep the council solvent. The relationship became strained. The Trustees felt that charges were not being increased realistically to meet expenditure and too much reliance was being placed on the existence of a large charitable trust; residents felt that they were being asked to meet essential expenditure which could have been borne by the Trustees with no noticeable effect on their income.

Each party attached different weight to other factors which complicated an apparently simple relationship. The community facilities provided by the Trust over the years were on a scale far greater than would be required by the residents on the estate. A service was offered to a much wider area and the involvement of its residents was essential to the financial viability of the council's affairs. The council represented only the New Earswick residents; but the many societies and sports clubs on whose activities income depended were administered by committees drawn from a much wider area. The unfortunate council was caught in the pressures from these organisations for more up-to-date facilities, and from the Trustees for financial prudence. Trustees were reluctant to accept the fact that the facilities themselves were hopelessly out of date; what had been in 1907 a community building which others came to see, attracted no admiration fifty years later from men and women accustomed in their homes, work places and places of recreation to higher standards of comfort and convenience.

The conclusion that more radical action was needed was explicitly recognised by the Trustees in 1959 at the meeting at which they were told that their Private Bill was about to complete its progress through Parliament. Two Trustees felt a special concern about relationships with the elected council; they sent to their colleagues a paper arguing that although the difficulties were always presented in financial terms, the real problems lay in the size and quality of the community buildings and in the change in the use of leisure which the advent of television, improved transport and higher incomes for younger people had brought. The impact of these changes, they believed, called for a new examination of the facilities provided on the estate. 'What Joseph Rowntree would do', they observed, 'would be to pull down the Folk Hall and plan something quite new, related to present, as distinct from past, habits of life'. This seemed a somewhat radical approach. It was, however, accepted that the Trustees had a responsibility both to their own tenants, and to housing authorities generally, to study the nature and implications of the changes that were taking place, and then to apply their findings to the renewal of buildings and equipment provided by their predecessors to meet the needs of an earlier generation. A small working party of council and Trustees sought the advice of the National Federation of Community Associations and soon reported that a study by an independent observer should be put in hand.

Thus began a joint exercise which was still making its impact on the life of the estate twenty years later. An advisory committee was brought together; its members included representatives from the Trust, the village council, the National Federation of Community Associations and some independent advisers. With the approval of this body the Trustees invited Dr Paul Morpurgo to undertake the study. He was a natural scientist who had taken advantage of the Nuffield Foundation Fellowship to read for a second degree in sociology and whose interests lay in the field of community organisation. Dr Morpurgo chose to live for six months as a paying guest in a family house on the estate. He was at first an object of curiosity. What sort of person was it who had come to study leisure time activities and the facilities needed to provide for, and strengthen them? His daily and nightly involvement in all that was going on soon made him well known, and to his credit, well liked; twenty years later his advice was still being sought and he was returning to look up former friends and colleagues. His report presented six months later had been prepared with the help of frequent and long discussions with his advisory committee. From it came the brief to an architect for the virtual re-building of the Folk Hall: a different constitution for a new village association; a recognition of the role of groups drawn from villages and hamlets beyond the New Earswick boundary; a new financial relationship between the Trust and the association; and a new understanding by all parties of the relationships between an elected local authority, an elected association of residents, and an endowed trust which, because its public accountability was expressed in a different way, would always be an uneasy partner to both.

Dr Morpurgo's recommendations were set out in twenty paragraphs at the end of his report. Agreement was reached between the Trustees and the village council that these recommendations would be studied by a series of working parties drawn from the village council; the Trustees and their staff would be available for consultation but would not themselves join in framing proposals for action. Four recommendations concerned with the structure and management of the Folk Hall were examined by three members of the council. Three recommendations were concerned with the interests of the main users of the Folk Hall for whom special provision had been made in the original design. These were remitted to the same group, strengthened by four additional members representing these interests. Seven paragraphs dealing with the constitution and finance of the council became the responsibility of four other council members; they were to take account also of a separate paper prepared by two members of Dr Morpurgo's advisory committee who had contributed the knowledge and experience of the National Association of Community Associations. One paragraph which recommended action by the Trust to improve the service to tenants was left to Trustees; the remaining five recommendations were deliberately postponed. These dealt with new building in the village, homes for orphans, the Trust's letting policy, the sale of alcohol, and a possible shift in the emphasis in Trust work from housing to social organisation.

The immediate outcome of this elaborate exercise in policy making was disappointing. Over a period of five years a series of minor proposals was

made to Trustees on structural and constitutional change, none of which was addressed to the critical questions which had led to Dr Morpurgo's appointment. In retrospect it is fair to say that the Trustees asked too much. A council unsure of its support in the community, and with no experience of the contemporary developments that had buttressed much of Morpurgo's analysis, was in no position to propose its own replacement, nor to hammer out a new financial basis for its work and for its relations with a Trust that had chosen to stand aside from problems which could not be resolved without its involvement.

On 17 March 1965, the architect's plans for the reconstruction of the Folk Hall, shown in drawings and on projected transparencies, were presented to a public meeting. There was instant furore. Dr Morpurgo's observations on the needs of the community, interpreted by an architect who took his report as a brief, had produced a design for the reconstruction of the hall more radical than either Trustees or village council had contemplated. The criticism focussed on the loss of the small hall; a building of some character in which the oldest residents could remember staging the first production of the *Pirates of Penzance*, and in which every club and association in the area had held its inaugural meeting. There was opposition, too, from the social club; the club had sole use of a large part of the building in which it provided a full-sized billiard table for a diminishing, but influential, group of older male residents.

The Trustees thought that time must be given for the debate to continue. Whilst progress with re-building the Folk Hall was in abeyance, they attempted to resolve the difficulty of drafting an acceptable constitution for the council. A suggested outline was prepared in the Trust office and sent to the council for comment. A year later no reply had been received.

The Trustees therefore decided an order of priority in which they were prepared to discuss the changes proposed by Morpurgo. First, a new constitution for the council should be agreed; second, an experienced person should be appointed to assist the council in its work; third, and only after agreement had been reached on the first two proposals, changes in the structure of the Folk Hall which were still in dispute could again be discussed. The Trustees appointed the Chairman of their New Earswick committee and their Director to meet the council and see if progress could now be made.

It was on constitutional matters that the views of the two parties had seemed furthest apart. The village council was encumbered with duties related to three different functions. Sometimes it acted, in effect, as a parish council; some of its members were elected both to the village council and the New Earswick parish council and the division of responsibility between them was by no means clear. Then it served as a tenants' association, bringing issues about housing management to the attention of the Trust as landlord. Thirdly – and this seemed to the Trustees its primary duty – it had day-to-day administrative and financial responsibility for a wide range of community facilities. Because of this confusion of roles, the council had difficulty in defining the duties of the person the Trustees wished them to employ; nor could they agree on the constituency they

should represent. It might be the tenants of the Trust's estate, those who lived in the parish of New Earswick or residents from a much wider area who sustained the organisations which used the Folk Hall, and met the fees and charges which were the council's income.

By 1967 a measure of agreement began to emerge within the council. Faced with the need to make a new appointment to their staff, and with the failure to find any acceptable alternative to the architect's plans for the Folk Hall, the council made two decisions. They embraced the first two requirements laid down by the Trust. The council would seek an experienced person to help in framing a new constitution and then to serve the council in its increasing responsibilities. Then it would look again at the plans prepared two years earlier for the reconstruction of the Folk Hall.

Rapid progress was now made. It seemed to justify the original proposal to appoint Dr Morpurgo as consultant and then to leave his report for five years whilst changes so radical to an established community could be discussed, adapted and absorbed within its traditional yet evolving structure.

Early in 1967 the council appointed an administrative officer. By the end of that year, enough progress had been made in framing a constitution for the proposed reconstruction of the Folk Hall to be brought back for discussion. With only small changes, the architect's plans were now found to be acceptable.

So in December 1967, work began on the new Folk Hall. As with the modernised houses, Sir Raymond Unwin's elevations remained unchanged; within the elevations, little was the same. Plate 6 shows both the original hall, around which so much loyalty to tradition was focussed, and the new plan which provides a new and inviting entrance, and a common meeting place and refreshment centre linked to the different parts of the building in which organisations and groups pursue their different interests.

Before the constitutional provisions and their outcome are examined, some account should be given of the completion of what Unwin had planned as the village centre.

Two new buildings were added. Each was designed by a different architect; both are deliberately modern in style, yet form an aesthetically harmonious group with the steeply-pitched roofs and elaborate detail of Unwin's Folk Hall unchanged by its internal reconstruction.

Plate 7 shows the new swimming pool linked with the Hall and sharing its common lounge and refreshment bar. The pool was needed by the primary and secondary schools on the estate and also by other schools in the adjoining communities, all of which had been dependent on swimming facilities in the city of York. But it was important to respond to the interests of local families as well, though this had to be achieved without employing staff to collect entrance fees and give supervision. A swimming association came into being offering family as well as individual membership; the association arranges a rota of experienced voluntary workers who take responsibility for safety and supervision. Technical maintenance is in the hands of the Trust's staff.

Conflict arises between the Trust's role as landlord for almost an entire

parish, involving quasi local authority functions, and as a charitable trust, seeking to demonstrate principles of site planning, design and housing management. It has no rate fund from which to bridge the inevitable gap between the costs of maintaining a swimming pool and the income it generates; yet it still feels uneasy about meeting these deficits from the income yielded by its endowment. If there were no Trust with resources to take an earlier initiative would public authorities provide for swimming and other community activities?

The second new building provides an answer to this dilemma which the Trust has always sought. For fifty years, the Trust had provided a public library within the Folk Hall. In the early days all the books were Trust property. As the public library service grew, supplies of books came from the county service, though the library was still staffed by volunteers and accommodated by the Trust. When the Folk Hall was reconstructed, discussions were already in hand for the building of a county library as an addition to the complex of buildings at the centre of the estate. The use for other community purposes of the space within the Folk Hall devoted to the needs of the library was part of the architect's plan, even though a date for the change could not be set. In 1972 an agreement was reached with the library authority that the Trust would convey on a long lease and at a fixed nominal rent a site on which a county library could be built. Mr Fraser of the Louis de Soissons partnership, who has been responsible for the modernisation of the estate, co-operated with the authority's architect in designing the building. Plate 8 shows how well this second modern building completes the provision for the recreational, social and cultural needs of a neighbourhood that extends well beyond the boundaries of the Trust's estate. The capital gift of land having been made, the cost of the library service in New Earswick, as elsewhere, falls on the responsible local authority. This principle had been applied with success to the primary school – originally an independent Trust venture and to sewage disposal and refuse collection – both formerly the responsibility of the Trust. Street lighting and road maintenance are similarly likely to pass from the Trust to the local authority.

The effort to apply these principles to the facilities for recreation was at the heart of the divisive debate on the constitution and finances of the village council. The structure that was introduced as the final stage in responding to Dr Morpurgo's report did not long endure. The root of the problem needs to be understood if workable relationships between the Trustees and the community they have created are to be firmly established.

The Morpurgo report identified and brought into open discussion the inadequacy in postwar conditions of the simple constitutional arrangements that had served for half a century. The community had grown in size; the population changed continuously; the Trust, with a greatly enlarged income, was looking to wider and different fields of activity; Trustees were no longer in day to day touch with a relatively stable group of residents taking responsibility for community affairs; staff were now employed for tasks which in earlier years had been undertaken directly by Trustees. Men and women, more conscious than before of civic rights, were unwilling to give time to local affairs if in the last resort decisions

were made by eight Trustees in whose appointment they had no voice. In administrative terms the task of running the estate demanded no exceptional management skill; it was the commitment to consultation and an increasing measure of genuine delegation that introduced difficulties and tensions. Had the Trust been established as a conventional housing trust, providing housing of quality but leaving services and community provision to the statutory authorities, the pattern of responsibilities would have been clear. Joseph Rowntree had set his Trustees a task which, fifty years later, was proving impossible to accomplish. Moreover, the simple and logical solution of handing over to the elected authority the structure of community services that had been built up, was no longer open. The scale of the provision, in relation to the size of the population which could benefit, was too great for any local authority. Nor was it realistic to try to stimulate fund raising within the community as a means of expressing independence from the Trust. Fund raising is not easy even when a real and urgent need can be presented; why become involved in it when the object to which the money is to be given could be achieved by a trifling increase in the expenditure to which the Trust was already committed?

The attempt to resolve these problems which emerged from discussions on the Morpurgo report introduced principles new in the history of the Trust. A formal constitution was drawn up along the lines of that recommended by the National Federation of Community Associations. It was accepted at a public meeting in 1968. The association thus constituted was registered as a charity. The membership of the council of the association was drawn in part from the parish of New Earswick – the estate itself was no longer the sole area of benefit – and in part from the groups and clubs which were the main users of the recreational and sports facilities. The association appointed Trustees through whom it could hold property. They accepted from the Rowntree Trustees a twenty-one year lease of the Folk Hall and sports fields at a peppercorn rent; the Trust retained responsibility only for the structure of the buildings and their external decoration. Otherwise the association was free to raise its own charges and, within the limits of what was charitable, to make its own decisions about the use of the land and premises. An initial grant was made by the Trust to put the association in funds and its financial stability was guaranteed for two years. The intention was recorded to transfer the swimming pool to the association on the same terms once some experience had been gained in its administration. At that early stage the finances of the swimming pool would otherwise have dominated the affairs of the new body.

There were certain safeguards. If the association were to be wound up, the land and buildings would revert to the Trust and would not be part of the association's assets. If the number of clubs and societies entitled to the representation on the council increased, then the number of elected members would also rise so that elected members would always be in a majority. This proved a critical decision. Then because of provisions in the Trust Deed of 1904, the sale of alcoholic drink in any of the premises included in the lease was forbidden. This, too, led later to strenuous debate.

One unusual provision had to be included in the new constitution. An

executive committee was to be appointed in which was vested responsibility for the land and buildings leased to the association. This committee was so constituted that residents in the estate would always be in a majority This would almost inevitably be the case, but the safeguard was needed to avoid a take-over by a group not representative of the estate community for whom, under the powers of the Trustees, these facilities had been provided.

As part of the acceptance by the Trustees of their role as a quasi local authority, they agreed to appoint to their staff an administrative officer who would then be seconded to the association and work wholly under its direction.

These agreements established relationships between the Trust and its tenants as near to those contemplated by the Founder as any previously achieved. The earlier days were, in fact, a period of enlightened paternalism, with which the postwar world was impatient. It would be difficult to find fault with the constitutional relationships now emerging which seemed precisely in accord with the principles enshrined in the Trust Deed and the Founder's Memorandum of advice.

Three substantial advances became possible at once which would have astonished an earlier generation of Trustees. First, the new association prospered financially. It took initiatives under its new powers which increased the income it received from the land and buildings it now controlled. With some satisfaction, its executive committee informed the Trustees that they would not need to call on the guarantee, and would in fact repay part of the initial grant which had been received. Second, the wish of the Trustees to broaden the management structure for the New Earswick estate was realised. This had been one of the arguments for setting up a separate Joseph Rowntree Memorial Housing Trust. At first the Chairman of the new association was invited to serve on the management committee in a personal capacity. Later, three representatives of the association were appointed for this purpose. Two representatives were appointed to a small committee responsible for the letting of houses; they worked with one Trustee, thus having a majority. Then thirdly the association raised the possibility of securing a catering licence so that the growing demand for the use of the Folk Hall for functions and small conferences could be better exploited.

Proposals involving the sale of alcoholic drink had been advanced over the years and had taken different forms. Some the Trustees had rejected because they felt them to be by any standards undesirable; one had been put by the then village council to the test of a ballot of the residents. It had been rejected by a large majority. The Trustees felt, however, that the new association had thought carefully about its proposals and that there were ways in which they could be accepted within the limits which the Trust Deed set. Broadly these were that any sale of drink must be so organised that no person or group should benefit financially from the sales; in other words there should be no financial incentive to boost sales; to provide alcoholic drink should simply be a response to the need for a service to the community. The oft-repeated gibe that an elderly gentleman in 1904 had forever prevented the residents of New Earswick from enjoying a drink

was untrue, indeed the provision he made was increasingly seen to be a wise solution to an admitted problem.

A professionally organised survey of opinion had served the Trust well when difficult problems of modernisation had to be settled, and the strength of opinion within the community was critical. The Trustees decided that the time had come to settle in the same way what was now becoming a contentious issue.

The British Market Research Bureau was again called into service. First a letter was sent to every resident by the Trust Director explaining in simple terms what it was the Trustees had to decide. The association wished to extend the use of the large community buildings; they would therefore offer the facilities of a catering licence to persons and organisations hiring accommodation and using the catering service which the association provided. Any surplus from sales would be separately recorded and used by the association for purposes of benefit to the whole community. It was no part of the intention of the Trustees or the association to open a public house within the Folk Hall. This would be contrary to the provision in the Deed of Foundation; it had been decisively rejected by an earlier ballot of all the residents; it would certainly be rejected by the licensing authority for there was no lack of such facilities in the area.

As on the previous occasion, each adult resident was individually consulted; Trustees thought this important because the issue to be settled had so often been misrepresented. A questionnaire was drafted and the investigators carefully briefed. Residents were to be asked first for their views on the proposals before the Trustees; then, if they rejected these, were there alternatives which would have their support? Separate replies were sought on the provision of these facilities at the Folk Hall, and at the sports pavilion, which in the view of the Trustees presented quite different problems. It was also made clear that, whatever the volume of support, a decision would need to be made first by the Trustees and then of course by the licensing authority.

In the outcome almost eighty per cent of the residents gave their approval to the proposals for the Folk Hall; the application for a catering licence was made and granted. The association's purpose in making the application seems to have been achieved and none of the social problems which some foresaw have been experienced. A much smaller majority was recorded for the sports field proposal; as substantial structural changes to the pavilion have in any event to be made, the Trustees thought the issues should be deferred. So what had become a controversial and highly emotive issue has passed into history; when equally earnest and determined rival groups each claim to speak for a whole community there is much to be said for putting the matter to the test. The Trust had the advantage that the cost of personal interviews could be met; as the Research Bureau's report shows (*Report on Survey of Residents' Opinions*, Joseph Rowntree Memorial Trust, 1978), this personal approach alone ensured that the answers given did in fact relate to the question which was put!

Ten years later yet another new start with constitution-making had to be made. The events are too close for a clear understanding of the reasons, though some weaknesses in the constitutional structure designed with

such care became apparent. The increase which was foreseen in the number of representatives of groups and societies on the council of the association did take place, and was a sign of vigour and health within the community. But under the constitution these representatives had to be matched by additional elected members; they could not always be found, and, more important, the size of the council became too large for effective administration. The administrative officer appointed at the Trustees insistence resigned, and the association decided, contrary to the advice of the Trust, that he should not be replaced. For both these reasons the number of committees grew rapidly so that the demands on the time of the association's executive committee and its officers became unreasonable. Inflation disrupted the association's finances; it became clear that the Trust would again have to intervene with the loss of the independence which all had laboured so hard to achieve.

The Trustees were anxious not to abandon the principles that had been introduced by the 1968 constitution. They proposed to the association that an independent consultant should be employed for six months to identify the weaknesses in the new regime that had led to so early a breakdown. Mr Derrick Adams, a Social Development Officer with the Liverpool Council of Social Service, was able to free himself to undertake the task. His terms of reference were defined thus:

'To review the development of the New Earswick village association since its establishment following the Morpurgo report in the light of changed conditions since that time and to make recommendations. The review should include the constitution of the New Earswick village association, the structure of its administration, the present and potential resources available to the association, the relationships between the association and the Trust.'

He was helped by an advisory committee to which the village association and the Trust each appointed three members. The report submitted in March 1978 was his own; he was not required, nor did he wish, to seek any advance support for his proposals from his advisory committee.

So, to the Morpurgo report and the two reports from British Market Research Bureau was added the Adams report. New Earswick residents could hardly claim that there was any reluctance on the part of Trustees to learn their views. The Adams report reflected the change that had taken place since Morpurgo in the structure and constitution of community associations. He identified three weaknesses in the structure of the New Earswick association. First, there was tension between council members nominated by clubs and societies, and those elected by the popular vote of people living in the area. Second, the massive committee structure was oppressive. Elected members found the work time-consuming and often unrewarding; many committees were dominated by club representatives with a narrow and special interest. Then third, the absence of any professional support from an executive officer left an impossible burden on the honorary officers; often there were no candidates for the posts and the loyalty of the staff employed to manage the Folk Hall was put under great

strain not knowing from day to day to whom they were responsible.

His conclusions were radical. The association should be wound up. To preserve continuity, those council members who served with Trustees on the New Earswick management committee, the lettings committee and other joint bodies should remain in office for six months to allow time to prepare a new constitution. A new village council should be small, all its members should be elected, one-third of them should retire each year and there should be a limit to the continuous service of any member. No person receiving any payment from the council should be eligible for election to membership. A full or part time administrator should be appointed to the council at the expense of the Trust. The council should concern itself with the needs of the whole community and should concentrate particularly on promoting good relations with the Trust and with the parish council as the statutory authority for the area.

On the administration of the Folk Hall, sports fields and other amenities, Mr Adams had firm views. They should be the direct responsibility of the Trust, whose staff should arrange all lettings to bodies wishing to use the Hall, including the council itself. Thus the balance between expenditure, fees from lettings and subsidy would be in the hands of the Trust which in the last resort had to find the money. To lay this task on a council which had neither endowment, nor the rate fund of a local authority, would in Mr Adams' view inevitably lead to renewed tension in the future. The Trustees should consult the users of the Hall through a standing conference two or three times a year. Mr Adams thought it was important, too, for the Trustees to have a part in maintaining a flow of new ventures in the community; they should appoint to their staff a social development officer to promote new developments in community work and thus counteract what Mr Adams saw as the stagnation since the resignation of the association's full time executive officer.

But the report was not wholly negative; the final paragraph read: 'There are fantastic opportunities for New Earswick. The community has so many advantages that are denied to other estates in the country. I hope the opportunity will be taken to re-build on the solid foundations existing and that any report made at the end of the next decade will make a valuable contribution to social development.'

Almost twenty years had passed since Dr Morpurgo completed his report. What is of concern to present day Trustees is whether the physical apparatus for social and recreational activities is so out of scale with the New Earswick community that no local and independent organisation can be created which would be able to bear its administrative and financial weight. The Morpurgo report profoundly influenced the relationships between the Trustees, the local community, and the wider area whose needs alone keep the New Earswick amenities in reasonable use. After years of discussion and a decade of trial, the weaknesses identified by Adams brought to an end what was beyond question a brave experiment. The energy with which Trustees and local representatives set about building a different structure based on Morpurgo as amended by Adams, but modified by local debate, shows that the search for a solution has not been abandoned.

Once more it seemed right to involve all the residents in bringing into being a representative body which would benefit from the experience gained following the Morpurgo report. A letter was sent to each adult resident explaining the outcome of the Adams report and asking for nominations for a committee of eight which would administer the affairs ordinarily falling to a representative body, and work with the Trustees in re-establishing a permanent organisation. Nominations were received and an election conducted which produced a committee of eight members; all, as it turned out, receiving support substantially greater than others on the list.

The new committee took up its work with determination and set itself the task of re-establishing an elected council under a revised constitution within a period as short as six months. Its members believed that much of the difficulty experienced by its predecessor arose because of a dual role. The former association managed the Folk Hall and other amenities; it also promoted a range of activities which depended on the use of the Folk Hall. The provisional committee therefore confined its duties to those of manager and landlord; promotion was left to others who were thus clients of the committee. It was common ground between the Trust and the committee that income from the use of the hall and other facilities should cover administrative expenditure and the running costs of the hall and other buildings. On the other hand, the scale of the provision was such that income and expenditure would be in balance only if substantial use of the hall by outside organisations could be successfully promoted.

In little over six months this simplified administration was operating well. The constitution then submitted to a public meeting and to the Trustees reflected the experience which the committee had gained. The new body was to be called the New Earswick Village Council; the concept of a community association had been abandoned. There were to be twelve members, all directly elected; representation by users of the facilities managed by the council was dropped. Specific provision was made for the preparation of budgets in consultation with the Trust's Finance Officer; earlier ideas to secure independence by leasing the property from the Trust to the council were also set aside. It had become clear that in the last resort the Trustees were obliged to intervene; deficits incurred by the council had to be met by the Trust; it was better, therefore, to establish a regime providing for regular consultation, than rely on draconian provisions for the dissolution of the council when debts could no longer be met.

The first elections under the new constitution were held in 1979; one third of the members retired in accordance with the constitution a year later.

The council is still new to its task. The constitution under which it operates is, it must be accepted, a compromise. For more than fifty years a similarly elected council had managed the social amenities of the estate with a relationship to the Trust which can not unreasonably be described as benevolently paternalist. The Morpurgo changes moved sharply towards independence. The association constituted following his report had independent legal status; it held property under the terms of a lease; it could not be dispossessed save for contravening the provisions of the lease;

the Trust surrendered as far as was possible any over-riding powers in respect of the management of property worth certainly not less than £250,000. This brave experiment ended in disaster. The agreed appointment of Derrick Adams, an outside adviser, to diagnose the cause and suggest remedies preserved mutual confidence; the respect which each party had for the other was never lost. The new constitutional provisions are nearer to the original pattern than to the Morpurgo design; they depend heavily on the quality of the relationships between, at one level, the council's honorary officers and the staff of the Trust, and at another between council members and Trustees. Critical to the successful working of the new provisions is the acceptance by both parties of the reality of the financial dilemma. The council can be self-supporting and independent only if it engages successfully in the commercial exploitation of the facilities it manages. It would then have to abandon any claim to charitable status. If, on the other hand, it directs its energies to the well-being of social organisations operating in the area, raises charges for the facilities it manages which are within the means of voluntary groups, and gives such bodies priority over any incidental use of the land and buildings by other bodies paying higher fees, then the council will need continuing, and probably increasing, subsidy. In the absence of any rate fund, the subsidy must come from the Trust and this is likely to reduce the prospects of grants from other statutory or voluntary bodies that exist to support community activity. The possibility of misunderstanding in such a relationship is considerable; both council and Trust must live with the results of splendid intentions defined at the beginning of the century which have proved to be incompatible with the independence which the Founder hoped his communities would achieve.

9   A Wider Service to Housing

The Rowntree Family Houses

The last twenty-five years have compelled Trustees to modify their views about the place of house building in their programme of work; it was also a period when their search for new fields of work found them in a mood to welcome and exploit new possibilities in housing, and with staff keen to respond. The first project outside New Earswick was the recovery for family use of, appropriately enough, their Founder's former home.

The early history of Clifton Lodge has been recorded by Ethel, Lady Thomson, one of three daughters of the Hon. Reginald Parker who bought the house in 1884 and sold it to Joseph Rowntree in 1905 (*Clifton Lodge*, Hutchinson, 1955). Joseph Rowntree lived there until his death in 1925. He added a large separate house linked by a communicating door on the first floor. It was called Rawcliffe Holt, and was occupied by his daughter. In later years the Lodge became progressively less suited to family occupation. A cottage at the rear became a riding school; rooms formerly used for domestic staff were adapted to serve as an improvised flat. Large areas of the ground floor in the main house were covered in dark panelling of no merit, giving the rooms a sombre and inhospitable appearance. Rawcliffe Holt, built for a style of living that had passed into history, was a rambling house on different levels; its sunken rose garden and tennis court were no longer maintained. Joseph Rowntree's daughter had built a thatched roofed pavilion in the large garden in which teas could be provided for small social organisations which were invited to hold their meetings and garden parties in the grounds. The ultimate use of the whole complex promised to be a daunting problem.

In 1955 the tenant moved from Clifton Lodge and decisions had to be made. Proposals were received by the Directors of Clifton Estate Ltd – the company wholly owned by the Trustees and created to accept the gift of the Founder's property – for its use as a youth hostel, a company office and a variety of institutional purposes. The large entrance hall and rather grand staircase frustrated attempts to divide the building into separate dwellings. A young architect had an inspiration. In the middle of the building, double doors opened on to a raised terrace above the garden. This became the main entrance. The room within became a foyer from which doors to the right and left led to rooms and hallways which were readily converted to large self-contained flats. The elegant staircase with its mahogany hand rail was skilfully turned through one hundred and eighty degrees to a third entrance door in the same new foyer. The building of a well-equipped kitchen in a former dressing room was the only change needed to complete the large five-roomed flat on the first floor. Plate 9 shows the terrace and door to the shared entrance hall.

The re-development of the whole property now went forward in stages. Mr de Soissons, on one of his regular visits to York, looked at the buildings and was asked to consider whether some new dwellings could be planned to occupy the dilapidated rose garden and tennis court. 'Yes', he said, 'I can see a three storey block of similar height to the present two storey buildings, "stepped" in three sections to fit between those fine mature trees and the shrubbery'. The carefully detailed elevations to the plans he produced merit the high praise they have received, and the constant demand for the flats, which were sold on a long lease with a nominal ground rent fixed for the term. There is one cause for regret. At that time leasehold flats were new to York. Professional advisers told the Directors that they would not find a market for twelve flats at a price in 1967 of rather more than £6,000. The Directors were confident that there was such a market for the flats on that particular site, which was unique in the city. However Trustees and Directors must exercise care if they are to reject strong professional advice in such a matter. The flats were 'shrunk' within the same elevations, saving about £1,000. By 1969 when the buildings were finished every purchaser would gladly have paid the additional capital sum for the larger area which is sadly missed in the flats as they were built. They have certainly proved a good investment for those original buyers who have sold their lease on moving elsewhere. Plate 10 shows Mr de Soissons' design, and the setting which determined the shape of the block and its elevation.

To associate the new building with the Founder and his family who had made their home there it was called Riseborough House – the name of the farm near Pickering below the North Yorkshire Moors in which Joseph Rowntree's grandfather John was born. John left Riseborough, the home of his father William Rowntree, and started a grocery business in Scarborough. His eldest son, also named John, followed his father in that business; a younger son Joseph started a grocery business in the Pavement in York. It was his two sons, Henry Isaac and Joseph, who joined Esther Tuke in her cocoa processing plant which grew to the company now known as Rowntree Mackintosh Limited and of which Joseph, late in the nineteenth century, became the first chairman, and in 1904 the Founder of the Rowntree Trusts. His brother Henry Isaac had died some years earlier leaving him to lead the enterprise alone. Riseborough House seemed an eminently suitable name for a new building in the ground of Joseph's home at Clifton Lodge.

The third stage in the shaping of the estate became possible when the riding school was closed. The area occupied by stables yielded space for garages badly needed in the area; the cottage was radically modernised along lines well tested on the New Earswick estate. Then in 1975 the Rawcliffe Holt was released from the institutional use to which it had been put for a number of years. Had the remainder of the small but beautiful estate not been so successfully transformed it is doubtful whether Trustees and Directors would have undertaken the elaborate and expensive work necessary to change the curiously planned house into acceptable modern flats. However it was the final stage in what had been a story of unexpected success. A large central staircase which dominated the interior of

Rawcliffe Holt, with a gallery above, had to be removed and an entire new floor built. The garden terrace was again put to good use by providing an entrance direct to the first floor. With these changes completed, conversion could follow familiar lines; two flats were built, though the day may come when the first floor flat may prove too large and a further division would be practicable. Two rooms remained which could not be incorporated into any of the dwellings. From them a self-contained one bedroom flat was built, entered from an external staircase. Rawcliffe Holt can be seen on the extreme left of Plate 9.

In all, twenty homes in a range of styles and sizes have been produced from the two large houses and their grounds. A decision to use them for some office or institutional purpose was so nearly made; it was averted by the imaginative planning of a young architect. Without it, a unique addition to York's stock of homes would have been lost.

The Trustees have been faced over the years with four other redevelopment problems in the Clifton area of York in which members of the Rowntree family in earlier years made their homes. The properties were Ouse Lea, a large house occupied by a second daughter of Joseph Rowntree, her husband, who was a doctor, and their family; the Homestead, built by Seebohm Rowntree as his first home, and subsequently occupied by his second son and his family, and Beverley House, purchased by the Trust because it adjoined Ouse Lea and connected with the latter and with the Homestead. Their extensive grounds ran down to the river Ouse or to the common land known locally as the 'strays', which stores flood water when rapid drainage from the moors upstream moves too slowly through the plain of York. The series of large houses – shown on the map of the Clifton area in Figure 7 – also included Haverford. This house was the home of a nephew of Joseph Rowntree, the son of his brother Henry Isaac, who had preceded him into the cocoa business. Haverford was damaged in an air attack on York in 1941; it was acquired by the Trustees who made changes in the boundary between Haverford and the adjoining Homestead, and then conveyed Haverford to the Youth Hostels Association. The building was adapted and later enlarged; the York youth hostel is one of the busiest throughout the year in the north of England.

Ouse Lea and its adjoining land passed into the possession of the Trust in 1960 when the Trustees exercised an option negotiated some years earlier with Joseph Rowntree's son-in-law, Dr MacDonald, who survived his wife. The Homestead was purchased by the Trust from Seebohm Rowntree when he moved from York to High Wycombe in 1936; the main purpose was to maintain the Homestead gardens as an attractive public park and children's play area designed and established by Seebohm early in his married life. His son who then occupied the property was a tenant of the Trust. These four properties included a large area of land extending from the River Ouse to the A19 road. Across the road, as Figure 7 shows, was the Clifton Lodge complex just described. The Trustees recognised that decisions made about the development of this large area must have a profound effect on the character of the Clifton area of York.

The first decision made was that the Ouse Lea house should be demolished. It was an undistinguished rambling red brick house with a cottage known as Sycamore Farm in the grounds. The cottage too was beyond recovery as an acceptable dwelling. Mr de Soissons was asked to consider the use of the whole area, including the Beverley House land and, if necessary for good site planning, some intrusion into the Homestead park. It was an interesting example of the truth of the principle insisted on

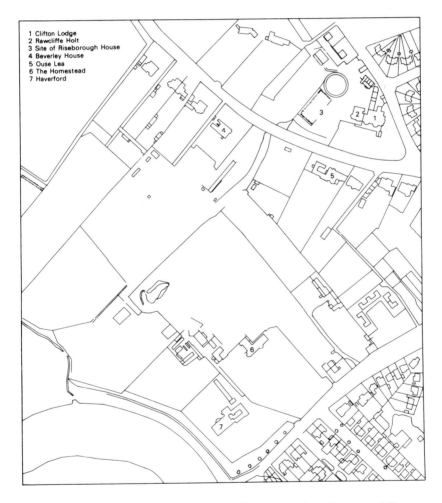

1 Clifton Lodge
2 Rawcliffe Holt
3 Site of Riseborough House
4 Beverley House
5 Ouse Lea
6 The Homestead
7 Haverford

Figure 7   The Rowntree family homes in Clifton now adapted to meet different needs. Based upon the 1961 and 1962 Ordnance Survey 1:2,500 maps with the permission of the Controller of Her Majesty's Stationery Office, Crown copyright reserved.

by Louis de Soissons when he agreed to advise the Trust many years earlier. 'I can do good work' he had said 'only when I have a good client; and a good client must know what he wants'. For the Ouse Lea site, the Trustees were not a good client; they were unable to decide what they wanted. The architect had no clear brief. His development plan which included a tower block on the lowest part of the site, and detached houses so sited in the remainder as to preserve the fine trees, might well have won distinction had it been built. But after long and expensive investigations of the market, drillings and soil tests, the Trustees, almost with a sense of relief, decided that the financial risks were too great and abandoned the idea of developing the site themselves. Negotiations with three national building companies followed; one reached the stage of agreed plans and the formation of a joint company to undertake the development of the site and the sale of the houses. In the event, the development company withdrew for commercial reasons almost as work was about to begin. For six years the cleared site remained to frustrate the gardening staff who resented caring for lawns, trees and gardens in what they described as 'dead land'.

The Trust's Director had been concerned with the discussions leading to the 1964 Housing Act and the establishment of the Housing Corporation to foster a movement in co-ownership housing. The Corporation's chairman was asked whether there was a housing society which would develop the site in consultation with the Trust, thus giving an opportunity to introduce this new tenure in a substantial way in the York area. Plate 11 shows the outcome. The development won a design award from the department of the Environment; it was however, a controversial scheme. The architect kept to a minimum the window area in the eastern elevation of the block of flats along the frontage with Shipton Road. The orientation of the building and the noise of traffic made this a right decision. But this elevation was the one seen by the passer by. The opposite elevation of the flats, with windows and balconies towards the south and west and looking across the Homestead gardens, won high praise. The rest of the site was used for houses of a wide variety of types and accommodation, from one bedroom flats to four bedroom town houses; there was garage space for each of the eighty dwellings on the site but distributed so that cars do not obtrude into the pedestrian access to and around the estate. It was part of the arrangement with the housing society that the Trust's staff should undertake the landscape work; the committee of owners which took over the administration of the co-ownership once the development stage was complete, have continued to use the Trust's services to maintain the dwellings and open spaces, and to arrange new tenancies.

It is sad that by 1978 an example of good design and of a successful application of a new form of tenure should be facing serious difficulties. Serious faults have been found in the structure of the Ouse Lea buildings; responsibility for these faults will it seems, have to be determined by the High Court. Remedial work is possible and is in hand, but it may well cost more than the price paid ten years earlier for the construction of the entire project. A complex of well-designed and beautifully situated homes will, however, remain when litigation and financial crisis have passed into history.

The Ouse Lea estate is likely to be affected, too, by the right given to co-ownerships in the Housing Act of 1980 to allow their members to acquire the freehold of the dwellings they occupy at a price determined by the amount of the original loan outstanding with the addition of any arrears of interest. Very large profits will be made by some co-owners. Probably – and this was foreseen when co-ownerships were introduced in 1964 – the properties would over time have passed into private ownership in any event. It has been the story of every attempt from the eighteenth century onwards to establish and maintain co-operative housing schemes. Unhappily the beneficiaries have rarely been the people whose devoted efforts established the project in the first place. Why this should be so in Britain is beyond the scope of this book; the promoters of co-ownerships in 1964 were warned that their work was unlikely to endure in the absence of new provisions in the law of property to introduce a saleable 'right to occupy' as an addition to the established freehold and leasehold tenures. However that may be, the Ouse Lea dwellings were designed to be managed as a group and will need corporate management. This is not necessarily excluded if the dwellings pass into individual ownership: a structure along the lines of the American condominium may prove useful to British housing.

In the immediate postwar years Beverley House was divided into three flats, each with a separate entrance. The Trust at that time had its simple headquarters in one room at the offices of the Rowntree Company. With the growth of the Trust's work and the recruitment of an Executive Officer and later of other supporting staff, some different arrangement became urgent. In 1948 the ground floor flat in Beverley House was vacant. The planning authority resisted the use of housing accommodation for offices; agreement was finally reached that the flat should itself be divided into two so that by the division of a very large room, three rooms became available for the Trust, and a barely tolerable separate flat remained. Progressively, as planning restrictions eased, the Trust had the use of the entire ground floor. It gradually became clear that Beverley House was capable of extension and that it could provide, given substantial expenditure, a gracious headquarters for all three Rowntree Trusts.

So it has become. Plate 12 shows the building today. Mr Fraser of the de Soissons partnership has so designed the additional wings that the enlarged building has a unity and sense of completion more satisfying than the original. Each of the three Trusts has office space; a boardroom, library and office machine room meet the needs of all. The large area of land in which the house stands now provides a small private garden to Beverley House, space for rearing trees and shrubs and bedding plants, and now an extension to the Homestead Park.

At intervals the Trustees reflected on the possible future of the Homestead. Next to Clifton Lodge, it had the closest association both with the Trust and the Rowntree Company. The Founder of the Trusts and the first chairman of the company had lived in the Lodge; his eldest son and principal partner in his Trust venture, and also his successor in the company chairmanship, had built the Homestead and lived there until his retirement. From the study in the Homestead, Seebohm Rowntree had

planned and organised his 'poverty' studies and other social enquiries. The public park which he and his father planned together was now maintained by the Trust and adjoined the Homestead. The house itself was large, but like the early New Earswick properties, the space was ill-suited to present day styles of living. The garden and grounds could not be wholly separated from the Homestead Park. This had become increasingly important in the work of the Trust; a succession of able head gardeners had raised its design and planting to a high standard which won wide appreciation. It was the only public garden and equipped children's playground in that part of York; a complex of greenhouses and propagation units had been completed which supplied the tens of thousands of bedding plants, shrubs and trees needed for the New Earswick estate, the Clifton Lodge site, the Ouse Lea co-ownership and the Homestead Park itself. A preliminary study of its possible use to the growing York University showed that it was both too small and too distant from the campus to have any place in the university's development plans.

What seemed to be the perfect solution came from what in historical and sentimental terms was the most appropriate quarter. The Rowntree Company, now Rowntree Mackintosh Limited, has become an international group of companies whose main board and immediately supporting staff were still housed with the now large manufacturing plant in the original buildings in York to which the company had moved more than eighty years before. The Company Chairman and his colleagues decided that the time had come when the central direction of the group of companies should move from the office buildings directly associated with the York factory. Should they move to London, to Brussels or some similar international commercial centre? The possibility of remaining in York where the business had begun, and perhaps adapting the Homestead which had been built by Seebohm and was owned by the Trust, was thought to be worth exploring. The Company Chairman was also a Trustee; the Trust was a charity and discussions had to be at arm's length. However there was no doubt about the attraction of the proposal to the Trustees. The elevation of the house would be preserved; they would have a voice in the adaptations; their own architect would be used by the Company to plan any extension; the unity of the whole area would be preserved since the Trust's gardening staff would be employed by the Company to maintain the extensive private grounds of the Homestead. Would the planning authorities, and more to the point, the Charity Commissioners give consent? And would the company accept a lease and not insist on buying the freehold in view of the large investment it was going to make?

One by one during 1978 the barriers came down. The planning authority, uneasy at the prospect of office development in the heart of Clifton's residential area, accepted that this particular office development offered the best chance of preserving the quality and integrity of the Homestead estate and ensuring care and sensitivity in the design of the additional building which any scheme would require. Indeed a financially viable development of the site for residential purposes would certainly have required more extensive additional building, whilst its quality would be

unlikely to match what the company had in mind. The Charity Commissioners were impressed with the arguments for a negotiated sale to the company and ready to depart from their usual requirement of open bids to secure the best terms for the charity; they needed, however, to be satisfied that the price was the full open market price taking account of the restrictions the Trust would have to impose on any purchaser. Valuers representing each party reached an agreement which they could recommend to the Commissioners and which the latter could accept. The greater concession was undoubtedly made by the company. To convert the large house to an entirely different purpose within the existing elevations; to equip an old building with the conveniences of air conditioning and the necessary standard of security; and to design to acceptable aesthetic standards additional buildings in the restricted area which the planning authority would allow; all this would certainly cost a lot more than building a new and efficient headquarters on a cleared site. Moreover, the company was required to accept a leasehold with restrictions on its disposal. And no-one could guarantee that when in later years difficult decisions might have to be made, the same understanding by each party of the claims and problems of the other could still be assumed. But there is a point at which commercial judgment must include the less ponderable qualities of faith and imagination; the deal was struck. The old building has been beautifully restored; its elevation opened to the view of the public coming to visit the Homestead Park and the gardens made lovely by the Trust's delighted gardening staff. Plate 13 shows the completed building. The best comment was made by one York mother to another as they brought their families along the drive to the public park. 'Isn't it wonderful what you can do with money'. If that were the only component needed the affairs of the Trust would present fewer problems!

Almshouses and Quaker History

The second series of commitments falling to the Trustees in their housing expansion beyond New Earswick was in service to an ancient almshouse trust and to the Society of Friends.

The York City Charities owned several groups of ancient and mostly dilapidated almshouses to which some modest improvements had been made with the help of improvement grants. One group of homes – the Ingram's Hospital – were of historic interest but, with a narrow winding stair in the thickness of the dividing walls, were quite unsuited to the needs of elderly people. These were exchanged for a site which adjoined the most modern homes owned by the charities – the Fothergil Homes built with a legacy to a high standard in 1936.

In two stages, completed in 1963 and 1974, the Trust's architect planned a substantial new development on this site, drawing on experience in building for the elderly in New Earswick and in the welfare provisions for the residents which were incorporated. On a quiet and attractive site, but within 250 yards of the busy shopping centre around Clifton Green, there are now forty-six dwellings with a family house for a warden and her

family. Apart from the development service which the Trust provided, it has contributed to the cost of the warden's house and to a two-way communication system between each dwelling and the warden. More recently, the Trust's architect has planned an extension to this house large enough to serve as a meeting room and social centre for the men and women who live in the homes. Almost the entire cost of the whole development has been met from private gifts and from the endowment of the charities which will be replaced, largely from housing subsidies, over a sixty year period. Now the modernisation of the original Fothergil Homes is in hand, with the prospect of five or six more homes on an adjoining site which the charities hope to acquire. The help of the Charity Commission has been critical, not only to the promotion of the Parliamentary Scheme which brought more than sixty ancient charities into a single trust with adequate resources, but to the sale or exchange of all the ancient dwellings in different parts of the city, none of which could be adapted to meet present day requirements for homes for older people. As the endowment is replaced over the years the charities should again have resources which will enable a future generation of Trustees to embark on some new venture appropriate to the time.

A new look has been given to an ancient site of historic interest in another part of the city. The Society of Friends owns a burial ground last used for interment more than a hundred years ago. It is still a place sought out by some visitors to the city because honoured figures in the Quaker story, John Woolman amongst them, lie buried there. The mature forest trees, mown grass and the enclosed quiet of the burial ground appeared in stark contrast to the dilapidated garages, warehouses and cottages which defined the boundary. A way was needed to replace these buildings by dwellings, using the ancient burial ground as a green setting for the new buildings and contributing to the improvement of a rather decayed part of the city.

There were a number of obstacles to be overcome. First, various legal complexities had to be resolved. Then the garages were in independent ownership but their site was critical to any building scheme. Even so, space was limited; the new buildings would need to intrude into the burial ground in so far as the ancient records identified areas not used for interments. The pieces started to fall into place when an opportunity came to purchase the garages; they were bought by the Trust and given to the Society of Friends which thus had the whole area in its ownership. The Charity Commissioners saw the possibilities of the proposed development and helped quickly and effectively in finding ways through the complexities of leasing the site to a specially constituted housing association, whilst preserving other rights and obligations defined in the surviving records. The new housing association adopted the name Tuke, in recognition of the number of members of that distinguished York family whose names appeared on the simple headstones in the burial ground. Mr Richard Fraser, the Trust's architect, designed a group of flats that have won general approval and contributed to the continuing restoration to its former distinction of a part of York which has decayed but which Lord Esher, in his report on the preservation of the city, identified as one that held great promise.

The Trust has continued to manage the property. More recently, in 1980, it has been of further service to the Society of Friends in using the Tuke Housing Association as an instrument to restore and convert some dangerously dilapidated, but listed, buildings adjoining the Friends Meeting House in the centre of York, thus releasing resources needed by the Society for the redevelopment of its too large Meeting House and contributing to the controlled adaptation of another part of York threatened by decay. Plates 14, 15 and 16 illustrate the three developments in different parts of the city undertaken for other charitable organisations.

A Partnership with Local Government

There was an air of exhilaration, even of excitement, within the Trust at the success of the modernisation programme at New Earswick. It came as a reaction from the depression left by the earlier decision that Unwin's houses would have to be demolished, and with them the evidence of the Trust's most distinctive work during its first fifty years. Could not similar principles be applied to some local authority estates, where both the arrangement of the site and the design of flats and houses seemed calculated to discourage any commitment by the residents to their homes and neighbourhoods?

From 1964 there had begun a series of changes in public policy which offered a quite new setting for the work of an independent housing trust. At first, loans from public funds began to flow to the voluntary housing movement not, as in the past, through local authorities, but through a central intermediary body, the Housing Corporation. In 1974 the Corporation's role was greatly extended. It became the main source both of loans and subsidies to housing trusts and associations, so that the movement became in fact what it had always argued it should be – a third component in the national provision of homes, complementing the work of local authorities which built for rent, and the builders and building societies which were making ownership available to a wider section of the population.

The dramatically successful work of housing associations working in areas of urban decay with the support of money raised by the Shelter campaign, was suddenly given official recognition; within a few years housing associations were becoming the largest operators in the rehabilitation of dwellings and the revival of neighbourhoods which under earlier policies would have been swept away under the disastrous clearance schemes.

The Trust moved cautiously again. It attempted to negotiate for the purchase of about one hundred terraced dwellings ripe for improvements to both houses and environment and mostly in the ownership of a single landlord. They were not for sale. The local authority in York was again approached; not this time about its own estates which remained a sensitive subject, but about older property in the centre of York, threatened with demolition, but which might be restored if the special powers and financial provisions applicable to a housing action area were applied.

So on 3 March 1977 a new period of work in housing by the Trust

opened. The Trustees received a report which recorded a welcome from the York Housing Authority for the Trust's involvement in a rehabilitation programme. The report drew a distinction between what could be achieved in a limited and defined area in the city of York and the work by associations in large conurbations often compelled to buy individual properties scattered over a wide area. The Trust could take responsibility for a neighbourhood, improving individual houses and their environment, and involving those who lived in them in the re-shaping of their community. Additional money could be added by the Trust to that available from central and local funds, to demonstrate, on the successful example of New Earswick, that old and attractive houses could not only be saved from demolition, but the renewed neighbourhood would prove more attractive to homeseekers than any new dwellings on a cleared site: the cost of radical improvement would also be less than that of redevelopment. Other possibilities were seen as the area allocated to the Trust was studied more closely. There was, for example, no need to turn a neighbourhood of mixed tenures into an estate of rented houses, dependent on large subsidies. The price of an occupied house, plus the cost of complete modernisation, reduced by the amount of the improvement grant, gave at the outset of the project a net cost which was below the market value of the improved house. An occupier who was a tenant could therefore be offered a unique chance to become an owner occupier. The Trust was able to offer temporary accommodation during the period of reconstruction; the Abbey National Building Society saw the possibilities of this new initiative and made funds available so that buyers were able to secure a mortgage, based on a proportion of the market value of the house, but equal to its total cost. There were clearly possibilities of exploitation; buyers accepted as a condition of purchase that the house should be sold back to the Trust if the original buyer left within a period of five years.

Within three years the benefits from this concentration of effort in a small neighbourhood were evident. Plate 17 shows what has been achieved. The re-arrangement of access roads and footpaths has yet to be completed, for time was needed to convince public authorities that these were as important to the renewal of the neighbourhood as improvements to its dwellings. Local interest – and pride – in a neighbourhood once threatened with demolition increased; young couples moved in, sometimes to take the place of elderly people who had been glad to accept the support of sheltered accommodation. Property values inevitably rose though houses at a fair rent remained for those for whom a rented house was still most suited to their needs.

The Trustees found themselves under pressure to launch similar neighbourhood improvement schemes elsewhere. There were other areas in York which invited attention. A number of experiments were made to see how far the procedures which the Trust had developed could be applied elsewhere in the north east of England. It was thought by some that the York property market offered opportunities that could not be repeated in Leeds, Hull or Nottingham. What had been achieved was particularly welcome to a new government in 1979 anxious to extend opportunities for owner occupation, and to reduce the high proportion of the cost of rented

houses that had to be met from public funds. The Trust was pressed to extend its operations to selected areas of decayed housing in Hull, Goole and Grimsby, whilst the Trustees' staff found themselves widely employed as consultants to advise other housing associations and local authorities on what was an entirely new field of service for the voluntary housing movement.

It is too early to draw conclusions on what may be the impact of this renewed housing activity on the further development of the Trust. In two respects discussed in the first part of this book the new work has already advanced the process of adaptation and change. Following the period of enquiry under Mr de Soissons' tutelage described earlier, Trustees reached the conclusion that they had no new contribution to make to the planning and design of houses which would justify a renewed deployment of resources in building on the scale of the New Earswick estate. Their authority to discuss and influence housing policy thereafter derived from the success of the modernisation of the early part of the estate and the initiatives in research related to housing policy which will shortly be described. From 1960 onwards the Trust was directly involved with the work of government committees concerned with housing policy; with national organisations, both voluntary and statutory, seeking new initiatives in British housing; and in personal and written consultations with ministers and their advisers. Increasingly the source of authority for this participation in policy making was derived from the knowledge and experience of individuals associated with the Trust rather than from any continuing corporate involvement in housing work. This being so, it seemed inevitable that the part which the Trust could play in the housing field would diminish. It is that trend which has now been reversed. Trustees and their advisers are increasingly involved in consultations at every level on housing policy and their authority again derives from the Trust's own experience. The Trust was established to raise the standard of housing by actually building homes of a quality which would influence public policy and practice. Any advocacy was to be based on achievement. It is that order that has now been restored.

The second problem which has plagued the administration of the Trust since 1950 is the incompatibility between the task laid on it by its Founder in the Deed of Foundation, and its status as a charity. There has already been told the story of the dramatic – and traumatic – intervention by the Board of Inland Revenue into the proceedings in Parliament on the Joseph Rowntree Memorial Trust Bill. Decisions by the courts had called into question the validity of the Trust's housing powers as a charitable purpose. It was the intention of Sir Milner Holland in his advice on the preparation of the Trust's private bill both to widen those powers and to remove any doubt of their validity as a charitable purpose. The effect of the Revenue intervention was drastically to narrow the Trust's housing powers. Later, on Sir Milner's advice, a separate Trust – the Joseph Rowntree Memorial Housing Trust – was set up without endowment and to it was transferred the entire housing enterprise. If its charitable status were called into question the Trust's endowment would be unaffected. A project such as the building of the Swedish flats was plainly outside the

powers of the Trust; the persons for whom they were intended could not be held to be 'poor' whatever definition might be given to that misused word. So the Board of Revenue was consulted. Strangely, they wished the project to be carried through. The building made no claim on charitable funds; those who were to occupy the flats were clearly essential members of any balanced community. So the Trustees' practice was upheld, though its powers remained inadequate legally to support it. In a report published in 1966 the Trustees recorded:

> If the Trust is to play the part in all this that the Founder intended, the Trustees believe that it is necessary to separate that part of their work which is properly charitable from that which in present day conditions is indistinguishable from the housing provision made by non-profit making societies. If this is not done, and if Trustees are required to administer their property within the present restrictions, it seems that New Earswick must gradually become a community of the poor, the aged and the handicapped. This would be contrary to the intentions of the Founder in establishing a housing trust; it would conflict with the lessons experience has taught about the evils of housing provision thus divided and it would be patently absurd when recent legislation has extended the taxation privileges formerly restricted to the housing of particular social groups.

Thus the authorities had reluctantly agreed to tolerate the Trust's administration of the New Earswick estate and its continued development. Once it began to mount an entirely new housing programme it was inevitable that the narrow terms of the Trust's housing powers would be enforced. So it has proved. But now the issues are wider; what is in dispute is the declared policy of a government, not the commitment of a particular trust. Ministers at the Department of the Environment find their legislative purposes frustrated by the application of the law of charity to work which makes no call on charitable funds and seeks no privilege in taxation not available to any registered housing association. All such associations build with the help of public funds. Their tenants pay fair rents settled by a rent officer; if they need help with those rents they seek a rent allowance from statutory funds. If the association by reason of accumulation of reserves or otherwise incurs a liability to taxation, that is cancelled under powers given to the Housing Minister in the Finance Act of 1965. All associations, because they use public resources, are expected so to frame their letting policies that they relieve housing need; a careful scrutiny of their tenants would not identify any different social or other group in the property of one association compared with another. Charity has become irrelevant to housing; the Trustees of an almshouse may make a maintenance charge which is as high as the fair rent charged by a neighbouring association operating under the general law.

In 1965 a Committee on Housing in Greater London was appointed by Sir Keith Joseph under the chairmanship of the late Sir Milner Holland. The Committee examined the work of housing associations in the London area and concluded with the following paragraphs.

It seems to us that if non-profit making housing associations are to make an effective contribution to the most urgent needs – and it is widely accepted that they should – then a rationalisation of the fiscal and legal provisions governing their activity is urgently needed; at present these seem to have the effect of discouraging the very associations which are equipped to give effective help in the area in which it is most needed.

Certain difficulties present themselves by reason of the importance of charitable status to societies raising money by public appeals or those having some income from an endowment. But we do not think that these problems applying to a small part of the movement should be allowed to perpetuate the anomalies to which we have referred.

From the evidence we have received we have formed the view that the future growth of the housing association movement is dependent on decisions of policy which it is not within our terms of reference to discuss. It is part of the larger question of whether the housing in London required by those needed to man the metropolitan services and by others earning comparable wages or salaries is to be provided exclusively by local authorities, or whether as in the other capital cities whose experience we have briefly considered, there are to be other serious contributions. If this is to be so, and if the contributors are to include housing associations and societies, then a quite new legal and financial framework for their activities must be provided.

Some progress has been made since 1965. More recently new initiatives have been taken by a small number of housing associations – mainly charitable – to improve decaying property and offer it for sale to those who could not otherwise hope to buy their own homes; or to enable elderly owner-occupiers to use the capital locked in their no longer suitable dwellings to secure a lease of a home designed to meet their needs; these bear the stamp of timely inspiration. Older houses are saved from decay; private assets are released to meet the changed housing needs of their owners; the housing stock is more effectively used; and public funds are conserved for those whose urgent needs for a dwelling can be met in no other way. The strict application of the narrow interpretation placed on the Trust's housing powers during the passage of its Private Bill through Parliament effectively excluded the Trust as a charity from carrying this work forward. Similar rulings have been applied to other charitable associations moving into these new ways of meeting housing need. The absurdity of the situation led to the invention, with the tacit approval of the authorities, of time consuming legal improvisations to ensure that the same people and organisations constituted as a separate association, are able to proceed with the work that so urgently needs to be done. Perhaps the enthusiasm of the government for so useful an application of skill, experience and resources will enable the task identified fifteen years earlier by the Milner Holland Committee to be completed.

Part III *Research and Innovation*

10 *Housing Practice and Policy*

The Rowntree Trust Housing Study

In June 1965 the Trustees held their first consultation with independent advisers as part of their search for a new field of work. Two of those advisers – Dr Michael Young and Mr Louis Moss – had suggested that the Trustees should start any new programme from the experience in housing work which they had built up over the previous fifty years. Seebohm Rowntree, ten years earlier, thought that the Trust had made insufficient effort to bring into public discussion the lessons of Unwin's work in site planning and house design at New Earswick. Otherwise their experience in trying to influence policy had been limited to the support given to individuals and organisations advocating and demonstrating the principles of planning defined by Unwin and Ebenezar Howard. In particular Sir Frederic Osborn and the Garden Cities Association – later the Town and Country Planning Association – had received substantial support from the Trust since 1920 for their campaign which led ultimately to the New Towns Act of 1946.

Their consultants' advice therefore found a ready response. The name Rowntree, through the work of Seebohm Rowntree, held an honoured place in the record of social change based on disciplined enquiry; the Trustees believed that the need for a similar contribution would continue. This was the reason for the long struggle to extend the powers of the Trust recorded in Part I. Now they were committed to embark on a research programme; housing had been their field of work for fifty years. In no other part of the national life was some new contribution to policy making more urgently needed. This is why research in housing policies and practice became the starting point for their new programme and why the series of studies described in this chapter occupied so significant a place in the Trust's work over the next twenty-five years.

David Donnison, then a Reader in the Department of Social Administration at the London School of Economics, wrote to the Trust asking for a grant of about £500 to study the results of the Rent Act of 1957. The Act was important in that it modified the system of rent control that had dominated the operations of private landlords, including organisations such as the Trust, since 1918.

This theme seemed to the Trustees too restricted; they wanted to examine the impact of legislative controls on the use, maintenance and improvement of the available housing stock. They knew from their own experience at New Earswick that if the upkeep of the estate had been dependent on the rents which were allowed under current legislation, the standard of repair and maintenance would have had to be reduced and the properties would be in a state of decay. In fact most of the income from

the low rents was spent on repairs and maintenance; interest on capital was negligible and nothing was available for its amortisation. A landlord without endowment who behaved in that way would long ago have been out of business.

So the Trust's Executive Officer was instructed to meet David Donnison and his colleagues to enquire whether, given adequate resources, a proposal for a more comprehensive study could be prepared. In a report prepared at the time the Trustees recorded their views:

> Much has been written and said about the state of homes in the United Kingdom; different and sometimes conflicting policies have been advocated to save older houses from decay, to give their occupants the opportunity of reasonable standards of hygiene and comfort and so to increase the total number of houses that people may be able to choose the kind of accommodation they want and move from one place to another whether for reasons of personal choice or changed employment. Much of this public discussion takes place as a part of political controversy, whilst little of it appears to be based on any adequate knowledge of the ownership and management of property or the effect of existing legislation and controls on its improvement and maintenance.

The proposal for an enlarged study which then reached the Trustees was accepted with little discussion. The work was expected to last five years; the Trustees hoped that useful information would become available during that time and that it would be published; they recorded, however, that they must resist any temptation to publish incomplete results which might only add to current controversies. In fact it became apparent early in the course of the work that however much might have been said and written about privately rented houses, very little was known about them. An inquiry into the ownership and management of such property became an important part of the national and local studies that were put in hand.

The national sample of houses which provided the base for the study took account of different local government areas, and of wards within those areas having different characteristics. The data obtained from the national study was supplemented by four local enquiries. Of these, one was in London under the control of David Donnison and his colleagues; others were conducted from the universities of Manchester, Nottingham and Exeter and were directed by Mr J.B. Cullingworth, Dr A.J. Willcocks and Mr P. Fletcher respectively.

This group of studies, which came to be identified collectively as the Rowntree Trust Housing Study, proved to be of profound significance in the development of the Trust, quite apart from their impact on housing policy. It set the pattern for the Trust's research work in three ways.

First, the Trustees appointed an advisory committee which could stand with a measure of independence between the research teams and the Trustees. For this committee they successfully sought the help of Professor R.M. Titmuss, Professor of Social Sciences and Social Administration in the University of London, who chaired the advisory committee for the

duration of the study; Sir John Wrigley, KBE, CB, formerly Deputy Secretary of the Ministry of Health and responsible for housing work in that Ministry and its successors until his retirement in 1952; Mr D.N. Chester, Warden of Nuffield College, who later resigned owing to the pressure of other commitments. Two other appointments were then made: Mr W.B. Reddaway, Director of the Department of Applied Economics at the University of Cambridge and Professor F. Laffite of the Department of Social Policy and Administration at the University of Birmingham. The Director of the Trust always attended meetings of the committee. In later years, a Trustee was appointed to such advisory committees. For this first venture, the whole advisory committee was invited at least once a year to meet the Trustees to discuss progress and to agree any changes in the plans for the work and in the resources needed to support it.

Secondly, the Trustees avoided a commitment to a single defined project but sought to promote inquiry into a series of issues related to policy questions with which they were already concerned. Working with the members of the advisory committee, they were willing to see the project developed and shaped as new issues of importance to housing policy were identified. The original estimate for the cost of the five year project begun in 1958 was £45,000, against the £500 which was the amount of the first application to the Trust. In fact more than £90,000 was spent before the series of studies was closed. On the recommendation of the advisory committee, two appointments were made to the team so that the role of the landlord in British housing could be examined; Dr R.A. Parker studied the local authority as landlord and Mr J. Greve examined the diminishing part played by the private landlord. In 1962 Miss D.A. Nevitt joined the group to study aspects of housing finance. She was concerned with the flow of capital to house building and the factors that govern it, the impact of taxation and subsidies on the number and type of houses built, and the real cost of these dwellings to the people who occupy them.

Thirdly, the Trustees looked for a continuing relationship with those whose work they were supporting. They hoped that the expertise built up through the series of studies would be of wider use as those engaged in the work established a reputation and found opportunities of wider public service. In fact within a year or so of the completion of this first series of studies, members of the research team were undertaking work for a number of the large housing authorities, for several independent research institutes and for the United Nations Economic Commission for Europe. Twenty years later, the Trust was still providing money for the research work of three members of the original team. The Rowntree Trust Housing Study and those involved in its work had a direct impact on housing policy; they were involved with the research programme of the government departments concerned with housing, with the work of the Central Housing Advisory Committee and its sub-committees; the Committee on London Housing (Milner Holland) and on some aspects of the work of the Committee on Local Authority Personal Social Services (Seebohm). All this was additional to the publications resulting directly from the studies; a series of articles and occasional papers was published from the second year

of this study in 1959; individual members of the team published books on the topics for which they had taken responsibility; an analysis of the whole study, placed in the wider perspective of international policy and practice, was published by David Donnison under the title *The Government of Housing* in 1967.

During the period of twenty-five years with which this book is concerned, the Rowntree Trust Housing Study under the general direction of David Donnison was the Trust's main contribution to the discussion of general housing policy. The series of studies to which it led, the range of which is shown by the list of publications which were produced, embraced the whole field of housing policy; not only so, but the studies led to the assembly by central government of a continuing flow of information about housing, published in a form which gave authorities and researchers a wealth of material about the supply and use of dwellings, and the condition of the housing stock, far richer than any that could be produced by a private trust.

In the twenty-five years since the Rowntree Trust Housing Study was launched, the Trustees have been involved in more than forty housing research projects, wholly or partly financed from the resources they control. The projects have been of three kinds. Within each of the three categories some projects have been initiated from within the Trust, others have been suggested to the Trustees, and have secured their support either in the form in which they were presented, or as modified in discussions between the Trustees and the researchers. First, there has been a number of studies of the finance and organisation of housing in Britain or elsewhere. Secondly, grants have been made to organisations in order that some new departure might be initiated, which could be sustained over a period, and carefully monitored. On occasion a new organisation was established to fulfil the Trust's purpose. Thirdly, some grants have been made to organisations and institutions to enable them to sustain or extend their established work during a period of change and growth.

The projects receiving support can also be divided by reference to the particular aspect of housing policy or practice to which they were directed. Eleven projects were directly concerned with the growth of the voluntary housing movement. The Trust itself had been established as an independent housing body; in more recent years such organisations found statutory expression as housing associations. The Trust became increasingly committed to the growth and extension of the work of housing associations, which came to be identified collectively as the voluntary housing movement and referred to by some as the 'third arm' in housing. Then a substantial group of projects has been concerned with the social consequences of housing policy. It is here that the Trustees have identified specific issues which seemed to them to call for changes in policy or practice, and have launched either a research project or experimental schemes designed to influence the practice of public authorities. The Trustees have been concerned with some broader issues of urban renewal and planning; their contribution has often taken the form of grants to established organisations seeking to influence public policy in these fields.

The Trustees have generally taken the view that if research has been

undertaken, or an experimental project launched, then the results ought to be made known. The reasons for failure to achieve the stated objectives of a particular project might be of at least as much significance to social policy as an enterprise brought to a satisfactory conclusion. The Trust's work in housing, as in other fields to be described later in this book, has therefore led to numerous books and reports which it would be tedious to identify in an account of the principal initiatives, which, under its extended powers, the Trustees were able to take. A list of publications and reports, in order of date of publication, is therefore given in Appendix VI; particular publications are referred to in this and subsequent chapters, only by way of illustration.

The Voluntary Housing Movement

The issue of policy on which the Trustees concentrated was the place of a voluntary housing movement in the British housing scene and the ways in which its work could be made more effective and greater in scale. They made their own enquiries about the role of voluntary housing bodies both in Europe and in the United States of America. The Donnison studies convinced them that whatever form the social and political debate might take, there was in practice little prospect of any revival of the private landlord as a supplier of rented housing. But the part he had played in meeting housing need was clearly one which was not being taken over by either of the other providers on which British families had become dependent for their housing. Neither private builders nor local authorities were producing an adequate range of types of housing, nor had they the flexibility of administration to meet the variety of need which was becoming evident and which went far beyond the traditional family house on which the other two providers then concentrated.

The only third provider in prospect was the voluntary housing movement. It was, however, in no shape to undertake the task which the Trustees felt to be necessary. For most of its history, it had been dependent upon private capital at low rates of interest, so that housing on any scale had resulted only from the activities of a small number of philanthropists. The Trust itself was in that tradition. Then, in the postwar years, there had been a more general growth, but successive governments had cast housing associations in the role of auxiliaries to local housing authorities. The number and types of dwellings they could provide were wholly dependent on the decision of the local authority in whose area they were working, and the opportunity for any new initiative, whether in terms of scale, or types of housing, was severely restricted. The statement by the Milner Holland Committee, quoted on page 90, reflected the views that had been formed within the Trust. If the Voluntary Housing Movement was to meet the need which the decline of the private landlord presented, then a legislative, administrative, and financial framework suited to its needs must be devised.

The Trustees therefore decided that they would initiate a widely ranging study on which government action might be based. Mr J.B.

Cullingworth had moved from his interests in the Rowntree Trust Housing Study to establish a Centre for Urban and Regional Studies in the University of Birmingham. He was invited by the Trustees in 1965 to undertake an enquiry which the Trustees identified as 'Statutory Procedures for Voluntary Housing'; a sum of money, at 1964 prices, of £12,000 was allocated in the first instance but the understanding with Mr Cullingworth, as with David Donnison some years earlier, was that the study might be developed and extended in the light of experience. Their hope was that reports would be produced which would identify the principles on which a new legislative, administrative and financial framework for the Voluntary Housing Movement should be based, and within which it could develop a life of its own, and make a substantial contribution to the nation's housing stock.

The Movement was represented by a central body called at that time the National Federation of Housing Societies. It had been established in 1935 under the Housing Act of that year, which authorised the responsible minister to make grants to a representative body bringing together the interests of housing associations and trusts. While Mr Cullingworth's work was proceeding, the Federation had itself taken the initiative in asking the Minister of Housing and Local Government to set up a committee to investigate the potential of the Voluntary Housing Movement and how that potential might be realised. The Trust was associated with this request; its hope was that the material produced by Mr Cullingworth would prove useful to any official committee that was set up, and thus influence policy more quickly and more effectively than would the publication of a series of reports, perhaps several years after the work had been completed.

In fact, a committee was indeed appointed, but it proved to be a disaster. The Chairman appointed by the Minister – Sir Karl Cohen – was wholly announced at the outset of his work that this was the principle by which he would be guided. The committee received a lot of valuable evidence. The research group formed by Mr Cullingworth at Birmingham was commissioned to prepare a report specifically to meet the needs of the committee; it also submitted other material which had been collected as a result of its research. The National Federation brought together a group of its members to prepare and submit to the committee an analysis of its experience over the years, and evidence of the ways in which, in its view, a substantial growth in voluntary housing might be encouraged. It was hardly surprising, however, that divisions within the committee became deep, and rendered any progress towards a report impossible. Indeed, some members of the committee were preparing to draft a minority report which might well have received the approval of all the members apart from the Chairman! There was no way of resolving this impossible situation, save by abolishing the committee, and this a newly appointed Minister hastened to do. In order that all might not be lost, a review of the evidence submitted to the committee was prepared within the department and published as a discussion document. This was a very different outcome from a report from an authoritative committee, which could become the focus of political debate and lead to a new departure in public policy.

The disaster did not end there. The Centre for Urban and Regional Studies had deferred any separate publication because of the opportunities which were expected to follow the appointment of a government committee. Much of its material had now been reviewed in the department's publication. What the Centre decided to do, with the agreement of Trustees, was to publish a full account of the three surveys its staff had undertaken, as 'A Further Contribution to Public Debate'. The three surveys were concerned with the constitution, work, and organisation of a sample of housing associations throughout the United Kingdom; a study of the attitudes of local authorities towards the work of voluntary housing associations; and an examination of the families and individuals who, in one region of the country, looked to housing associations for their homes, the reasons why they did so, and the results of their experience. To supplement these three studies, the Centre had examined the origins and expansion of one large national association: the result was published as a case study. In order to draw on experience from other countries, it also published an account of voluntary housing in Scandinavia. The addition of these publications to the available literature about housing associations was of value; the project, however, failed to focus discussion and lead to action on the scale which the Trustees had hoped.

The task to which the Trustees had set their hands still remains to be done. In the years since 1971, when the last publication by the Centre for Urban and Regional Studies on this topic appeared, the Trust has limited itself to lending strength to organisations and pressure groups promoting the work of the Voluntary Housing Movement, and giving specific support to particular associations undertaking work which seemed to the Trustees to demonstrate in valuable ways the potential of the movement. Over a period of a decade, the support given by the Trust to the National Federation of Housing Societies (later the National Federation of Housing Associations), though modest in scale, gave the organisation sufficient certainty to expand the service it was able to offer to its membership, and develop an expertise which made it increasingly effective as the spokesman of the movement in such policy discussions as successive governments initiated. The Trust was in close touch also with the Shelter campaign, which successfully brought to public notice not only the decay of the privately rented property on which many families in inner city areas were dependent for their homes, but also the pressures being put upon the most vulnerable families to leave their homes, because of the profits to be made by new owners if they were able to secure vacant possession, and take the property out of the market for rented housing. Direct support was given for a period of years to the Shelter Housing Advice Centre, which not only devised ways of helping a large number of homeless families to find accommodation, but analysed the flood of information which reached its staff, and published material which demonstrated beyond dispute the reality of homelessness in inner cities.

To give further practical expression to their commitment to those for whose needs Shelter had become spokesman, the Trustees, unusually, gave a grant to a large established housing association, to enable it to extend its work into three additional London boroughs. It believed also,

that there was a limited, but useful, role for the development of co-operative housing in the United Kingdom. It established an action-research project for this purpose in the University of Edinburgh; it gave both advice and money to a newly-formed co-operative, which brought together people from different races, and purchased, adapted and managed property in a very needy area in co-operation with an experienced housing association and a local authority. In later years when the Department of the Environment, in association with the Ford Foundation, wished to examine the possible contribution of the co-operative movement to the management of estates in areas of special housing difficulty, the Trustees became a third partner in an exchange of visits between the United Kingdom and the United States of America. So that such limited experience as there was could be shared, and those taking part in the exchange could apply their knowledge to practical developments in the areas in which they worked, the Trustees offered grants to housing managers from three areas where co-operative principles might be applied to the management problems of existing estates. In the years since 1970, recognition of the need to fill the void created by the departure of the private landlord, and disenchantment with a continually increasing local authority sector, has led to government action in a variety of ways to extend the output of the Voluntary Housing Movement. In so doing the Movement has gained a new confidence and, in some respects, a new independence. The extended powers of the Housing Corporation granted in 1974 have demonstrated the value, indeed the necessity, for an independent and central source of finance of the kind which the Trustees' studies had shown to be an essential component in the growth of voluntary housing organisations on both sides of the Atlantic. However, the comprehensive approach to these problems which the Trustees had in mind when they launched the studies in 1964 has still to be achieved, though the Movement now has resources of experience gained through government sponsored growth, and from the range of initiatives by individual associations that have characterised the last fifteen years.

The Social Consequences of Housing Policy

In the immediate postwar years there was a widely accepted view that the problems of dense populations in urban areas could in part be solved by building to heights much greater than those traditional in the United Kingdom. Through its support over more than thirty years of Sir Frederic Osborn and the Town and Country Planning Association, the Trustees had helped to oppose this view. Sir Frederic argued what is now widely accepted; quite apart from the social disadvantages of high-rise flats, there was not, in fact, any saving in land. His view was by no means new or original. Ebenezar Howard, Raymond Unwin, and Barry Parker, had all argued the same case. However, flats in large numbers were being built in tall structures inelegantly referred to as high-rise flats. In 1960 Mrs Eirene White asked the Trustees to support a small investigation into the problems created for mothers having very young children, who were housed in

PLATE 9   Clifton Lodge and Rawcliffe Holt. The new entrance to the flats in the Lodge is in the centre of the picture; to the left is the door to the upper flat in the re-constructed Rawcliffe Holt.

PLATE 10 Riseborough House occupies the site of a tennis court and sunken rose garden in the grounds of the Holt.

the upper storeys of high-rise blocks. The report of this group was published in 1961; it had an immediate impact. A cartoon in a London newspaper gave its publication an initial boost. Lord Snowdon had just been invited by the Royal Zoological Society to design an enclosure for birds at the zoo. On the day that 'Two to Five in High Rise Flats' was published, a picture appeared showing a block of flats some twenty storeys high, at the top of which was a curiously shaped enclosure forming a cage, in which numbers of very young children were shown playing happily. One worthy councillor was shown remarking to another: 'so we asked for the help of Lord Snowdon'!

The report received wide circulation on both sides of the Atlantic and soon had to be re-printed. It led Lady Allen of Hurtwood, who was one of Eirene White's advisers, to publish three pamphlets on the design and care of playgrounds for young children in urban areas, under the title 'Design for Play'. The Trust met the cost of the original enquiry, the publication of the report, 'Two to Five in High Rise Flats', and then later the cost of the three pamphlets, each describing facilities for play related to the needs of a particular age group.

Pearl Jephcott, of the Department of Social and Economic Research in the University of Glasgow, then proposed a more sophisticated study of the social implications of domestic housing in high blocks, which she defined as those with six storeys or more. The city of Glasgow presented an interesting and particularly acute example of the extensive use of high blocks of council housing. These were some 245 blocks already occupied, approved, or proposed as a result of the magnitude and urgency of Glasgow's housing needs. The Trust had become convinced of the importance to family life of the work begun by Eirene White and agreed to support a three year study of the massive high-rise development in Glasgow. Miss Jephcott's work was helped by an effective advisory committee and her report confirmed and elaborated the earlier conclusions. The concern first expressed by Eirene White, developed in the way described, had undoubtedly begun the rapid retreat from the policy of building high-rise flats. But for the foreseeable future many high-rise blocks will remain, and pressure on the supply of dwellings will compel some families with young children to live in the upper storeys, however careful and enlightened may be the management policies which housing authorities pursue. It was for this reason that the Trustees followed up these studies, by joining with the housing department of the Birmingham Corporation in employing staff under Pearl Jephcott's guidance to find ways by which those families with young children, compelled for a time to be housed several storeys above ground level, could be given special help and support, so that the damage to family life might at least be reduced.

The interest which this series of studies generated, both within the Trust and beyond, led to a consideration of the needs of other groups which seemed to be left at a disadvantage by the ordinary operations of the housing market. How far was housing and transport policy based on the assumption that most families and individuals would have access to a motor car, and what was the effect of this on the personal mobility of those without a car? How far did housing policy affect opportunities for

employment; what was the relationship between the market for houses, and the mobility of labour within, and between regions? Two studies were supported to elucidate these questions. The first brought the Trustees into a close working relationship with Political and Economic Planning; the study was supported by an advisory committee under the chairmanship of Lord Sainsbury. This partnership, as a later chapter will show, led in later years to one of the most important departures in Trust policy since the Trust was formed. The second study of housing and the mobility of labour was undertaken in University College in London. A limited study was undertaken of the housing needs of another group – the newly married – a significant number of whom found it difficult in their early married years to achieve an independent home. Following a pilot study supported by the Trust, the subject was later taken up in a more substantial way by the Department of the Environment. The importance of the issue has been confirmed from evidence that not only do the problems which lead to marital difficulties often have their beginnings in the early years of marriage, but are significantly more likely to occur for those married couples who spend more than two years before they enjoy the privacy of an independent home.

The Trustees received evidence too, that the return of some men to prison, only a short time after they had completed a previous sentence, was related to the virtual impossibility of securing a home in which to rebuild their lives with their wives and families. A housing association, having the support of the prison authorities, was established with financial help from the Trust. It used the labour and skill given voluntarily by prisoners for the rehabilitation of dwellings for those about to be discharged. It is now a national organisation. Similar considerations seemed to apply to men apparently unable to live an independent life outside an institution and therefore to gain a livelihood. In co-operation with other trusts and foundations, a scheme for group housing and supervised employment was attempted, and has proved capable of considerable extension.

The Trust has played its part in supporting research into the needs of the elderly as a later chapter will show. Its own experience as a housing organisation seemed, however, to show that many of those needs did not arise for elderly people living in a house suited to their needs. For this reason support was given in its early days to the National Association of Almshouses, through the efforts of which the great majority of ancient almshouses in this country have been modernised or replaced, and now provide a high standard of accommodation for those who live in them. One of the contributions of the Voluntary Housing Movement to housing policy has been to demonstrate how effective in bringing comfort and independence to older people are the different kinds of sheltered housing, with which associations have experimented. The Trust supported a number of such ventures. But the relationship between the support which sheltered housing provides, and the services available generally for the elderly, needed examination if the best use was to be made of limited resources. After discussion with several universities and research institutes, Professor John Greve, of the University of Leeds, who in earlier

years was associated with the Rowntree Trust Housing Studies, agreed to direct a study likely to cost some £90,000 over a period of four years. Here the special experience of the National Corporation for the Care of Old People (now the Centre for Policy on Ageing) was highly relevant; the National Corporation was willing to contribute to the cost of the study, and to help in the work of the advisory committee set up to offer guidance to Professor Greve and his colleagues. The Trustees were fortunate in the high standard set by the research team and the quality and commitment of a widely representative advisory committee. Papers immediately relevant to the work of those providing sheltered housing were published throughout the enquiry: a final report was presented to the committee and to the Trustees in 1981 in accordance with the time table agreed at the outset. Few research projects achieve their intended purpose so precisely and there are sometimes good reasons why this should be so. Trustees and their advisers must be allowed their glow of satisfaction at this unusual experience.

Two studies supported by the Trust were concerned with the social and practical problems which arise when an area of housing is demolished, the population temporarily dispersed, and a new neighbourhood created on a cleared site. The difficulties experienced by those who were compelled to move were examined by a group based on Cambridge House. They were concerned not so much with the familiar picture of the slum which was to be destroyed, and the new estate which arose in its place; instead their study concentrated on the period of transformation, which might span most of the childhood years of some residents, the entire retired life of others, or the critical early years of marriage for yet another group. On the practical side, it seemed from evidence presented to the Trustees that the loss in the number of available dwellings during the period of demolition and rebuilding could be varied quite dramatically by the way the work was organised. If the whole area was first cleared, plans for redevelopment gradually matured, and then the new estate built as a single operation, the greatest possible loss of accommodation would occur. On the other hand, the completion of redevelopment plans in advance, and the careful co-ordination of demolition and reconstruction might, it seemed, substantially reduce the loss of accommodation at any one time, and thus reduce the disruption to the lives of those affected by the clearance and re-development. A group based on the Architectural Association School of Architecture was enabled to work on this problem, with the idea of producing practical guidance to authorities involved in clearance and redevelopment schemes.

These studies contributed to the formation of policy in ways different from those intended by the parties to the research. They added to the much greater volume of evidence from other experience that clearance and redevelopment should be the exceptional, and not the accepted, practice in dealing with urban renewal. The Trust played its part in developing a different approach as the last chapter showed. It can make no claim to have provided the leadership and vision, for lack of which so great a price has been paid.

In their own business, Seebohm Rowntree and his colleagues were

known for the importance they attached to the selection and training of
men and women for particular tasks. Training whether in housing management, social work in its different branches, or in home making, has
been a principal interest of the Trust. In the Trust's early days, the work of
Octavia Hill in the management of housing was making some impact on
the practice of the 'improvement societies' in large towns but was largely
ignored by the new and growing housing authorities. For many years the
Trustees provided bursaries so that women, and later men, could, after
experience in other fields, move into housing management and benefit
from the training provided by the Society of Housing Managers. Later
that society merged with the Institute of Housing, and what had been two
streams of professional training were brought together. However, the
Trustees concluded that a private initiative was needed at a different level
of training. Directors of housing employed by large authorities were no
longer managers of local authority estates. They needed different skills if
they were to discharge effectively the comprehensive responsibility for all
housing in the area that was now seen as the local authority task. The
Trustees therefore asked Brunel University if a higher degree or diploma
in housing management could be established for qualified housing managers with substantial experience who wished to prepare themselves for
the wider responsibilities now falling on the profession. The offer was
accepted; finance was provided by the Trust for the additional staff
required; senior fellowships were created so that men or women in middle
life who might have family responsibilities could be enabled to take
advantage of the training thus provided.

At a very different level, the Trustees co-operated with the Association
of London Housing Estates in examining the work and potential of tenants
associations in the management of the estates in which their members
lived. Four different schemes to enable tenants to participate in housing
management were examined and the results published by the association
as a guide to their members and to housing authorities.

Urban Renewal and Planning

Of the remaining projects in which Trust resources were invested, most
were concerned with the broader questions of urban renewal. Indeed, the
number of applications for the support of research into problems arising
from the rehabilitation of urban areas was so considerable, and seemed
often to cover ground so similar, that the Trustees asked Mr Cullingworth
of the Centre for Urban and Regional Studies at Birmingham to review
the work already completed or in progress in this general field, and thus to
identify what direction any new research should take, or how the results of
the research already completed could be made accessible and usable by
local authorities involved in urban renewal schemes. The Trustees made a
grant to the Centre to enable an examination along these lines to continue
for about two years.

The report suggested that priority in the use of Trust resources should
be given to the second question. For the most part public authorities were

slow to apply the available results of research to work they had to do. The Trustees decided therefore to make a general grant to the Centre, to enable it to provide a consultancy service to local authorities. Often the cost of this service might be met by local authorities seeking to use it. Independent finance would, however, be needed so that security of appointment could be assured for the staff who would provide the service, and sometimes to finance the investigation of particular problems that might be presented to them.

The Trust could not permanently finance the service to local authorities; they wished to learn from the experience why it was necessary for them to intervene.

> The proposal made by the Trustees was therefore expressed as follows:
> It would be useful, the Trustees think, to identify what are the constraints on local authorities in accepting a service of this kind from an academic group, in what ways these have been overcome at the Birmingham Centre and what are the advantages and problems which are met when an academic consultancy service of this kind seeks to offer guidance to the very differently constituted administration of a local authority. We thought in our discussion that there might be certain aspects of this review which would need to be included in providing a paper prepared for the Trustees, and this would be very helpful. We hope, however, that you will also have in mind the possibility of a more general paper recording the experience, which could be published as a study document and thus help to promote this kind of co-operation between universities and public authorities.

The Trustees' experience of intervention in these wider issues has not been encouraging. For a private foundation to involve itself in a large area of general policy such as urban renewal, without isolating a particular aspect on which limited resources can be concentrated, is likely to result in substantial expenditure and absorb a lot of staff time, with little of consequence to show for the effort. In 1962, for example, the Trustees responded to a request from the Ministry of Housing and Local Government, the Liverpool Corporation, and Liverpool University, for the establishment of a Housing and Development Unit. The purpose was to identify the principles and methods by which a large and attractive area of distinguished but dilapidated buildings in the region of the University could be brought into present day use; a condition of the Trust involvement was that the effectiveness of these principles and methods should be tested by actual work on the site. The study was supported for five years. In retrospect it is difficult to identify what benefits have resulted, either to planning policy generally, or to housing in Liverpool in particular.

Part II of this history shows how the Trust's own housing work owed its merit to a continuing association between the Trust and a few distinguished men. Raymond Unwin, Barry Parker and Richard Fraser have between them designed all but two or three of the Trust's housing

projects, small and large, in New Earswick and beyond it. That is not to diminish the role of the Trust as client; it was Louis de Soissons who first emphasised the importance of that role before he agreed to advise the Trust; near the end of his life he paid what is perhaps the highest compliment that the Trust has ever received. 'I have had many clients' he said 'in all parts of the world. I think the Trust has been the best'. It was a remarkable tribute; the scale of the Trust's commissions had been relatively small; what he had valued was a clarity of purpose on the part of the Trust and the willingness on both sides to agree and to disagree in finding ways to implement it. So in research and innovation in the housing field the Trust has been willing to give an apparently gifted and determined individual an opportunity to develop his or her ideas in ways that would not have been possible without private support. They responded to a request for a grant so that the history of the famous Quarry Hill flats in Leeds could be recorded and evaluated before they were finally demolished. They enabled an architect to explore the possible use of unused space above shops in the inner area of York as student accommodation. They enabled two young men to experiment with Primary System Support housing and assembly kits to simplify methods of building construction. They gave small administrative grants to a gifted and determined group that pioneered the movement to enable the elderly to use the capital locked in their unsuitable dwellings to provide themselves with well-planned homes and support in their later years. They similarly carried the administrative expenditure for two groups building hostels for particularly disadvantaged groups so that their work could be carried to the point when these costs could be met from revenue.

There were others too. Some of this work is unrecorded; some led to publications included in Appendix VI. It is important that a private foundation with substantial resources should not exclude experimental ventures of this kind. Sophisticated procedures for the selection of projects to be supported by a foundation have their place; the Trustees have always felt free to take risks with ideas whether generated from within the Trust or suggested by others. The broad programme of research and development in housing, of which a short account has been given here, has affected housing policy and practice, and the housing opportunities available to individuals, in important ways. Had the Trustees not been willing to accept the risk, and indeed the certainty, of occasional failure, there would probably have been little of lasting interest to record.

11   *Planning a Research Programme*

The Trust has made rather less than 240 grants, large and small, over the period of twenty years since the Joseph Rowntree Memorial Trust Act received the Royal Assent. Forty of these related to housing; they have been described in the previous chapter. About a similar number have been made to organisations and institutions in Yorkshire; an account of these and of the support given to the University of York will be given later. How did the Trust select and carry through the 150 or so other projects on which the greater part of its net income was spent between 1959 and 1979?

On the agenda paper for any given meeting of Trustees there may be up to one hundred applications for financial help which have been rejected by the Trust staff under delegated powers. They are, however, reported in some detail so that any decision made can be questioned and if necessary reviewed. There may be another dozen or so proposals which fall outside the criteria for the use of delegated powers, and therefore await attention at a Trust meeting, but which, because the outcome is not in doubt, are presented in a separate section of the agenda paper.

This method of working is important. The Trustees do not regard themselves as presiding over a grant making organisation; the rising flow of applications continues despite vigorous efforts to reduce it. The speed with which decisions affecting large sums of money and substantial projects are made, reflects the continuing thought and discussion within the Trust about the areas of interest in which it should operate, and the persons or organisations it hopes to draw into partnership. The concentration of substantial resources in a few fields of interest, developed in partnership with others sometimes over quite a long period of years, has meant that the Trust has had an impact on particular aspects of social policy, which sometimes appears to be out of proportion to its size.

Because the Trust was established to undertake the executive task of building houses, it was part of its habit of thought to expect to see results from decisions made and expenditure incurred. The Trustees have therefore tended to choose projects likely to have early and identifiable results in terms of social policy and practice, and to be concerned with the evaluation not only of their own work, but also of the policies and activities to the development of which it was seeking to make a contribution. There is a danger inherent in this practical approach to research and innovation to which the Trust may be prone. The occasions when there is a direct and identifiable relationship between a project in social research or development, and a subsequent new direction in policy and practice, are infrequent. What Trustees may hope to do, is to discern the issues which at any given time are likely to shape policy and practice, and initiate studies or experiments through which they may hope to show the ways in which the

public welfare is likely to be most effectively advanced. Moreover, the Trust will be but one amongst a number of agencies contributing to the formation of policy; in today's complex society any given advance is likely to be the result of thought and action by many individuals and corporate groups. This account will necessarily relate particular Trust initiatives to hoped-for, and indeed realised, changes in social policy and practice. This is not, however, to argue *post hoc ergo propter hoc*, it shows what in the view of Trustees have been the particular policy issues to the elucidation of which they have wished to make a contribution.

More than two years before the Trust's Private Bill became law, the Trustees were already considering specific projects in which they might become involved, on the assumption that, in one way or the other, they would secure the wider powers they were seeking. In January and February of 1957, when they considered issuing a public statement of their intentions, they recognised the difficulties they found in their new enterprise and recorded:

> There is not an unlimited number of projects of the highest quality awaiting financial support. At any given time, the number of people capable of such work is small; they naturally seek as partners in their work organisations which have established a reputation for supporting work of quality. The Joseph Rowntree Village Trust is not yet known in this field.

Of the possible fields of study suggested in later paragraphs of the paper from which that extract is taken, there are three which have become the focus of continuing Trust effort over a quarter of century. First, they wanted to explore the possibility of identifying criteria by which to assess the effectiveness of the rising volume of public expenditure on different social services. The scale of consumer demand for services in health and welfare, was, they noted, virtually unlimited; some measure, however crude, of the results achieved by this expenditure seemed essential if available public resources were not to be overwhelmed. Years later the president of an American foundation committed to studies of health care wrote:

> The effects of personal medical care are limited. And, as we move through this decade, there is a growing sense that the vast number of dollars being poured into the American health care system is not improving the health status of the population. Nevertheless, our costly technology proliferates, and there are no limits to the resources that can be consumed by it. All these new developments are often used without valid criteria for need or efficacy.

The Trustees felt similar misgivings about the part they might take in the promotion of social services; there was a parallel responsibility to identify 'valid criteria for need or efficacy'.

The second field was concerned with the training of social workers. Two suggested projects were concerned with specific aspects of family life; this led to the Trust's third field of interest. It brought the Trust into

partnership with a company of persons and organisations concerned about the pressures of economic and social changes on family life, believing that the family is still important to the quality and stability of society.

The concern with the development of social work led the Trust, in partnership with the Nuffield Foundation, to establish what came to be a permanent institution – the National Institute for Social Work Training. The decision to pursue studies concerned with social policy as it affected the family, led first to the establishment of small units within universities, which bore the name of the Trust, and later to the idea that the Trust should itself establish a centre through which it could develop those interests. Thus, a second permanent institution – the Centre for Studies in Social Policy – came into being. The concern for the evaluation of publicly and voluntarily provided services has not in the same way found any institutional expression, but has led the Trust to initiate a number of substantial projects, which in more recent years have together been a significant element in Trust expenditure. The development of these fields of interest and the establishment of the permanent institutions to which they led are the subject of the next four chapters.

There was another component in the practice of the Trust over its first fifty years which helped to determine its approach to its new task. The Trustees had not directly employed any staff. They had close personal relations with Unwin and Parker and themselves directed their work. Their minutes and accounts, the employment and supervision of building and maintenance staff, and the clerical duties necessary to all this work, were provided from within the Rowntree Company of which the Trustees were Directors. The Housing Manager when appointed reported directly to the Trust Chairman and attended Trust meetings as needed. When in 1946 a first appointment of an Executive Officer was made, he was engaged first in the postwar search for a new role for the Trust, then in the temporary return to a housing programme, and thereafter until 1959 in the negotiations for extended powers for the Trust which led to the Private Act of that year. Trustees then in office were heavily committed in business or professional life; they now needed a different service from their staff – a change that was marked after a few years by the use of the title Director. But they intended to remain closely involved in the work of the Trust and did so. No further addition to the staff was therefore made, now that the three areas of research just identified were added to the continuing commitment to research and innovation in housing. Before embarking on the story of the Trust's development of this research programme, some account should be given of how the human resources available to them were strengthened so that they could continue to fulfil their Founder's intention that they 'should themselves direct and guide the appropriation of the Funds'.

For more than a decade they used the generously given help of academics, administrators and professional men and women. The chapters that follow will show how often they met in the evening or sometimes over a weekend to reflect on issues they wished to pursue and had the help of individuals and groups from whose advice new departures in their work came.

About half way through this twenty year period the Trustees decided that they should attempt to evaluate their own work. It followed from the way they operated that no internal review could be effective; they must submit to the scrutiny of an independent assessor. His work, as will be seen, had an important influence on the Trust's policy and practice.

The review of the Trust's work which led to this exercise in evaluation led also to a quite new use of a consultant. He was added to the staff for one third, later increased to one half, of his time and was given the title Associate Director. He served the Trust in this capacity until 1976 when a successor was appointed also for half time, and with the same title, for a period of three years. These appointments profoundly influenced the shape of the Trust's programme, as indeed was the intention. The decision to make such unusual appointments, and the choice of consultants, are worth examination.

The Fourth Report of the Trust was due to be published in October 1969, and drafts of the various sections of the report were before Trustees in the course of that year. These recorded the wide range of apparently unrelated projects in which part of the Trust's resources had been deployed. There was a clear need for a new examination of the role of the Trust, as wide ranging as that undertaken when the Trustees decided to extend their powers by the promotion of private legislation.

On 10 September 1969, Trustees received a paper from their Director concerning the changed conditions in which the Trustees would be operating in the next five to ten years. This paper was considered at their meeting on Friday 10 October; the minute records the main considerations which were discussed by the Trustees at what they felt to be a preliminary stage in their review. These considerations were:

a)   Although the Social Science Research Council was allocating substantial sums for research in the social sciences there was some evidence that less orthodox types of research received little encouragement. There might, therefore, be some important fields of research in the social sciences which still required independent support from foundations.

b)   It was likely that the Trust would work more effectively if fairly substantial commitments were accepted to a limited number of programmes or projects; this need not exclude smaller grants in particular circumstances but the latter ought not to absorb more than a small proportion of the Trust's resources.

c)   The tradition of the Trust was that its Trustees should be closely involved in, and committed to, the work which they were supporting; the emergence of a consensus of view about the main fields of operation was therefore important before substantial commitments were accepted and if necessary decisions might have to be delayed to allow this consensus to emerge.

d)   Certain specific fields of work were mentioned; it would be useful to continue to build up a range of possibilities in order to test the views amongst Trustees about the direction in which the Trust should move.

Thirteen widely ranging possibilities were listed in the minute, simply to demonstrate the breadth of the field open for consideration by the Trust. The minute concluded with the following paragraph:

> However, at this point the Trustees were more concerned with the central issue of whether large resources should be concentrated within a limited field or whether encouragement should be given to a large number of researchers and social workers unable to find support from university or public funds. The Trustees agreed that a further paper developing the proposals made at the meeting should be circulated and that a separate session should be held after supper at their next meeting which was likely to be held in London.

On 22 January 1970, the Trustees met in London to discharge the ordinary business of the Trust meeting; they then dined together and spent the remainder of the evening in less formal discussions on the future role and activities of the Trust, taking this up from the point at which it was left by the discussion recorded in the minute just quoted.

The administration of the Trust was now a considerable undertaking. There was an executive task of administering the Trust's housing estates, which included the modernisation programme, carried out by direct labour, and a continuing addition to the estates by new building for purposes chosen to incorporate an element of the experimental in the service offered to individuals and families with special needs. Then the Trust was directly responsible for a growing number of research projects, and provided resources for others through institutions, so that day to day communication had to be maintained with a range of universities, research institutes and authorities. The standing and reputation of the Trust in the field in which it was working, meant that requests were received by the Trust's Director to serve on a number of national bodies and government committees. It had always been the policy of Trustees to encourage such service; they believed that this was an important way of contributing its experience to the development of national policy, and itself benefiting from direct involvement nationally with problems of policy to which it was seeking to make a contribution. But the most important task falling on the Director of the Trust, was to bring to the Trustees proposals for new work in social research and practice, which would use effectively and constructively resources already in 1969 approaching a half a million pounds a year, and likely to increase rapidly. It was clear in the light of the experience revealed by the Trust's Fourth Report, that another mind was needed to reflect on the areas of social policy in which the Trust should become active, and that there might be advantages in securing this additional help by a consultancy, leaving any new appointment to the staff of the Trust until the shape of future development became clearer.

An opportunity to secure the needed help was quickly found. The governors of the National Institute for Social Work Training were beginning to think about the changes they would need to make in the administration of the Institute on the retirement of Robin Huws Jones, who was the Institute's first principal in 1961. There had been close links over nearly

a decade between the Trust and the National Institute, whilst the office of Principal brought the holder into touch with current thinking about social policy in universities and institutions in the United Kingdom, the United States, and generally in the western world. The Trustees thought that their immediate needs would most suitably be met if the Principal was able to devote about one third of his time, not to any executive responsibility for Trust activity, but as a consultant during what was felt to be a critical period in the development of the Trust's work. The proposal seemed likely to be welcome to the governors of the National Institute, in offering a period of transition to the changed field of work which the Institute was likely to enter. Trustees believed that at least £150,000 a year could be devoted to new initiatives in the Trust's programme, from which might be expected to grow a range of continuing and developing commitments no less significant in the work of the Trust than, at an earlier time, were housing, social work training, and social services overseas. A part of the minute of record of this informal, but important discussion, read:

> In considering the fields of work open to them the Trustees felt they should stress in their future work the importance of giving effect to the results of research and expert reports; it would be consistent with the traditional work of the Trust to take up particular recommendations resulting from committees of enquiry or research reports and to implement these in a way which would enable experience to be gained of a service in operation and a judgment formed about how far it should continue to be part of the publicly supported services in Britain.
>
> The modernisation at New Earswick and the continued development of the estate, both physically and socially, would continue to be a central interest of the Trust. It was expected also that Trustees and their Officers would continue to make available the experience of the Trust by the service which they gave to outside organisations in whose work it was right for the Trustees to have a continuing part.
>
> The Trustees own programme should continue to be concerned with questions of housing and planning; several substantial projects had been discussed with the Trust's Officers and details of these would be included in the agenda for the April meeting so that progress with the development of this part of the Trust's work would continue. There was an increasing concern for the care of the community for its members, and this included the right expression of that care, whether through centres established by the local authority or organisations such as Councils of Social Service bringing together those sharing a common concern. Much work needed to be done, however, in identifying in present day conditions the purpose of these organisations and institutions, and it was hoped that the Trust, which had initiated some work in this field, would develop it and that the consultant would include this in his interests.
>
> The Trustees considered very briefly also the difficult questions, which were bound to become more urgent, on the right ways of financing social and health services and the problem of using efficiently

the resources which the country was able to devote to these services. This would be a difficult field of research but ideas about it were not lacking and it ought to find a place in the Trust's programme.

Three years later, Robin Huws Jones finally retired from his duties as Principal of the National Institute of Social Work Training, and the Trustees thought that their staffing needs could best be met by offering him a half time post, as Associate Director of the Trust, with particular responsibility for the development of its research programme. This part-time appointment continued for a period of four years. By then the Trustees' responsibilities had greatly extended; they had accepted responsibility for the Family Fund, which is described elsewhere, and the income available for their programme of social research and experiment seemed likely within the next year or two to reach a million pounds a year. The demands made on the staff of the Trust by outside organisations had also greatly increased. But the Trust's Director was within little more than three years of retirement; he had carried the main responsibility for the Trust's development since the search for a new role began immediately following the second world war. An additional appointment at a senior level to the Trust's staff at that stage might well inhibit the different approach to the Trust's work that would be expected to follow the appointment of a new Director. Thus, the Trustees sought the part-time help as Associate Director, of Mr H.R. Poole, secretary of the Liverpool Council of Social Service who, as a later chapter will recount, had played a major part in the development of the Trust's programme of work in East and Central Africa. A new range of interests were opened during his three year appointment. But the way was left clear at the end of that period for Trustees, advised by a new Director, to decide their pattern of work for the 1980s; by the beginning of that decade, an income approaching one and a half million pounds a year had to be deployed.

12 *The Profession of Social Work*

Perhaps another two decades will pass before the role and contribution of professional social workers to the health of society can be assessed. The demonstrable concentration of the help of social workers on those who are deprived, who have low incomes, or who have inadequate housing, suggests that the needs in our society for professional social workers is of a different sort, than for example, our need for medical care with which, perhaps unfortunately, social workers have chosen to compare their contribution and training. Although the Trust's quantitative contribution to the development of professional social work has been marginal, in the political debate it has been critically involved.

The earliest consultations with men and women prominent in the fields of work in which the Trustees wished to operate included several who were associated with the Tavistock Institute of Human Relations, and with the promotion in this country of concepts of social case-work developed by schools of social work in the United States of America. The Trustees created a number of fellowships at the Tavistock Institute for men and women, professionally qualified in social work, who had carried substantial responsibilities, and who were willing to return for a year's further training in advanced social work. In their first weekend meeting at Oxford, to which reference has already been made, the Trustees devoted a session to discussing with Dame Eileen Younghusband and her colleagues, what further part they might play in the development of professional social work, and in its practice. The Carnegie United Kingdom Trust had taken the lead in this field in establishing working parties on the training of social workers under the chairmanship of Dame Eileen; the second of their reports argued the case for a staff college to serve as a focus for a higher level of consultative training. The Younghusband report particularly commended this development to the interest of foundations. It was not surprising therefore, that both the Rowntree Memorial Trust and the Nuffield Foundation, each of which had interests in this field, should join together and establish at Mary Ward House, what came to be known as the National Institute for Social Work Training.

Mary Ward House was purchased and beautifully restored by the Nuffield Foundation, then probably the largest foundation in the United Kingdom. The Foundation and the Rowntree Trust accepted responsibility for providing essential running costs for a period of ten years. It was the longest commitment, and the greatest in amount, that the Trust had ever accepted. Robin Huws Jones, as recorded earlier, was appointed Principal of the new institution. Under his leadership, the Institute built up a national, and indeed an international, reputation for the quality of its courses and consultations; it also developed a research programme impor-

tant in its own right but so designed as to contribute to the training and consultation which were the primary purposes of the Institute. Two other initiatives vigorously developed by the Principal and his colleagues added to the quality of its reputation and to the wide dissemination of its service to the profession of social work. It built up a specialist library used not only by students attending the courses it organised, but by a much wider circle of students, researchers and scholars who were given the privileged status of 'readers'. In co-operation with the publishing firm of Allen & Unwin it began its own series of books. Some were specially commissioned; some arose from the Institute's research programme; some were edited versions of lectures given at the Institute by staff or visiting consultants. The Principal was responsible to a widely representative governing body to the chairmanship of which the two Foundations succeeded in appointing Lord James of Rusholme, the Vice-Chancellor of the University of York. In 1965 he was succeeded by Lord Seebohm, Chairman of the Joseph Rowntree Memorial Trust who in turn handed over the responsibility in 1973 to Peter M. Barclay. Peter Barclay had represented the interests of the Mary Ward Settlement, from whom the premises were acquired, and guided the negotiations which secured acceptable accommodation in which the Settlement's work could continue. He was a member of the new Institute's governing body and became a Trustee of the Rowntree Memorial Trust.

The Trust's experience as a founder and joint major supporter of an institution brought lessons that shaped its future policy. Hitherto the Trust had made grants for relatively short periods; Trustees could plan how they should end as well as how the work should begin. The Institute was promised support for ten years; no shorter period was possible when a building had to be acquired, a considerable staff brought together from other employments and the process of building new and experimental courses, related to the needs of a new profession, begun. Ten years seemed a long time; how the work could be sustained at the end of the period – indeed whether it would still be relevant at all – could not be seriously discussed. As the end of the period of assured support approached in 1972 the Trustees recorded this note in their report published in that year:

> For both the Trusts this was a commitment which in terms of size and duration was exceptional. It has shown, however, the great advantages which are secured when a new venture can be established with adequate resources and with a sufficiently long period of security to attract and hold experienced members of staff and win the confidence alike of central and local authorities and academic institutions.

The Trust's support for the Institute was different in another respect from other commitments the Trust had accepted. It could not be extended for a single year to provide a little more breathing space whilst longer term support was organised. In their report, the Trustees reflected on the problem:

> It had been expected that by the end of ten years the training of social

workers at different levels would have become part of the continuing work of other institutions and universities with one of which the Institute might have become closely associated. For a variety of reasons this has not happened; nor in the light of changes in the social services which follow the Seebohm Report would it necessarily be an advantage that the Institute as an independent body should end at the present time. The Trustees believed when they embarked on this venture that the training of social workers, especially at the senior level, would become of increasing importance to the community and it was a service to which they were willing to remain committed. Their view has not changed; indeed this view has been confirmed by the experience of the Institute and by the new demands on it which are constantly being made. The basic support provided by the Trusts has enabled the Institute to undertake a variety of research for which finances from other sources have been readily available. This has not only been of value in itself but has contributed to the quality of the training which the Institute provides.

A new structure of support was devised which the Trustees were ready to continue for a further eight years. It had to take account not only of increased costs but of the wider range of work beyond training which the very success of the Institute had made unavoidable. To mark that expansion the Institute adopted the title National Institute of Social Work. The Rowntree Trust almost trebled its contribution; the Nuffield Foundation ceased to pay any direct grant but undertook to make Mary Ward House available on terms which represented a very handsome subsidy indeed. The Department of Health and Social Security which had contributed to the cost of the Institute's research programme now agreed to accept a share of the responsibility for its general work; in particular the Department helped to bridge the gap between the cost of providing courses for officers from local authorities and related voluntary organisations and the fees that could be paid by students.

Three intractable problems faced the Institute's governing body as this new period of support drew to a close. First, the prospect of incorporation into a university institution grew so remote that it was abandoned after prolonged and intensive negotiations. Universities were having sufficient difficulty in maintaining their existing work from their allocation from the University Grants Committee; that body was in no position to allocate additional funds for a new enterprise in social work training. Second, the period of great inflation itself threatened the Institute's work; the Rowntree Trust responded by further increasing its annual payment and even extended it for two further years, and the Department of Health and Social Security acted similarly. Even so, the work of the Institute became restricted. Third, the two sponsoring foundations had reached the end of the road. The Rowntree Trust gave formal notice that its grant would not be further extended; the Nuffield Foundation gave notice that it would now require a rent for the premises in Tavistock Place which would be determined by the market. The Foundation's own financial strength had been gravely reduced through the dramatic decline in the fortunes of the

car industry from which Lord Nuffield's endowment had been derived.

The later story of the Institute cannot yet be written nor is it any part of the history of the Rowntree Trust. The immediate rescue operation involved the purchase of the building from the Nuffield Foundation. The Rowntree Trust contributed £100,000 to the appeal fund and other large gifts were received. Even so, the purchase was made possible only by the intervention of the Department on which the Institute now became dependent for its premises as well as a large part of its income. The Trustees drew two lessons from the twenty years experience; it remained convinced of the special value of a long term commitment of this kind, and it did not forget how traumatic was the ultimate withdrawal.

The Seebohm Committee

Phoebe Hall, in her book *Reforming the Welfare – The Politics of Change in the Personal Social Services* (Heinemann Educational, 1976), a study financed by the Joseph Rowntree Memorial Trust, discusses the origins of the Committee on Local Authority and Allied Social Services. She shows how the National Institute for Social Work became a focus for those pressing the government to institute an enquiry, before proceeding with the proposals for a family service based on the Ingleby Report on Children and Young Persons. Lord Seebohm, Chairman both of the Joseph Rowntree Memorial Trust, and of the National Institute for Social Work, was appointed Chairman of the Committee which in 1965 resulted from these representations.

In the pressures brought to bear on the Trustees following the publication of the Committee's report in 1968, two quite different policy issues became confused. The main recommendation of the Committee was that 'personal social services' should be administered within new departments to be set up by local authorities. This, in due course, was accepted by the government. There was great anxiety to see this part of the report implemented quickly, particularly as the reorganisation of local government was under consideration by a Royal Commission under the chairmanship of Lord Redcliffe Maud. The Trust met the expenses of a group of members of the Committee who gave time to arguing the case for the early implementation of the Seebohm report. The sum of money involved was trivial. But the decision is important; it is the only example in the Trust's history of the difficult distinction between making known the results of research and enquiry, and advocating a policy. Sir Milner Holland had stressed the point when advising on the draft of the Trust's private Bill nearly twenty years earlier. The current vogue for the creation of pressure groups has caused the Charity Commissioners to stress the same principle in more than one of their annual reports.

By the end of the period covered by this review, the direct link with the National Institute for Social Work had come to an end. Through the newly established Policy Studies Institute, the Trust was resuming the difficult but important task of assessing, in the light of experience, the effectiveness of the structure of social care developed since the Seebohm

Report, and the place within it of the professionally trained social worker. From 1959 to 1979, however, the development of the profession of social work and its place in the social services was in financial terms the Trust's biggest commitment apart from housing. Whilst its interest was centred in the National Institute it took other initiatives elsewhere. It met the cost, for a period of years, of the appointment of a staff tutor at Liverpool University to develop teaching in community organisation; it had supported the Northumberland and Tyneside Council of Social Service in establishing a social work training unit; and it had financed in Scotland a working party on the role and structure of the Departments of Social Work established in Scotland earlier than in England. From its own experience as well, the Trust became interested in the process by which advisory committees are appointed by governments and how and why their recommendations may be implemented, rejected, or left in limbo. The Seebohm Committee offered the opportunity of a case study. After some discussion, Professor Roy Parker of the University of Bristol, agreed to accept a grant for the study, and Phoebe Hall was appointed to conduct it. Her report was published under the title *Reforming the Welfare – The Politics of Change in the Personal Social Services*, to which reference has already been made.

Over a quarter of a century, trusts and foundations have had a decisive influence on government policy for the organisation of social services and the development of the profession of social work. The broad structure which has emerged may be widely approved, but many critical and difficult questions remain. The Joseph Rowntree Memorial Trust has retained this field of work as a central interest. In 1975 the Trust expressed its unease about the outcome of the policies it had helped to shape: a paragraph in its report published that year read:

> The Trust may claim over the last twenty years that, with others, it has contributed to the training of social workers and to the growth of a view of their role in society that has found its expression in the report of the Seebohm Committee and its implementation in the Local Authority Social Services Act. But it seems now that the structure of the new Social Services Departments and their relationship to the profession of social work is resulting in a deployment of limited resources that will need to be reconsidered within a relatively short time. The manpower (or perhaps person-power) which is currently projected has implications for training resources and for local government expenditure that do not seem to have been adequately considered in relation to other equally compelling demands. There is already evidence that it may be the immediate need of the citizen that is the first casualty of over-committed or ill-directed resources. What part can a trust take in assessing the effectiveness, for the citizen in need of help, of the present organisation of the social services, and of the training prescribed for the social worker? What is the relationship between that training and the administration of highly complex and wide ranging public services? There are lessons to be drawn from the history of the medical officer of health, on

which the Seebohm Committee received evidence, which the zeal of the new profession of social work seems to have overlooked. Trusts are not lacking in techniques and procedures to draw official attention to gaps in our social services; to warn effectively of the dangers of too single minded a concentration on the very course which they have advocated, calls for different skills which they have yet to develop.

The Trustees persisted in their efforts to throw light on the problems raised in their report. Their support for the work of Tilda Goldberg, described in the next chapter, was a first outcome of this resolve.

13   *The Family and the Community*

The Trust's records for the years from 1959–79 identify some thirty-six projects in research and social experiment, which are directly in the field of family and community life. There are another fifty-three which are concerned with such matters as health and child development; the special needs of the elderly; penal questions; matters of employment; and general support to institutions concerned with social policy. It is with this large group of projects that the present chapter is concerned. Many of the reports made to the Trust led ultimately to the publication of a book; a list of these publications is given in Appendix VI.

When the extension of the Trust's powers by Parliament was assured, discussions began with the Institute of Community Studies which, with the help of the Nuffield Foundation, had been undertaking studies into aspects of family and community life in the East End of London. These discussions were not directed to the support of any particular project, nor at that stage would the Trustees have been willing to consider such a proposal. What was being proposed was, in effect, a partnership to extend over a period of years, within which the Trustees would provide a general grant, equal to a substantial part of the Institute's financial requirements. The Trust would consider and comment on the programme of work which the Institute intended to promote, and Trust representatives would join in an advisory body concerned with the details of the specific projects which the Institute would launch. The Trustees saw this as a development in the field of family and community life, comparable to the initiative in housing research which launched the Rowntree Trust Housing Studies. The existence of an independent Institute, with its own body of governors, marked, however, an important difference in the part which could be played by Trustees in the work they were supporting. Successive Directors of the Institute of Community Studies, and their colleagues, have recognised the influence of this unusual and early relationship with the Trust on the development and work of the Institute. Trustees, however, have been more conscious of the impact of the partnership with this group of workers on the thinking and development of the Trust. It is fair to say that the Rowntree Trust Housing Studies, and the Institute of Community Studies, together exercised the most significant influence on Trust policy and development after the decision to promote private legislation had been made. Sometimes the Trustees could still, in the words of their Founder, 'guide the appropriation of the funds', and this they hoped to do in substantial measure. A rising proportion of the available funds would, however, need to be deployed in some different way, and to the Trustees, their involvement in the Rowntree Trust Housing Studies, and the Institute of Community Studies, represented the best available alterna-

tive which most nearly fulfilled the spirit of their Founder's intention. Twenty years later, the Trustees were still working with a number of those with whom they had been in partnership in these two enterprises; satisfaction with these early arrangements was undiminished; and they continued to be a bench mark against which relationships with other individuals and groups were judged.

Lessons can be drawn, too, from the other projects recorded in the Trust's first report published in 1960. The Trustees agreed to support a study of family life in Swansea, with particular reference to the interests of the elderly; this they undertook in order to complement the studies of family life in East London. They established an advisory commitee, on which Trustees served, and which was based on the experience gained with the two series of studies in housing and family life. For similar reasons they agreed to establish in the University of Edinburgh a research unit to study family life and social development on a large housing estate. The Chairman of the Trust regularly attended meetings of the advisory committee established to guide this study. Then, at a different level of Trust involvement, small grants were made for the support of Home Advice Groups, and for the development of the Family Service Units. Individual Trustees, and the Trust corporately, had been involved in the development over a period of years of these two movements. Support for their further development was, therefore, consistent with current Trust policy even though no initiative by the Trust was needed, nor did the Trust grant mark any new departure in the work which was receiving help. At a greater distance from the Trust, grants were made to the National Citizens Advice Bureau, to improve and develop the information service on which local bureaux were dependent. Then, still more remote from Trust influence, a first grant was made for a survey into perinatal mortality. This had already been planned and executed, but had run into difficulty because inadequate arrangements were made for the analysis of the data brought together. A single contribution was made based on scant information and little enquiry. Twenty times as much was ultimately paid as the scale of the problems facing the organisers of the research became clear. This proved to be a study of great importance to child development; not only was the quantity and quality of detail on each live birth during a chosen week unique; the progress of the cohort through early childhood, school and beyond, was recorded and related to the original data. The National Child Development Study had been founded. But the role of the Trust was no more than to fill a financial gap. It had no contribution to make to the planning or implementation of the study; it had no expertise or experience in the medical or social issues which were being considered, and the work added nothing to the competence of Trustees, or of their staff, to use effectively the growing resources for which they were responsible.

Some new decisions were then made which reflected the response of Trustees to the pressures resulting from their deliberate policy to make as widely known as possible the existence of the Trust, the scale of its resources, the fields of interest in which it wished to operate, and its readiness to work in partnership with others active in the same fields.

Mr J.B. Cullingworth, a member of the team which was completing the Rowntree Trust Housing Studies, had accepted in 1960 an appointment in the University of Durham. Following consultations in which members of the advisory committee for the housing studies were involved, the Trustees agreed to support a series of studies in Durham. They hoped to develop with that University, a pattern of co-operation as fruitful as that with the London School of Economics for the housing studies, and with the Institute of Community Studies, for the studies in family and community life. The purpose of the new research unit was to examine the problems in the county arising from declining communities based on industries now obsolescent. In these areas, the structure of the population, the possibilities of employment, and social conditions generally were different from those in the north eastern region as a whole, and in the United Kingdom. New towns had been developed at Peterlee and at Newton Aycliffe; the studies were designed to compare these with the declining areas from which their populations had been drawn, in order to identify the social and economic consequences of this policy. As with the Institute of Community Studies, it was the general direction of the research programme that was agreed, leaving the details to be developed as the work made progress. The lesson learned by the Trust from this new attempt to establish a research team in partnership with a university, was that success depended heavily on a continuing relationship between the Trust and the originators of the project. David Donnison for the housing studies, and Michael Young for the research into family and community life, remained the Trust's partners for the whole period of the work and beyond. At Durham, the leadership of the Unit changed over the years; the direction and emphasis of the research followed the interests of the leader of the team; the role and significance of the advisory committee changed in ways that did not always retain the commitment of those whose help the Trustees had sought at the outset. However, twenty years later a new team at Durham University, guided by a new advisory commitee, was considering another aspect of social policy of direct interest to the Trust, and was making available for publication material from the original research programme which had not been brought to completion earlier but which was of more than contemporary interest.

Two other new commitments were accepted during this period, which, like the perinatal mortality survey, cannot be fitted in to any coherent framework of policy. They were not related to the Trust's declared fields of interest, nor did they fulfil its commitment to direct involvement in the deployment of Trust funds. A grant was made to the Selly Oak Colleges, to enable them to bring the salaries of their senior staff into line with academic salaries elsewhere. It was argued that only if the gaps were bridged for a period of years from independent funds, given for this specific purpose, would the new level of remuneration become accepted as part of the ordinary financial structure of the colleges. In those terms the project was a success. Then, the Trustees made a grant to the Institute of Race Relations, in circumstances which were to cause much heart searching in future years. The Institute expressed an interest in three relatively minor pieces of research, which might well have been undertaken without

any intervention either by the Institute, or by the Trust. The application arose from the search by the Institute for a new role, and a desire to secure support from the Trust as a means to improve its position in negotiation with other authorities. The Trust failed to come to grips with this central problem at the time. As a result it was drawn into discussions about the future of the Institute of Race Relations, and into support for particular aspects of its continuing work. In so doing the Trustees were postponing changes which had become inevitable. Their investment, both of time and money, had no impact on race relations in Britain, nor, save in the very short term, on the future of the Institute which had been responsible for distinguished work in that field. It was the first salutory lesson that acceptance of the role of a grant making trust would require different skills, a much greater commitment of time by staff and by Trustees in examining the work of appellant bodies and persons, and different criteria for decisions. The Trust had not been established to deploy resources in that way and it was neither staffed nor equipped for such a purpose. The record of expenditure in this period too, shows an increase in the number of small and even trivial grants made to organisations on the grounds that their work impinged on the Trust's own interests. Of a group of six such grants, all of a value of less than £1,000, only one, so far as the Trustees knew, resulted in a development of any importance. This grant was directed to the establishment of a series of occasional papers on social administration, by an editorial board under the chairmanship of Professor Titmuss. This series provided a medium at the outset for the publication of a number of papers arising from the Rowntree Trust Housing Studies, and later for a large number of other papers, which have been important to the formation of social policy, but which would not have achieved early publication through ordinary commercial channels.

In the middle years of the first decade in which the Trust was able to deploy its extended powers, the number of small grants for purposes unrelated to the general interest of the Trust declined. There was a new recognition that only by positive action could their declared intention to concentrate their resources in a limited number of fields of interest of their own choice be achieved. The Trustees returned to a method that had served them well twenty years earlier; they convened a series of discussions at which consultants with wide experience of developments in social policy, and of the research related to them, were invited to discuss with Trustees what were likely to be the aspects of social policy to which they might most effectively contribute.

It was as a result of one such evening discussion that Professor Mac-Gregor was invited to present to the Trustees proposals for a study of legal institutions since the middle of the eighteenth century. The Trustees decision was based on the proposition that one approach to a better understanding of current social problems might be to consider more thoroughly the forces and influences by which society has been shaped. These have found expression in social and legal institutions which have been the response of the community to needs of which it has become aware; once established they make their own impact on the community's development. The longer term intention of Professor MacGregor and his

colleagues at Bedford College, was to establish a Centre for the Study of the Sociology of Law. The building up and development of such a centre would be beyond the resources which the Trustees could allocate to it, but they were willing to help launch the enterprise by financing a series of studies of legal institutions which was likely to extend over a period of five years. The growing concern with law reform, and the appointment of commissioners for that purpose, added importance to studies of the social consequences of legal institutions. There was concern, too, about the way the system of legal aid was developing and any review of this needed to take account of the history of access to the courts by poor persons. Questions then current about public morality and the incidence of sexual offences needed to be considered in relation to the development of family law. In these and similar issues, historical and comparative studies were needed if public concern was to lead to social reform. The central purpose in establishing the Centre which most commended itself to Trustees, was to bring together lawyers and sociologists with, as time went on, other disciplines in the social sciences.

As things turned out, the significance of the Trustees' involvement in the establishment of the Centre, was in the long term, related to developments outside Bedford College. A series of discussions began under the chairmanship of Lord Scarman, involving representatives of the Social Science Research Council, those concerned with the new centre at Bedford College, and the Trustees, which led, before the end of the period of the Trust's grant, to the transfer of the work to Oxford. There a Centre for Legal Studies was established within Woolfsen College, supported by the Social Science Research Council; the Trustees made a direct contribution over a period of years, to give the committee responsible for the new centre a degree of freedom in the development of its work, greater than would ordinarily have been possible in a research unit under Social Science Research Council auspices. The Trust's interest in the relationship between law and society, however, remained. Towards the end of the decade, the Trustees met the cost of a feasibility study, to see how far court records could be made available for a substantial enquiry into the impact on family life in general, and on the needs of children in particular, of the changes in the law relating to divorce introduced in the 1970s. The study showed that there would be wide support from the court authorities for such a study, and that it would have the support of the Lord Chancellor's Office. So a Rowntree sponsored research unit was established at yet another university – the University of Bristol. Its immediate task was to analyse the new procedures for divorce and their social consequences. The head of the department at Bristol University in which the Unit was established – Dr Roy Parker – first worked with the Trustees in the Rowntree Trust Housing Studies, and was later concerned with some aspects of its interests in the training of social workers. An advisory committee was appointed to bring together Trustees, the University, the Lord Chancellor's Office, and independent members with experience to contribute. The new agreement with Bristol University, although concerned immediately with a study of the social consequences of the new divorce procedures, was designed to promote a continuing partnership in

other fields of work of common interest to the Trust and to the University. It was another example of a joint enterprise concerned with a defined field of study, established in a chosen institution, and with academic staff with whom the Trustees were able to develop a relationship based on shared confidence and concern.

An attempt to establish another similar partnership was made when the Trustees decided to deploy a substantial part of their resources in a new study of poverty. Seebohm Rowntree's second study – *Poverty and Progress* – had been published in 1936. In 1951, and towards the end of his life, he had undertaken a more limited study within the city of York, to examine how far the social conditions identified in the 1936 study had been changed by the introduction of the series of measures corporately referred to as the welfare state (*Poverty and the Welfare State*, Longman Green & Co, 1951). That third study, however, had not attempted to measure the extent of poverty in Britain in relation to criteria as rigorous and objective as those which Seebohm Rowntree designed for his earlier historic studies. Proposals for a national survey for that purpose, presented jointly by the University of Essex and the London School of Economics, were welcomed by the Trustees, and resulted in the largest grant for a single project ever made by the Trust.

For reasons which could not have been foreseen, the work came to be concentrated in the University of Essex; over a period of years the information revealed by the study was the basis for continuing and sometimes controversial contributions to discussions about the incidence of poverty, and the effectiveness of social security and related benefits in reducing its impact. It was not until 1979 – nearly fifteen years after the study was launched – that a substantial volume was published bringing together the results of the largest and most comprehensive study of poverty ever attempted. The delay was a great disappointment to the Trustees; they were not inactive, and made continuing efforts to secure the completion of the analysis and the publication of the data brought together by the survey. The authoritative advisory committee which had been assembled at the outset, was inevitably dispersed before the real work for which it was appointed began; the report itself, however valuable as a record, was based on data gathered so many years earlier that any impact on current social policy was greatly reduced. The Trustees drew the lesson that too close a relationship between social research and the desire of researchers directly to influence social policy, not only drew the Trust itself into areas of political controversy, but was likely to reduce the value and relevance of the research. Particular parts of the analysis might be brought into early public discussion because they seemed relevant to an issue of current political concern, whilst a considered discussion of the outcome of the whole project might be deferred until it had largely ceased to be relevant.

The issue is not simple. The value of the study of sheltered housing at the University of Leeds already described was greatly increased by the publications and contributions to seminars by the researchers throughout the course of their work. The effectiveness of the poverty study on the other hand, and of a three part investigation into homicide and capital

punishment, were greatly reduced by the use of data to respond to current political controversies. The publication of the first was, as already noted, delayed for more than a decade: the second was abandoned altogether.

It had been the intention of the Trustees to complement this large national survey of poverty with two smaller studies, one based in York, and the other in Newcastle. The purpose of the York study was to examine the widely held view that poverty in our society is, to a significant extent, chronic and cyclical. It recurs in the same family from one generation to the next. But the extent of such cyclical poverty and the reasons for it, had not been adequately examined. The study at Newcastle was of particular interest to the Trustees because it seemed to complement the work being undertaken at Essex. It was concerned with clarifying the concept of poverty; it sought to identify for different families the critical income point at which any reduction would involve the sacrifice of important items of expenditure. Neither of these studies was brought to completion, although at Newcastle a substantial survey was undertaken, and the results partly analysed. These experiences were critical to the decision to commission an analysis of the research projects in which the Trust had been involved over a decade. The results are discussed in a later chapter.

A third substantial commitment accepted by the Trustees during this period, neither had roots in earlier Trust interests, as did the poverty studies, nor did it lead to any new continuing commitments, as did the studies in law and society. A proposal received from the Centre for Contemporary Cultural Studies, which was part of the School of English at Birmingham University, evoked an immediate response. Values in society were changing; the standards by which personal and corporate conduct was judged were clearly different from those applied thirty years earlier; the extent of the change and its implications for the social and economic development of the community were matters of debate. Those responsible for the work of the Centre for Contemporary Cultural Studies, wished to examine journals and newspapers published during the last fifty or sixty years, and to identify and define the changes which had taken place in the values presented. The project was thus to be concerned with the part which the press has played in reflecting, mediating and shaping social attitudes, assumptions and values.

The work continued over a period of about five years. The amount of material collected, and the complexity of its detail, led to the decision that the full report should be prepared as resource material for later researchers, and this should take precedence over any attempt to reduce it to popular form for general publication. A voluminous report under the title *The Popular Press and Social Changes 1935–65* was lodged in the libraries of a number of universities. The Trustees, therefore, have no measure of the usefulness of their expenditure, either to researchers or to those concerned with framing social policy. They did, however, argue strongly for the preparation of a shorter report for general publication, if only as a means of drawing attention to the unique store of material deposited in university libraries. In 1975 – some ten years after the project was initiated – a book about the study by A.C.H. Smith was published by Chatto and Windus, under the title *Paper Voices*.

The last three years of the decade appear in retrospect as a period marked by a lack of conviction as to where the main thrust of the Trust's efforts should be directed. There were new developments in the Trust's chosen field of housing, and in social work training, which are recorded elsewhere. An overseas programme continued. Otherwise, expenditure was distributed over a range of projects in the choice of which it is difficult to detect any settled policy or consistent principle. Of sixteen new projects which were initiated, only one owed its origin to a concern felt by the Trust, and for which a partner in a university or research institute was sought. This project was identified in Trust discussion as 'The Social Implications of Educational Change'; the Trustees were concerned with the process of selection for different forms of higher education, and in particular with students at the borderline of entry to university. In a period of fierce competition for entry to universities, it seemed from the records that a difference of one place in the A level grade in a single subject could determine whether a student should have the opportunity to graduate in a university. These critical distinctions were not drawn at the same point by different universities; nor was there any established correlation between so fine a distinction in A-level results and the level of achievement at the end of three years undergraduate work. Ultimately, the Trustees were successful in entering into an arrangement with the Department of Educational Research at the University of Lancaster, to undertake a four year study, broadly along the lines which the Trustees had wished to promote.

Otherwise, the range of activity was wide. There was a commitment to a community centre in Scotland fostering music and traditional crafts in restored stone buildings; a large contribution to a training college providing short courses for the handicapped; a study was initiated into the construction and administration of adventure playgrounds; the Outward Bound Trust was helped to analyse its experience in establishing Outward Bound Schools over a period of years; support was given to a study into the involvement of young people in community service, and a parallel study into work which was being successfully developed with 'unattached' youth; a study was supported arising from the recommendations by the Plowden Committee that educational priority areas should be established; strangely, as it seems now, a grant was given to a School of Dentistry, towards a series of sociological and aetiological studies of dental ill health. There was another incursion into the field of education through the support given to a study of the effects of limited linguistic ability on the capacity of children to benefit from the educational opportunities open to them. The Trustees commitment to the University of Durham was extended to include two studies in urban sociology; there was an examination of the impact of newly established local radio stations, and of the claims that local radio can, through an increase in knowledge of local affairs, secure better recognition of the responsibilities and opportunities of local citizenship; there was a follow up study of a group of children, aged eighteen to thirty, who had been in foster homes, designed to relate the circumstances in the home in which the child was fostered to the child's development in later years. None of these projects led to any continuing interest or commitment on the part of the Trust. A number

were not brought to a successful conclusion; reports on other projects were secured only after strenuous and time consuming efforts on the part of the Trustees' staff to secure an analysis of data gathered at considerable expense in the course of field work.

One substantial project which attracted one of the larger grants made by the Trustees during the second half of the decade illustrates the pressures on a Trust with substantial resources, even when it has sought to define and make known the boundaries of its interest. The Trustees had decided, after their experience with the Institute of Race Relations, that they should not become involved in the growing field of research and action generated by the presence in the United Kingdom of an increasing number of immigrants. They had no special experience or expertise to contribute; a number of organisations and charitable trusts were deploying large resources and expertise in a difficult field of work in which specialisation seemed essential. The Home Secretary, in whose Department government responsibility for these matters rested, had established two bodies to deploy the funds which the government was making available. A Race Relations Board kept watch, and took action as appropriate, over discrimination against coloured people in ways which were contrary to statute, whilst a Committee for Commonwealth Immigrants, under the chairmanship of the Archbishop of Canterbury, had been established to promote good community relations in areas in which Commonwealth immigrants had settled in large numbers. The Home Secretary and the Chairman of the Race Relations Board, had received a proposal from the Ford Foundation that there should be a substantial study of race relations in Britain, the cost of which would be met by the Foundation. This proposal, which affected closely the work of the Archbishop's Committee, was reported to that body at one of its regular meetings. Members of the Committee from their local knowledge questioned the wisdom of launching such a study under the auspices of an American foundation, when its success would depend on securing the active co-operation of coloured people living in Britain. One or two large British foundations had already taken initiatives in this field, and it seemed strange, without any consultation, to launch a substantial national survey under the auspices of an American trust. These suggestions were not welcomed by the Home Secretary and his colleague from the Race Relations Board; they observed however, that there might be work resulting from the large national study which could be taken up by British foundations if they so wished – an observation hardly calculated to secure co-operation from the bodies to whose representatives it was addressed.

Within two or three days of that meeting, the Director of the Joseph Rowntree Memorial Trust received a telephone call from the Chairman of the Race Relations Board. This disclosed that the Ford Foundation had itself expressed strong reservations about the propriety of proceeding with a national survey of race relations in Britain, under the sole sponsorship of an American foundation. The Ford representative raised the possibility of the cost being shared with a British foundation. In the difficult situation thus created the Director of the Trust was asked if the Trustees would be willing to join with the Ford Foundation in financing the survey, each

meeting half of the total cost. An immediate decision was required. Trustees had to be consulted by telephone but consensus rapidly emerged. First, the Trustees had settled their policy, and had no wish to become involved in the sponsorship of a large national survey of race relations. Secondly, even if they were to undertake the work, it seemed to them inappropriate to become involved in such a sensitive area in partnership with an American foundation. The sums of money involved were large, but in no way beyond the resources of those British foundations which had already entered the field of race relations. Thirdly, the Trustees recognised that, however unnecessarily, the Home Office and the Race Relations Board had committed themselves to the promotion of this study, and detailed negotiations with a survey organisation were far advanced. The resources on which they had depended were now suddenly removed. In the course of the discussions both the concern and the competence of British foundations had been impugned. It seemed important to future relationships between British foundations and the government, that the response of the Trust to this unexpected impasse should leave no hint of wry satisfaction at the problems to which an unwise course of action had led. The Trust Director was therefore instructed to telephone the Chairman of the Race Relations Board, making clear first, that the Trustees were not departing from their general policy about involvement in race relations, but were acting solely to resolve the difficulty with which the authorities were faced; secondly, that the Trustees would not regard it as appropriate in such a venture to act in partnership with an American foundation, although they had gladly so acted in other fields; thirdly, that in all the circumstances the Trustees would meet the entire cost of the proposed survey should the Home Secretary and the Race Relations Board still wish to proceed with it. In the event, the offer was accepted; the survey proceeded under the direction of Political and Economic Planning; the results were published under the title *Survey of Racial Discrimination in Britain*; the Trustees paid the bill but had no part in the planning or execution of the project.

Advised by the first of their part-time consultants, the Trustees launched a series of projects concerned with the outcome of the reorganisation of the social services following the Seebohm report. What place in the new structure would there be for the work of volunteers and voluntary organisations? What would be the impact on the quality of the service available to the family?

Councils of Social Service, which represented the interests of volunteers and voluntary organisations in most urban areas, needed to adapt their structure, their finances and the services they offered, in the light of the statutory changes. Grants were made to a number of councils to assist in the period of transition and to gain experience which might be of service to others. The resources of bodies such as Community Service Volunteers and the Blackfriars Settlement were strengthened to see how far the better use of professional supervision could both increase the number of voluntary workers engaged in social service and extend their work into more specialised fields such as mental hospitals. For the first time in the Trust's experience the Department of Health and Social Security took part in these

developments, contributing to their cost and ensuring that the experience gained would be monitored and used. So many new initiatives were being launched throughout the country that the Trustees responded to a proposal that some central register should be organised so that mistakes were less likely to be repeated, whilst successful ventures would be exploited by others. It met with only partial and temporary success.

From the small and tentative involvement by the Trust in the changing work of local Councils of Social Service there developed three substantial projects undertaken with other foundations and with the National Council of Social Service – shortly to become the National Council of Voluntary Service. With the Gulbenkian Foundation the Trustees gave support to a Community Council Development Group formed from the Community Councils of Cheshire and Lancashire and the Councils of Social Service for Liverpool, Manchester and Salford. They covered an area with a population of nearly seven million. The purpose of the group was to initiate and guide the re-construction of community organisations in the north west. The two foundations were equal partners in the enterprise, which had the support of the National Council of Social Service, not least because the study would be of importance for other regions of the country

The Trustees joined with the Carnegie United Kingdom Trust to sponsor a national enquiry, under the chairmanship of Lord Wolfenden, into the role and function of voluntary organisations in the United Kingdom in the last quarter of the twentieth century. There had been no study of the voluntary sector on this scale since Lord Beveridge published his review in 1948. The two trusts undertook wide consultations which included ministers, shadow ministers, representatives of voluntary organisations and local authorities, and a wide range of individuals with experience in this field. A committee of enquiry into voluntary organisations would, the two trusts were advised, benefit from sponsorship by independent charitable trusts; the alternative, and more usual, course would have been the appointment of a departmental committee by a minister. The government, however, associated itself with the study by the appointment of the head of the Voluntary Services Unit at the Home Office as an observer; the observer's principal role was to bring together the evidence which government departments might wish to place before the Committee. The experience and views of government departments were recorded in a memorandum which proved to be a document of importance in its own right, quite apart from the impact which it made on the work of the committee. It was, with the approval of the Home Office, included as an appendix to the committee's report.

Lord Wolfenden's committee published its report in 1978. The Trustees found some of its recommendations relevant to their own continuing programme and committed themselves to the support of three projects, which together involved expenditure of the order of £500,000. Each was designed to test and develop the concept of what the committee had called 'local intermediary bodies'. First, they established a small Voluntary Organisations Research Unit. The committee had commissioned a series of local studies to examine the scale and type of voluntary activity in a number of representative areas, and the relationship between these

activities and those of the statutory authorities. As its first task, the unit would analyse and publish this material which had not been fully used in the preparation of the committee's report. The unit might prove of wider use to other bodies later on, and the Trustees therefore agreed to provide support for a small central staff for a period of five years. Then, secondly, they made available to the National Council of Voluntary Service a sum of £100,000, which could be drawn over a period of years to develop the work of councils of voluntary service in the large metropolitan areas. They hoped that other trusts and foundations might also be willing to contribute to this central fund to enable the National Council to initiate and sustain a planned transition to a more permanent method of financing these bodies which, under the Wolfenden proposals, were crucial to the structure of support for local voluntary organisations. The total sum was to be drawn on at the discretion of the National Council, which would discuss its programme at intervals with the Trust's Director, and would submit a report each six months on the use made of the Trust's grant. Thirdly, £240,000 was given to promote specialist intermediary bodies, bringing together, in local centres, the resources available in the community to respond to social needs. Some vigorous initiatives had taken place in Bradford, Barnsley and Stoke-on-Trent, and groups in each of these areas were working together to use the combined resources more effectively. The three groups were willing to accept an independent assessment of their work and proposals for monitoring the group of projects as a corporate venture were presented to the Trust. A grant of £10,000 a year for each of five years was made to each of the three projects; a further grant of £30,000 for each of the three years was made to the Northern College to monitor the development of the three projects and to publish an assessment of the outcome.

For the Trust, half a million pounds was a lot of money to invest in formal structures designed to promote voluntary activity; it demonstrated their commitment to the issues of social policy examined by the Wolfenden Committee. But what of the neighbourly help given and received every day with little regard for organisations, voluntary or statutory, and which, in the aggregate, might make a greater impact than the formal structures which Wolfenden and his colleagues had examined? Professor Philip Abrams of the Department of Sociology at Durham University submitted a proposal for an analytical review of the literature on the meaning of 'neighbourliness' and the factors that seemed to encourage or deter it. Three field surveys were designed to identify patterns of neighbourly care in different types of local communities. The quantity and quality of care might be determined by social class, by the extent of hardship, by kinship, by religion, by race or by age. Professor Abrams had the help of an advisory committee under the chairmanship of the Vice-Chancellor of Durham University.

The report on this study suggested that there were severe limits to what could be expected from unpaid neighbourly volunteers in providing help to those in need in the community; it was not a lack of goodwill; it was the combination of willingness, ability and available time that was scarce. The report was the subject of wide debate.

Two projects were initiated by the Trust designed to explore the possibility of extending the range of a local authority service in order to see how far those needing help could be better served and the call on other services reduced. For both projects the Trust worked not only with the local authority but with the Department of Health and Social Security, each partner bearing part of the cost.

The first venture of this kind examined the possible advantages of a substantial extension to the Home Help service. In a large urban authority two comparable areas were chosen, in one of which, at the expense of the Trust, the number of home helps was greatly increased. The object was to assess the extent of unmet need for home helps; to observe how far pressure on other services might be relieved by an increase in the provision of home helps; and to discover whether an increase in the home help service would provide positive gains for the families helped, as well as for the community, in terms of a reduced cost for its services generally. Over a period of four years, and at 1974 prices, the Trustees provided £60,000 towards the services provided by the local authority social services department; the Department of Health and Social Security added £30,000 to meet the cost of devising and testing research instruments and techniques by which to evaluate the project; the local authority contributed £45,000. In addition, the authority accepted responsibility for phasing out as necessary the increased allocation of home helps in the chosen area, in a way which would recognise the commitment accepted to a number of households.

The expansion of the service in the selected area changed the attitude to their work of the home helps themselves; they used the time spent in the homes to which they were allocated in different ways; they developed a different relationship to social workers and community nurses involved with the same households; there was a different pattern of demand on other local authority and health services. Critical to the significance of the project was the sophistication and thoroughness of the monitoring and evaluation throughout; this was made possible by the substantial research component provided by the Department of Health and Social Security. An analysis of the experience was published in technical journals and subsequently as a report by the Coventry Social Services Department.

A similar pattern of co-operation was secured for a second project. This was designed to discover how far adults who were dependent on the help of others could be taken into foster homes if support were given to the hosts by experienced social workers. If such homes could be found, it would follow that the need for residential care provided by public authorities would be reduced and a continuing home life with increased independence could be offered to men and women who might otherwise have to seek refuge in an institution.

It was a new and difficult venture and progress was slow. The three years for which the work was planned was extended, at the request of the advisory committee, to four. Social workers with the experience and interest which the work needed were not easy to recruit for the limited duration of the project and with no sure prospect of the outcome. Three groups were involved for each foster home that was arranged – the

PLATE 11 Part of the co-ownership estate built on the site of Ouse Lea.

PLATE 12   The headquarters of the Rowntree Trusts at Beverley House. The first extension on the left can still be identified; to the right a second extension is nearing completion. Details of brickwork, windows and roof in the original building have been faithfully followed in

families who were to be the hosts; the frail or handicapped person for whom help was needed; the social workers planning and operating the new family care service. To explain the scheme proved a difficult and complex task and progress was slow. Those monitoring the work hoped that light would be thrown on four questions: Is family care possible? Is it worthwhile? What does it cost? What is involved in planning and operating a family care service? Some of the complexities of the work become clear from a summary of the numbers of guests and hosts involved during the four year period. Some 363 people were referred to the project for whom a home with a family was thought to be suitable. More than half the number were in some form of residential care. The largest group – about one-third – were mentally ill; nearly as many were mentally handicapped. There were smaller numbers of physically handicapped and a few defined simply as elderly. Enquiries were received from 204 families about the possibility of providing a foster home. In the result thirty-eight people were received into the homes of twenty-nine families for longer or shorter periods. There was a surprising proportion of mentally handicapped amongst those regarded as having being successfully placed. A detailed report of the whole experience was prepared for the Department of Health and Social Security which financed the monitoring and research; a summary report was made available by the North Yorkshire Social Services Department; the project was described in technical journals.

There are now a number of such schemes in operation in different parts of the country. Any more substantial report should take account of the experience in other areas; tentative answers were given from the North Yorkshire experience to the four questions posed by the research staff but larger numbers and different methods of operating need to be brought into the analysis if a judgment is to be made on family care as a different and, for some, more acceptable way of helping those who need continuing care.

The need to assess the outcome of the growing expenditure on publicly provided social services was referred to in almost every policy paper submitted to the Trustees after their powers were extended by the Joseph Rowntree Memorial Trust Act. A theme of the Trust's published reports had been the possible role of trusts and foundations in evaluating the services which this expenditure supported. An opportunity to act on this intention came with the retirement of Miss E.M. Goldberg, formerly a scientific officer with the Medical Research Council, from the research unit at the National Institute for Social Work. She was persuaded to accept a senior fellowship at the Policy Studies Institute, giving two-thirds of her time over a period of three years. She thought that her study should not be directed to a review of the effectiveness of social *work*, but to a more pragmatic examination of the effectiveness of social care, widely interpreted and related to the particular needs of the elderly. The importance which the Trustees attached to this study is shown by the authority of the advisory committee they were able to appoint. It included a Professor of Sociology and a Professor of Social Psychiatry, the Director of the Central Council for Education and Training in Social Work; the Director of Social Services of a London Borough, who was also a member of the Chief Scientists' Research Committee at the Department of Health and Social

Security; the Chairman of the Trust, and another Trustee who was also Chairman of the governing body of the National Institute for Social Work; the Senior Research Officer of the National Bureau for Child Care; the head of the Thomas Coram Research Unit within the Institute of Education at London University; and an Assistant Director of Social Work Service in the Department of Health and Social Security who, more than two years later, was to be selected by the Trustees as the successor to the Directorship of the Trust, although no one had foreseen this at the time. The committee also included a member in the United States, where similar problems were under investigation, who contributed to the study by correspondence.

In the course of the study a workshop was arranged on recent trends in evaluative research in social work and the social services. The participants were drawn from the United States and Europe. The Trust financed the gathering as an addition to the main project; the papers presented were subsequently published. The results of the main study on evaluating social care for the elderly was completed in 1980 and published the following year – more than a decade after the Trustees had first decided to commit themselves to this difficult field of research and begun their attempts to launch a first project.

Another ambitious venture in partnership with a local authority had to be brought to an end within a year of its opening. The terms of reference of the Wolfenden Committee had drawn a sharp distinction between the work of voluntary organisations and the deployment of volunteers. The committee was concerned with the former. The Trustees were, however, also concerned to assess how effective could be the contribution of volunteers in the statutory services and a large metropolitan authority agreed to join in an action research project designed to assess the benefits and the costs of using an increased number of volunteers within the Social Services Department. The conceptual and technical difficulties of quantifying benefits and costs in this way were undoubtedly substantial. It soon became clear that there were differences in the approach of the Trust, the authority and the staff recruited to direct the project, that made any joint project impracticable. Without any criticism of their partners, the Trustees thought it best to recognise that an investment over four years was unlikely to bring useful results and the enterprise was abandoned. It was a decision unique in the experience of the Trust.

Two other studies concerned with the development of social care were initiated from within the Trust in which advisory committees played an important part and which led to publications likely to have continuing relevance to social policy. It was estimated that ninety per cent of severely disabled children in the United Kingdom were cared for at home with their families; in some other countries the pattern was different – a high proportion received care in institutions. There was evidence that the same might be true of the elderly. Responsible families wonder whether they are doing their best for their handicapped members by keeping them at home; would standards of material care and expert treatment be higher in hostels, residential homes or hospitals? If even five per cent of the families who now look after severely dependent members were to ask statutory

authorities to take over the responsibilities, the pressure on the social services, at least in the short run, would be calamitous. So the Trust wished to initiate a study of the changing patterns of family care. For this they were successful in interesting an American scholar who came with his family to London for a year to review the influences at work in Britain, the experience of one or two similar countries, and to attempt to forecast trends with some consideration of their social implications. A year's work along these lines might at least show where it would be useful to dig more deeply. The results of the survey were published with that purpose in mind.

Finally, the Trustees became convinced of the need to launch a study of day centres. For well over a decade they had received applications from voluntary organisations for help in establishing day centres for the elderly, or for adults who were mentally or physically handicapped. They had been impressed with the wide variation in the services offered, in the way the centres were staffed, and in their relationships with other services. The Trustees were under constant pressure to extend the range of the study that was eventually launched and it proved difficult to contain both its scope and its cost. To bring it to completion was a difficult task for the advisory committee. The report is an important guide in a field of activity in which very substantial capital expenditure is being deployed.

This was a period of high morale within the Joseph Rowntree Memorial Trust. The introduction of a part-time consultant familiar with the work of the Trust, and accustomed to work with it, brought an increased capacity to identify the issues which the Trust should examine, and initiate in partnership with others the studies which would illuminate them.

A second new field of work was opened by the Trust during the later years of the decade. It was introduced by the second consultant, appointed to maintain and strengthen the capacity of the Trust in research and innovation, in the period immediately prior to a change in its directorship.

In November 1976, a discussion paper was considered by the Trustees concerned with what was identified as 'Structural Unemployment in Inner Cities'. It took as its starting point, the assumption that when the hoped for upturn in the economy took place, certain areas which suffer from structural unemployment might benefit marginally, but were likely to be left with their endemic problems. A variety of initiatives had been taken over the previous ten years to anticipate such problems, but their combined effect had not been in any way spectacular. The initiatives included the creation of educational priority areas, the urban programme, the introduction of community development schemes, and the series of inner-area studies, with their own particular style of operational research. The discussion paper suggested that although the solution in the long term must lie in a combination of education, training and new employment, there may be scope for private initiative in building on some of the vigorous neighbourhood groups in order to establish small scale enterprises in inner-city areas, which, given a sheltered environment in which to operate for about three years, might well prove commercially viable. Some established businesses in these areas were already doing valuable work in placing employment opportunities within the communities of

which they were a part; it was argued that an additional component was needed, having an agency or brokerage role, to bring together knowledge about sources of aid, training opportunities, and marketing and commercial expertise.

Both the needs and possible ways of meeting them were discussed at more than one meeting of the Trust. In the outcome, the Trustees agreed to embark on a series of five projects over a period of about three years, which together would be likely to absorb about £200,000. The most Trustees could hope to do, would be to draw attention to the nature of the problems that needed to be resolved, and suggest, by practical demonstration, some principles which might be capable of wider application.

They first decided to strengthen and expand an initiative already taken by business and community leaders in Merseyside. There is probably no area in the country where the impact of changes in established patterns of industry and commerce has been greater. The physical, economic, and social consequences are there to be seen by even the most superficial observer. Resources from the Trust were made available, over a period of three years in the first instance, to a group constituted as an Action Resource Centre, competent to assess the feasibility of new initiatives in business and manufacture, to decide how best to inject technical or financial support, and so to monitor these new developments that a body of experience would be built up enabling decisions on these matters to be made with a greater degree of confidence. The advisory committee brought together to forward the project was larger than that appointed for any other Trust venture, and was drawn from a wider range of people from universities, community organisations, commerce, industry, the press, and nationalised industries. A parallel initiative was taken in supporting an Action Resource Centre in Glasgow.

The second project to receive support was concerned with the evaluation of the job creation programme. Some initiative in this matter had already been taken by the University of Stirling, which had brought together representatives from the Manpower Services Commission, from the local authorities, from employers and from the trade union movement. There were, at that time, fifteen thousand jobs in Scotland within the job creation programme, and the study was to be based on a sample of one thousand people employed within the scheme. The purpose was to enable judgments to be formed on the experience of those employed within the programme, and their subsequent experience in seeking employment.

Thirdly, the Trustees wished to examine the attitudes of students at universities to their future employment. The general statement was often made that students preparing for a first degree were prejudiced against industry and tended to favour the field of public service, including the universities themselves. The University of Lancaster was, therefore, supported in a study aimed to assess the factors which determine the attitudes of graduates to different kinds of employment. A number of university and polytechnic departments were identified, which had high and low proportions of male graduates entering industry. Within those institutions, attitudes to public service and industrial employment by undergraduates at different ages, and from different social backgrounds, were

assessed, and changes in attitudes were identified which might take place whilst a student was at university or polytechnic. The analysis, the researchers expected, would show how far these changes could be related to the structure of the courses which undergraduates decided to follow.

The fourth development in the field of employment which attracted the attention of the Trust, was concerned with common ownership and the growth of co-operative enterprises in a local economy. In 1960 there were twenty co-operative enterprises in Britain; by 1977 it was thought that there were about one hundred and seventy. Local authorities were seeking new powers to assist and influence industrial development, and some were discussing extensions of co-operative enterprise, which might well prove successful, particularly in areas of high unemployment. Other questions which needed to be examined included the availability of capital, the influence which could be exerted by central and local government, and how far the increase in the number of co-operative enterprises reflected the measure of success in achieving their economic objectives. The Centre for Environmental Studies, which had designed the study, was concerned that it should be at a very practical level and that the results should be presented in a form designed to be of immediate use to those who would have to make decisions affecting the future development of co-ownership and co-operative enterprises.

The last in this series of projects came to the notice of the Trustees as a result of initiatives by a group of schools in the York area. Their representatives made no claim to be initiating a new venture, but saw their work as a local response to the growing and desirable trend amongst educational and industrial institutions to work and think and plan together. There were five secondary schools in the group – a grammar school, a mixed secondary modern school, and three mixed comprehensive schools; with them was associated a college of further education. If, later, other secondary schools in the York area saw advantages in the work of the group it was open to them to join it. The contribution of the Trust was to provide funds so that a liaison officer could be employed for three years to work with the schools and with industry. The local authority associated itself with the project by providing accommodation and secretarial services. One major employer released an experienced person for part-time to work with the liaison officer, helping, in particular in the early stages, in securing the right relationships with local industry. The immediate aim of the project was to offer a service of advice to young people and to industry. Part of the Trust's interest in the project was that the experience was to be carefully monitored and recorded as a piece of educational research. Whether or not the outcome of the venture would show the need for a permanent organisation and attract the funds to support it, had to depend on the analysis of the practical results for young people and for industry.

This group of five projects was broadly within the field of community development which at an earlier stage the Trustees had excluded from their programme. Thus the Trust had no direct experience to contribute; they offered support to initiatives already taken by others which needed resources beyond what were available to the initiators, if the possibilities inherent in their work were to have a chance of realisation.

At the end of the period covered by this account of the Trust's work, interim or final reports had been received on each project in this new series. For some, a report was unimportant save as a mark of account-ability whether by the researchers to the Trustees, or by the Trustees to the public on whose behalf they administered the Founder's bequest. Action Resource Centres in Merseyside and in Glasgow had to justify the funds and time invested in them by what they achieved for men and women without work and often without hope. How far the new workshops would lead to new sources of employment it is too early to say. The conditions in those areas make the task immensely difficult. But the immediate impact on men and women able to use their skill and initiative in producing useful goods often from salvaged materials is there to be seen; it is a risk investment of a sort that trusts exist to make. The York and District Schools and Industry Project started slowly but at the end of the three years for which Trust support was given it could show a record of new and constructive links between teachers in different disciplines and those in industry using the skills they taught. The Trust was asked to extend support for a single year and to allow the money to be used over a longer period as the expected longer term money from other sources came in. The expectation was fulfilled. Then there were the three evaluation reports. The Lancaster study of Undergraduate Attitudes to Employment was complete; the outline of the report which would be published had been received by the Trust. Important changes in the attitudes which were being examined had clearly taken place during the period of the study – the outcome of a depression unexpected in its severity when the work was planned. The University of Stirling had published its evaluation of the job creation programme. The examination of co-ownership and co-operative enterprises by the Centre for Environmental Studies was complete and the results published. Again the findings about the conditions required for such projects to flourish were more sharply relevant in 1980, when new enterprise was so desperately needed, than the researchers could have foreseen when the work was planned.

In Chapter 15 there is an account of the attempt by the Trust to evaluate the public significance of its own work over a decade. One of the hypotheses it wished to test was that projects initiated from within the Trust were more likely to be brought to a conclusion within the time allocated, and to lead to positive results, than those which came as unsought applications for financial support. This series of projects was started after the decade covered by that evaluation. Should the Trustees pursue their intention to repeat that evaluation, these projects would be important amongst the evidence to be examined. They were outside the field of the Trust's established interests; there was no corporate experience within the Trust of the problems they considered. But they were the outcome of a second part-time appointment to the Trust's staff made with the deliberate intention of introducing new outlets for the Trust's resources. They might well rank high in the 'rating scale for outcome' devised for the Trust's assessment of its work.

14 Centre for Studies in Social Policy and Policy Studies Institute

On 9 October 1970, the Chairman introduced another discussion on the future role of the Trust. He is recorded in the minutes as introducing his statement by observing that over the previous twelve months it had become clear to Trustees that the main thrust of their work should be concerned with the implementation of social policy. Much was being done, to which the Trust had contributed, in identifying policies in different fields of social and community work which could profitably be deployed. There remained, however, a gap between this and the implementation of those policies. The Chairman went on to tell his colleagues that he had been involved in a number of discussions about the possible establishment of a Centre for the Study of Social Policy. Any involvement in such a project by the Trust would need to take account of four considerations.

First, American experience tended to show that work along these lines would need to be developed in an international context.

Second, the Trust had resources to make a substantial contribution to such a centre, thus enabling it to have a voice in the direction of its work, but other and 'more substantial' resources would be required, whether from the British government, or from the specialist agencies of the United Nations, which were concerning themselves with this same field of work.

Third, preliminary enquiries from those within and outside government, who had experience of such developments, led to questions about the scale which would be necessary to make such a centre effective, and what its relationships would be to other institutions which in part filled a similar role.

Fourth, it would be desirable, so far as the Trust was concerned, that any project of the kind discussed should be complemented and supported, by a range of smaller and continuing projects related to the same theme of the implementation of social policy.

All Trustees could say in response was that the idea of initiating an international centre of this sort held great attractions, but clearly presented issues of great complexity, and called for a leisurely discussion at a meeting convened with little other business on the agenda paper. The Trustees decided to devote their January meeting to this topic.

On 15 January 1971, the Trustees made the decision to establish a Centre for Studies in Social Policy. The Trustees recorded in their minute 'In establishing the centre, the Trustees would be initiating a major commitment, of a different kind from anything previously undertaken'.

The wider consultations which were thought to be essential at the earlier

discussions came after the decision to proceed had been made. The 'more substantial' resources from other contributors referred to in the Chairman's statement were not on this occasion considered; the Trust decided to proceed alone. No serious thought was given to the financial implications; there were eight items of expenditure in an outline budget which added up to the amount which the Trustees had earlier decided that they could allocate to new developments. Any developments other than the proposed centre were by implication excluded, though the need for a series of related projects had been stressed. The lessons to be drawn from the Trust's experience in founding the National Institute for Social Work Training were accepted; no term could be set to a commitment involving the establishment of a new institution. Indeed the permanence of the Trust's support was seen as the critical distinction between the project now launched by the Trust, and those which, it was understood, had been considered by other organisations. There was a permanent source of income available to sustain the centre and to ensure its independence. The Trustees hoped that other organisations, including government departments, would wish to make use of the facilities which the new institution provided, and commission studies or research on policy issues which were of current importance. But the support of the centre itself, its premises, its upkeep and its core staff, would remain a responsibility of the Trust and the centre would be the Trust's instrument.

The decision presented a number of practical and philosophical questions. The Founder, in the Memorandum printed in the opening pages of this record, had discouraged his Trustees from passing the resources of the Trust to other bodies, who would decide how they should be used; they should themselves take responsibility for the deployment of the funds of the Trust. This requirement, though it had no legal force, still commended itself to the Trustees as one of the most valuable principles which the Founder had built into his bequest; it strengthened the Trustees in their resolve to create an institution which should be their own instrument, and in whose work they should, as a group, be intimately involved.

It was the practical application of this resolve, however, that presented difficulty. The Trustees took the view that their purpose would be met if all Trustees approved the objectives of the Centre, and three or four of their number, who might rotate, were included in the membership of any governing body. It was appreciated that Trustees could not provide a majority of any governing body; it must have considerable independence of the Trust if men and women of the experience and calibre required were to give their time to the Centre's work. But once an institution is launched with its own governing instrument, with a council or governing body which is wider than the initial sponsoring body, and with a director and senior staff appointed by, and responsible to, that governing body, then the sense of direct responsibility to the founding Trustees must progressively diminish. There is adequate experience of the development of institutions to show the tensions and strains inevitable in such a constitutional and administrative structure. The difficulties were increased for this new institution because the amount of money which the Trustees were setting aside was relatively modest, and could cover only the costs of a

very limited programme. The point was emphasised in the wider consultations that were now put in hand. The Centre would therefore be dependent, if it were to make its mark in its chosen field, on securing substantial funds from other organisations.

In less than a decade, the Trustees were obliged to make new and no less radical decisions about the future of the centre. The positive advantage which it had increasingly brought to their work was the wider range of experience and expertise available as they considered the use of growing resources. They had underestimated some of the difficulties. It had not been possible to purchase premises of a kind which could be identified with the Trust. The centre was housed in rented premises the price of which was subject to periodic review. To recruit a research staff in the social sciences of the calibre needed if the Centre was to establish the international standing that its work required was hardly possible given the limited resources available for its work. Half way through the decade the Trustees noted in a published report:

> It is undoubtedly a momentous decision; the development of the new Centre, its relationship to the Trust, and the impact on the Trust's own programme will all be watched with care over the next decade. It may well be that the income of the Trust will continue to grow, and that the new departure will prove so successful that other centres similarly constituted may be established to pursue particular areas of work which the Trustees believe should be supported from Trust resources. On the other hand, the links with the parent Trust may prove difficult to maintain; or the area of direct activity left to the Trustees and their staff may be unduly limited. To sustain the life and vigour of a trust requires the continuing pressure and challenge of increasing resources to be used in ways relevant to the changing life of the community. This stimulus cannot be replaced by reports, however interesting these may be. Time will show whether the Trustees have found a successful instrument through which to deploy rising resources in ways consistent with the wishes of the Founder, but relevant to the times in which the Trust has to operate, or whether other and different methods may have to be sought.

By the end of 1977, decisions were made which meant that the Centre for Studies in Social Policy, as an independent body wholly dependent on the Trust for its resources, was about to come to an end. The Centre now absorbed a larger proportion of the Trust's income than had been contemplated, but the scale of its operations was still small. The relationship between the work of the Centre and the projects which the Trustees initiated, was tenuous in the extreme; each organisation necessarily reflected the interests and skills of those who directed the work, so that each had developed on distinct lines. No satisfactory means had been found of involving the Trust corporately in the work of the centre. Trustees were a minority on the governing body, and the involvement of the remainder of the Trustees was limited to hearing or reading reports on the Centre's work.

How these problems would have been resolved, had there been no other reason for change, it is not possible to say. The experience had been a salutary one, and it is probably safe to predict that the Trust would be unlikely to embark again on the establishment of an independent institution, wholly and permanently dependent on Trust resources. Apart from any other consideration, the costs of such an institution rise with the general level of costs in the community. There can be no guarantee that the income of a foundation, at least in the short term, will keep pace with inflationary trends in the same way. It follows that it is then upon the Trust's own programme that restrictions have to be concentrated.

Comparisons are sometimes drawn with an institution – the Outer Circle Trust – established by the Joseph Rowntree Social Service Trust, the non-charitable Trust established by the same Founder for the reasons given in an earlier chapter. But there were important differences that make any comparison of little value. The Outer Circle Trust was set up from funds not subject to the laws of charity to examine a range of policy issues, and then to undertake political discussion and negotiation to achieve the legislative changes which research showed to be necessary. The director was supported by two research assistants and secretarial staff; financial commitment was little more than one-third of that accepted by the Memorial Trust for the Centre for Studies in Social Policy. The Outer Circle Trust was given support for five years to achieve defined objectives; the problem of securing a director for so short a period was overcome by offering an additional year's salary at the end of the five year term to allow adequate time for the holder of the post to move to the next stage in his career. In fact he left, and the Trust finished its work before the end of the five year term; other members of its staff found other posts, perhaps helped by the period of intense political work in which they had been engaged. There was no intention to involve members of the sponsoring Trust in the work of the institution; the objects having been agreed, the staff pursued their research and political lobbying from day to day in the most effective way they knew. They achieved considerable success.

The immediate cause for a review of the Memorial Trust's relationship to the Centre for Studies in Social Policy was the announcement by the director of his intention to return to the civil service and to a new post to which he felt strongly drawn. The vacant post was advertised, but before any appointment could be made the Trustees as sponsors of the Centre were drawn into a new and different venture.

One of the arguments which led the Trustees to initiate the Centre was the influence and prestige of the Brookings Institute in the United States. Some experienced observers advised at the time that the scale on which the Trust could operate could not conceivably reproduce in the United Kingdom a comparable institution. Now, however, the Director of the London School of Economics and Political Science, Professor Dahrendorf, began a campaign to secure the establishment of a European institution which would be comparable to Brookings. He argued that the four institutions in the United Kingdom, which partly covered that field of work, should come together, and then seek substantial additional resources, from the United Kingdom and from Europe, so that a new

institute could be launched. The four institutions he had in mind were: The Royal Institute of International Affairs, better known as Chatham House; The National Institute for Economic and Social Research (NIESR); Political and Economic Planning (PEP); and The Centre for Studies in Social Policy (CSSP). Some of these institutions received substantial public funds, and there were indications that these might be transferred to a new institute along the lines now proposed, and withdrawn from the specialist bodies to which so far they had been paid. The view of those responsible for these bodies was that, in the United Kingdom setting, there were advantages in having separate institutions of reasonable size, which could concentrate on a sphere of interest of which they had knowledge and experience, but collaborate in initiatives which called for shared resources, and were related to a common purpose. The three older institutions, Chatham House, NIESR, and PEP, had already had some preliminary discussions about the policy they should adopt towards Professor Dahrendorf's ideas. CSSP was drawn into the discussions at a later stage.

It immediately became apparent that two of the four institutions, Chatham House and NIESR, were of comparable size, each deploying resources equal in 1978 to about half a million pounds a year. PEP had resources of about half this amount and were conscious that this was inadequate to sustain a body of research work in their chosen field. That was a difficulty experienced also by CSSP, the latest arrival in the field; moreover the Centre was active in a field of work which had much in common with PEP. The latter raised its money from a variety of sources of which industry and commerce were the largest part; CSSP enjoyed a secure income from the Trust. Thus, the logic of the discussion soon became clear. If CSSP and PEP could merge, then there would be three, and not four, institutions each deploying approximately similar resources. One, Chatham House, would broadly represent the field of international affairs, the second, NIESR, would concentrate mainly, though not exclusively, on economic research, and the third, which would be a combination of CSSP and PEP, would apply itself particularly to the field of social policy.

There followed a concentrated round of discussions to see in what way a new development along these lines could be initiated. From the experience with CSSP, the Director of the Trust argued that Trustees should take this unexpected opportunity to discharge their continuing commitment to CSSP by a new and different agreement with the institution to be formed by the merger of CSSP and PEP. There would first be an obligation to provide a permanent endowment equivalent to about £100,000 a year – the amount of their original commitment to the centre. At the outset, the Trustees would have a moral obligation to finance projects costing a further £150,000 a year, thus bringing their total annual contribution to a quarter of a million pounds a year, and matching the resources brought to the joint venture by PEP. But this project money should, as quickly as possible, be identified with particular projects within the field of the Trust's interest; as these were brought to completion, future contributions to the programme of the new institution should result from initiatives

which the Trustees wished to see taken, or which had received their specific approval as being within the programme they wished to develop. Whether in the outcome the Trust's involvement was limited to their original capital gift, or whether sums much larger than any contemplated for CSSP would be deployed, would be determined by the usefulness of the new institution to the developing interests of the Trust.

Premises were found at a rent of £75,000 a year; the Trustees undertook to provide these for a period of twenty years, meeting any additional rent which would be negotiated in the course of the lease. The Trustees hoped in due course to buy the freehold of the building if it proved suitable for the work of the institute, and make it available without charge. They would retain the right to use the building for other purposes, or to recover their capital, if for any reason the work of the institute was brought to an end. The balance of £25,000 a year from their twenty year commitment would be indexed in relation to the level of retail prices and thus meet a substantial part of the cost of engaging a Director and his immediate personal staff. At the level of the Trust's income in 1978, the permanent contribution could readily be absorbed without substantial impact on the development of the Trustees own programme. Thus, a critical period in the Trust's history ended in a more constructive way than at one time seemed possible.

15 *An Evaluation of the Trust's Work*

The review of their programme which the Trustees undertook at the beginning of the 1970s, led first to the appointment of a part-time Associate Director as already described. There was, however, a second part of the Trust's review which led to an independent assessment of the Trust's work probably unique in the history of foundations.

The principal reason for the review was that the Trustees had been responding to a larger number of requests to support research originated by outside bodies, rather than from within the Trust. There seemed to be a greater difficulty in bringing such projects to a successful conclusion, than had been the case when the Trustees initiated the greater part of the work which they supported.

In a report published in 1972, the Trustees recorded:

> A disproportionate and wholly unjustifiable expenditure of time, as well as of other resources, has been devoted to the effort to secure the completion of some projects which have come to be supported in this way. The contrast over the whole field of the Trust's work between these projects and the work resulting from initiatives within the Trust is clearly marked. Too often grants are applied for and accepted, research staff engaged, field work planned and carried through; from all this no one but the researchers benefits. The more demanding task of recording and publishing the results is delayed, correspondence and visits of enquiry multiply, whilst not infrequently the original researchers have dispersed to distant and more immediately attractive assignments.

The Trustees, therefore, decided that they should finance an investigation which they hoped would throw light on these problems, and which would itself be something of a new departure in the practice of private trusts. They invited Dr J. A. Heady, a statistician, to consider the social investigations financed by the Trust since the passing of their Private Act. The terms of reference finally agreed between the Trustees and Dr Heady, are of some interest. They were:

a) To review the policy, practice and experience of the Trust in selecting and supporting research projects in the social sciences with special attention to:

    i) a comparison between the projects initiated from outside the Trust and those arising in part or wholly from within it, and

    ii) the fact that difficulties have been experienced in ensuring that

studies are completed and their results made available to interested professionals including administrators.

b) To discover the experience of other grant-giving bodies supporting similar work in so far as it is relevant to the problems of the Trust.

c) To identify:

   i) the methods of selection and administration of projects and of promulgation of their results which have most reliably resulted in a useful product, and

   ii) the aspects of the relationship with the Trust which have been particularly helpful or difficult for the research workers.

d) To make recommendations to the Trust.

Although a wide definition was given to the term 'research projects', the terms of reference excluded a substantial part of the work of the Trust, and this was deliberate. For example, the institutions supported by the Trust were not included; nor for the most part, was the work overseas. In fact, as Dr Heady recorded in his report, his investigation represented about one-third of the Trust's total expenditure on grants in the period. But this was the element in the Trust's expenditure which presented most uncertainty to the Trust; it was, as this record shows, well able to assess the relevance and the legitimacy of the other major developments which it had sustained, and to adapt its policy in the light of its judgments. Sixty-two projects were included in Dr Heady's study, and these covered five main fields of interest. They were: housing, the community, the personal social services, poverty and the family. Table 15.1, which is taken from Dr Heady's report, shows the amount of money spent under each of these headings, and the proportion of each to the total sum deployed. Two further categories are included in the table, which the Trustees undertook for special reasons; they are distinguished because it is in the first five categories where the Trust's traditional interests mainly lie.

Table 15.1 *Expenditure in each of the selected fields of interest*

Subject of Study	£	Percentage of Total
1 Housing	290,000	27
2 Community	370,000	34
3 Personal Social Services	127,000	12
4 Poverty	85,000	8
5 Family	38,000	4
6 Penal/delinquency/legal	87,000	8
7 Socio-medical	78,000	7
	£1,075,000	100%

Dr Heady was able to approach those who had held grants from the Trust, to seek, in confidence, their views on their relationships with the Trust, and in particular with the Trust's Director, and how far these were

helpful or inhibiting to them as researchers. Details of each research project, together with a statement of the outcome, were then subjected to assessment by three separate judges. Dr Heady devised a simple four point scale, by which the outcome of the projects could be assessed.

Rating Scale for Outcome

1 No result at all.
2 A report produced – but no publications, or influence on practice.
3 Publication or publications which have attracted little attention or failed to influence practice.
4 *Either*
Publication or publications which have attracted attention or influenced practice to a significant extent.

Or
Work (e.g. in association with a housing department) which, though not resulting in a publication, has noticeably influenced practice.

The ratings were made first by the Trust's Director; secondly, by a panel of outside judges; and thirdly, by Dr Heady himself. Most of those who were approached to serve on this panel of judges responded willingly; the demand on the time of each was limited, because they were chosen as people who would almost certainly know of the projects referred to them. Each was sent an abstract of the topic, and, unless the judge himself had access to a good library, he was also sent the publications and unpublished reports arising from the particular study. Most of the judges, in accepting the remit, said that they were willing to take part in what was an unusual exercise, and were indeed glad to do so, because they felt that foundations should undertake this kind of enquiry into their own procedures. From start to finish the analysis occupied more than six months. It resulted in the classification of all but four of the topics; for one reason or another, the judges concerned did not feel qualified to make an assessment of these four. The result of the investigation was published privately by the Trustees, but the report was widely circulated amongst foundations and others concerned with the management of social research; every request for a copy of the report was met. The Trustees saw no reason to keep the report confidential; but it was not a publication which would have been regarded as suitable for the commercial market. It is appropriate here to quote the final paragraph of Dr Heady's report, which, in broad terms, brings together the results of his interesting enquiry:

> To sum up, the record is that a quarter of the projects which have been reviewed were unanimously judged to have had a substantial impact, and more than sixty per cent produced a publication of some sort. Very few produced no report at all and some of these are on the way. So far as the writer knows there are no comparable figures by which this record can be assessed, but it does not appear to require any apology. There have, of course, been difficulties and several suggestions are put before the Trustees in the next chapter for consideration

as ways of reducing the delays and frustrations. They must, however, be set against the increase in administrative work and red tape which they would cause. As has been stressed, the yardstick of likely success is not put forward as the only or even the main criterion, on which potential projects should be judged. Difficult problems require experiment and risk-taking, but there is no harm in reducing the risk as much as possible by suitable procedures of selection and administration.

It may be of wider interest also, to quote in full the specific suggestions which Dr Heady made to the Trust in the light of his enquiry, and to which reference is made in the summary paragraph just quoted. There were twelve recommendations which he thought Trustees might consider.
The Trust should:

1　Continue to use a high proportion of its resources to support work originating outside the Trust because it is one of the few remaining non-government sources of such support.
2　Continue to make occasional small grants in spite of their relatively high risk of failure.
3　Consider more frequent consultation of referees.
4　Continue its policy of setting up advisory committees in suitable situations, but not inevitably, especially where there is strong institutional support.
5　Consider the institution of a system of regular reporting at least where there is no advisory committee which makes this requirement.
6　Consider the re-introduction of a standard form of agreement at the outset of a study which clarifies the expectations of the Trust in terms of reports, publications and time-table.
7　Consider publication in a leaflet, or in some other form which could be widely distributed, of a list of those subject areas where it wished particularly to concentrate its resources.
8　Consider the possibility of short-term grants to cover the planning and pilot stages of large studies.
9　Make specific and large allowances in the time-table for writing-up of studies.
10　Consider holding infrequent one-day or weekend meetings at which grant-holders of the more important studies could report progress directly to the Trustees.
11　Consider the possibility of entering into a relationship with a university press or similar publishing house in order to ease the present difficulty of publishing the results of studies which it has supported.
12　Consider placing grant-holders under a more specific obligation to keep the Trust informed about publications arising directly or indirectly from studies which they have supported, and to follow this requirement up with reminders in the few years after publication of the main report.

A small point of some interest is to compare the ratings in the Rating Scale for Outcome given by each of the three judges. The Director of the Trust had rather fewer projects recorded under the first category of having produced no result at all. The reason for this was simply that he knew of publications in the course of preparation, on which information was not necessarily available to the other two judges. Then, he rated a substantially larger number of projects under category three – projects where the publication or publications attracted little attention, or failed to influence practice. The outside judges were more optimistic about the impact of the work which the Trust had supported, whilst Dr Heady came mid-way in his assessment between the Trust Director and the outside panel of judges. The Trust Director was more pessimistic in the award of category four – projects having had a substantial impact on practice; the Director awarded this classification to only one-third of the projects, whilst the outside judges thought that fifty per cent deserved this classification and in this category Dr Heady was slightly more optimistic than were the outside judges.

The Trustees found the exercise of great value. They recorded their determination to repeat it in respect of a range of comparable projects, initiated during a second and later period of their activity. The analysis itself and the recommendations which were made, have certainly influenced the Trustees' procedure and practice. But the involvement of the Trust office in this disciplined examination of the work for which it had a large measure of responsibility, had perhaps as much impact on the development of the Trust's programme as did the report itself.

Part IV *External Responsibilities*

16 *The Family Fund*

A New Government Initiative

The Wolfenden Committee on Voluntary Organisations discussed the role and importance of national and local intermediary bodies. The solution they provide to the problem of distributing government funds to support voluntary organisations is described in Chapter 13. Wolfenden found an example in the Housing Corporation, which allocated £400 million in a single year for approved projects to the 3,000 disparate, but registered, housing associations, which make up the voluntary housing movement. It noted also the Development Commission, which recommends allocations from the Development Fund; the University Grants Committee, which in its heyday presented to government its estimate of the financial needs of universities, and then distributed what was forthcoming among individual universities in accordance with its judgment of the needs of each. The Committee included in these intermediary bodies the Arts Council, the Countryside Commission and the Commission for Racial Equality. For some purposes, on the other hand, a government department will make grants direct to independent agencies; the Department of Health and Social Security, the Department of the Environment, the Home Office and the Department of Education and Science, all make grants to voluntary organisations. The centre of the problem of allocating public funds directly to independent bodies is *discretion*; how far can civil servants have freedom in making allocations which may greatly extend the scale of one organisation, maintain the work of another at the same level, and make certain the early demise of a third?

The administrative structure described by Wolfenden was concerned with the support of organisations. Payments to persons are governed by different principles. The merits of any system to allocate grants and allowances to individuals, if the reports of the Supplementary Benefits Commission are taken as a guide, lie in the *absence* of the need for the exercise of discretion. The system should produce standard allowances for which there is clearly defined entitlement. The Commission, to pursue that example, is neither organised nor staffed, nor could it be, to undertake an eleemosynary distribution on the scale required, if standard allowances were to be substantially replaced by benefits paid at discretion.

On one occasion, when the problems of discretion were particularly acute, the Trustees themselves accepted the role of an intermediary body and became responsible for the distribution of public funds. It was not an easy decision; the use of a powerful independent organisation to discharge public duties brings the organisation itself into political controversy; it may be difficult to safeguard the integrity of the work for which it exists.

The task was accepted by the Trustees with reluctance and subject to conditions which they did not expect the government would find tolerable. From the public standpoint, it was a departure in public administration for which there was no clear precedent; from the Trust's point of view it involved risks of political involvement from which, in the event, the Trustees have been unable to escape. So in the history of the Trust for the last decade, the administration of the Family Fund has an important place. The Family Fund was the name given to the resources placed by successive governments in the control of the Trustees, from which help was given to families having the care of a very severely handicapped child.

The origins of the Family Fund can be briefly stated. In September 1972 an article in the *Sunday Times* brought into public discussion the tragic results for 500 or so families of the use by the mother during pregnancy of a drug made in Germany, but marketed in the United Kingdom by the Distillers Company, under the name Thalidomide. The drug was withdrawn in 1961 but not before several hundred children had been born with terrible, and sometimes grotesque, handicaps. With the legal complexities which attended the efforts of the parents to obtain compensation, this record is not concerned. The sense of public outrage was expressed in debates and questions in Parliament, leading on 29 November to a motion tabled by the opposition and seeking the establishment of a fund for the children. Sir Keith Joseph, at that time Secretary of State for Health and Social Services, gave reasons for the refusal of the government to intervene in ways that might affect the responsibility in law of the Distillers Company, but drew the attention of the House of Commons to the needs of the much greater number of families carrying comparable burdens for whom no compensation from Distillers or any other source was available. In winding up the debate, Sir Keith Joseph told the House:

> I have something to say which the House will want to hear before I sit down. I must say again, so that I do not lose the thread of the argument, that compensation is for the company and that the offer indicates active negotiation.
>
> The government must recognise that there are others born with desperate congenital disabilities which gravely burden their families and which are as severe as the loss of limbs due to Thalidomide. Such families are inevitably involved in all manner of special needs. Many of these needs are the responsibility of statutory authorities but there are other forms of help outside these responsibilities which could improve the life of a child and reduce the burden on its family. The government accept that more needs to be done for children with very severe congenital disability whether or not caused by the taking of Thalidomide.
>
> In many cases the parents need more help in shouldering the various burdens which caring for these children entails. I have already paid tribute to the remarkable achievements of many of the parents concerned. The government have therefore decided to make the sum of £3 million available for this purpose, virtually at once. It is not intended that this money should be by way of compensation for being

disabled, but rather that it should serve to complement the services already provided by statutory and voluntary bodies to help the families concerned.

With this in mind the government will begin at once to consider, in consultation with the statutory and voluntary bodies likely to be concerned, what arrangements they can set up so that the money can best be used for the benefit of the children and their parents. The House can be assured that this will be carried out as quickly as possible. Further, in the light of experience with this operation and as soon as the cases are no longer *sub judice* the government will consider whether to provide a similar further amount of money in trust.

On the following day, 30 November 1972, the first approach was made to the Joseph Rowntree Memorial Trust to enquire whether it might be willing to take on this responsibility; on 6 December there was an exchange of views between officials of the Department and officers of the Trust to explain why the choice had fallen on a Trust which had no direct experience either of allocating money to individual families, or of the particular needs of handicapped children, and how, if the Trust agreed to take on the work, the Fund might be administered. On 11 December, the Trustees met for one of their ordinary meetings; the following evening the Chairman of the Trust, Lord Seebohm, and its Director, met Sir Keith Joseph to explain the conditions which the Trust would have to set if it were to administer the Fund. Three days later the House of Commons was told that agreement had been reached and the establishment of the Fund under the direction of the Trust would proceed.

Questions had been raised about how this unusual way of administering public funds would work. The Secretary of State in replying to these questions in the House of Commons identified some principles which were critical to the way the Trustees set about their task. It would not change the duties which statutes lay upon public authorities; it would complement them. Nor would it be concerned with compensation. The words he used were:

The House has generally welcomed the government's decision to make available virtually at once, as soon as we can make the necessary arrangements, a fund of £3 million. I emphasise again that this is not compensation. Its purpose is to ease the burden of living on those households containing very severely congenitally disabled children.

These children and these households look, above all, to the local authorities and the statutory services for the help they need. We intend to help from this fund to complement the statutory services available.

We have it in mind – this answers a question asked by my Hon. Friend the Member for Clapham (Mr William Shelton) – to try to find a set of trustees of an existing trust with responsibilities sufficiently wide to cover beyond Thalidomide the other very severely congenitally disabled cases. We hope that we shall be able to put this into

action very soon. We believe that the trustees should have power to spend income and, where they judge fit, capital.

I do not wish to overstate this case, but I suggest that those households which are under particular strain and about which we are, above all, worried during the period of waiting for a satisfactory settlement will be able to be helped to some extent by the trustees of this new sum.

Hon. Members asked me about the second £3 million to which I referred. I emphasise again that this also is not for compensation. It is intended to benefit, via the same channel, if our experience of handling the first £3 million is satisfactory, the same limited but rather wider than Thalidomide group, by the same means – namely, the use of income plus capital as the trustees judge fit.

Outside Parliament, reaction was varied. Some commentators deplored the decision of the government and of the Trust; this was no way for the community to discharge its responsibilities to some of its most needy members. Others produced figures to show that the total sum – whether £3 million or £6 million – would be totally inadequate to achieve the government's purposes. Those representing the interests of groups of families likely to benefit asked by whom were decisions on the allocation of the money to be made and to whom could a dissatisfied family appeal. Who would settle difficult questions about the entitlement of this child or that to be accepted as 'very severely handicapped' or as suffering from a condition which was 'congenital'? Reflecting on the range of such problems, one thoughtful contributor to the debate asked 'How can the unfortunate Trust cope?'

There were more fundamental questions of policy to which students of social administration were drawing attention. What was to be the future of the fund? Whether the lessons learned from its administration were to be used to develop and shape the public service, or whether the Fund was to be a continuing complementary instrument, had not been discussed. Was this a new mechanism to overcome the rigidity and slow response often inseparable from a service shaped by regulation and circular, and was it one which might for similar reasons be extended to other fields – the aged, for example, or children whose handicap is not congenital? If so, what were the implications for social policy of the creation by government of an alternative source of this kind to supplement statutory provision and reduce the inequities inherent in the unevenness of local administration?

The Trustees had themselves pondered these and other questions when they met on 11 December to decide their response to the Secretary of State's request. There was certainly no sense of rejoicing around the committee table in York when Trustees considered what action they should take. They were not staffed for such an enterprise; there was a danger that they would be drawn into controversy, not only about the individual decisions which they would have to make, but about the rightness of governments to resolve an urgent public problem in this way, and about their own wisdom in making this solution possible. Both the diversion of administrative resources, and their involvement in political

controversy, could prejudice the main work of the Trust which was to deploy a substantial income in housing and social research and experiment. Against all this, the Trustees would have been less than human had they not felt a certain satisfaction at being asked by the government to undertake so unusual an enterprise; the prospect of making available immediate help to a large number of very deprived families ought not, they thought, to be rejected save for quite overwhelming reasons; and the Trust's interests in social policy might be carried forward in unexpected ways by involvement in what was clearly a new departure in public administration.

On that afternoon they made one central decision which their Chairman was instructed to convey to the Secretary of State the following day, and on which their agreement to proceed with the scheme depended. The entire pattern of administration of the Family Fund over the next five years followed from that one decision. It was, that the Trust could not act as an agent of government. It could, under its powers, accept from the government, or from anybody else, a sum of money small or large, which it would agree to devote to a particular field of work. The Trust would be willing to negotiate broad guidelines within which the money would be used. But the money would become part of the Trust's fund and decisions about individual grants would be made by the Trustees alone. Because the money became part of the Trust's fund they could not delegate their responsibilities and there would be no possibility of appeal against their decisions. Perhaps to their surprise, this view of the responsibility of a body of Trustees was at once accepted by the Secretary of State. The Trustees raised two lesser conditions which presented no difficulty. The first was that their administration of the fund should be limited in the first instance to a period of three years, and second there should be some phasing in the introduction of the fund so that they would have time to assess what administrative resources would be necessary.

A formal letter was sent to the Department of Health and Social Security on 13 December 1972, indicating that the Trust was willing to administer the Family Fund on the conditions agreed with the Secretary of State. Eight days later the Department responded with a letter to the Trust's Director which set out what came to be known as the guidelines, agreed between the Department and the Trust, for the day to day decisions the Trust would have to make. Essentially the guidelines defined the families who would be eligible for help from the Fund, and the area of discretion within which the Trust was expected to operate. First, the geographical limitation of the Fund were to include England, Scotland, Wales and Northern Ireland. Secondly, help could be given to particular parents, or others with parental responsibility, having the care of a child under the age of sixteen, who in the opinion of the Trust, was very severely congenitally handicapped. Definition of these terms was for the Trust and would be settled in the light of professional advice.

Then, the guidelines stated that the parents must, because of their social and economic circumstances, be in need of the help which the Trust considered should be provided. There were two matters of importance which arose from the application of this principle. First, it was clear from

the outset that the Trust could not, and would not, attempt to operate a means test; it would form a judgment about the impact of the handicapped child on the social and economic circumstances of the family and provide help accordingly. Then, in judging the kind of help which should be provided, it would seek to relieve the stress on the family whilst the handicapped child is cared for at home. This concept of stress has been central in the administration of the fund.

The remaining guidelines dealt with lesser matters. The Trust was able to continue to help an eligible family after the child had reached the age of sixteen; it could take the initiative in offering help to a family even though no application had been received; the Trust could seek advice, information, and assistance, from any other organisation; and it could give help to a family notwithstanding that it was within the power of the statutory services to provide the help it was offering. This last point was important and was one that the Trustees stressed to the Secretary of State. They were anxious not to be in a position where 'the buck' was constantly being passed. If what they had in mind to do for a particular family was within the powers of a statutory body, the Trustees were willing to ask that body if it was proposing to act. If, for whatever reason, the answer was no, then the Trustees claimed the right to proceed to give the help they judged to be necessary. They had no status to police the work of statutory authorities; the most they were willing to do was, in exceptional cases, to tell the Department if a local authority seemed to them to be neglecting its duties because the Family Fund existed.

The guidelines themselves were not unchangeable over any defined period; it would be open either to the Trust or the Department to seek a review at any time.

How the Fund was Managed

Having settled these principles the Trustees then turned their attention first to the administrative arrangements that they would make within their own organisation to carry out the day to day work of the Fund; these had to be capable of expansion at short notice as knowledge of the Fund spread, and the pace of applications increased. Second, they wished to establish a framework of consultation so that, even though decisions finally rested with the Trustees themselves, the decisions would take account of professional advice and the views of organisations more experienced in the needs of the handicapped than were the Trustees themselves. Thirdly, they had to consider how in the longer term the experience that they would gain could be of benefit to the government and the community, both in building a better understanding of the needs of families having the care of handicapped children, and in testing a new departure in social policy which might be extended to other fields.

It is convenient to deal first with the last of these. The Trustees believed that the experience to be gained from this new task might prove hardly less important than the immediate help they would give to families in distress. No precedent came readily to mind for a government thus using an

independent trust to administer at its discretion £3 million of public money. Nor was there another example of a trust being asked to operate from public funds a centrally directed service parallel to that locally directed by statutory authorities. How this came to be, and how the scheme developed, ought to be recorded as part of the history of social administration. Then, the Department had itself stressed that lessons would be learned about the needs of the handicapped. The Trust had a duty carefully to monitor the applications it received and the grants which it made, in order to learn more about stress in these families, and the extent to which it was relieved by the help which the Trust could offer.

With these things in mind an approach was made to the Vice-Chancellor of York University. The Trust offered, and the University accepted, a Research Fellowship, for a period of four to five years. The Department of Health and Social Security offered to contribute to the cost of this research, but the Trust at first preferred to regard the project as part of its own research programme which it might well have wished to sponsor regardless of its own part in the administration of the Family Fund. However, the statistical analysis essential to the research project was also needed for the effective administration of the Fund. The cost of the unit established within the University's Department of Social Administration and Social Work was therefore divided between the Department and the Trust to take account of its role in the administration of the Fund. The Family Fund Research Project, as it came to be known within the Trust, proved to be amongst the most successful research operations which the Trust initiated; it takes its place in importance with the Rowntree Trust Housing Study of which an account has already been given. Jonathan Bradshaw, who was appointed to the research fellowship, published in June 1980 *The Family Fund – An Initiative in Social Policy* (Routledge & Kegan Paul, 1980); it is an analysis of the experience gained in administering the Fund during the first three years. His work continued, financed directly by the Department of Health and Social Security, as the Social Policy Research Unit, within the Department of Social Administration and Social Work at the University of York. If the Trustees needed a justification for their original decision to accept the administration of the Family Fund, it could readily be found in the outcome of the research project which they initiated. A unique body of data has been brought together, and a research unit established, which will continue to influence policy decisions affecting families with handicapped children, and the administration of the services which are set up for their benefit.

The Trust's second task was to set up a framework of consultation. They devised four components designed to reconcile their inescapable responsibility as Trustees with their commitment to administer objectively and intelligently a sum of money derived from public funds. Their Trust Deed enabled them to appoint committees, which could include members from outside the body of eight Trustees, and which could be authorised to make decisions within a defined field, subject to the final authority of the Trustees. Acting on this power, the Trustees set up a management committee for the Family Fund; it included four of their own number, one of whom was chairman; a consultant paediatrician; a director

of a local authority social service department; and a former principal of an institution concerned with the training of social workers. To these were added observers from the Department of Health and Social Security and from the corresponding departments in Northern Ireland, Wales and Scotland. The Director of the Trust attended the meetings of the management committee and provided the secretariat.

This management committee in turn appointed three other bodies with specific advisory tasks. First there was a consultative committee, chaired by a member of the management committee, all of whose members were *ex officio* members of the consultative committee. To it were appointed men and women experienced in the needs of different groups of handicapped children; some who were concerned with research; and others from social work and social administration. They came from a variety of voluntary and statutory bodies but were appointed in a personal capacity, not as representatives. Thus there were no alternate members save by special arrangement. The terms of reference of the consultative committee were widely drawn; they included publicity, relations with voluntary and statutory bodies, the types of help which the Fund might give, and questions of definition. The consultative committee, as its name implies, was not executive; its recommendations were addressed to the management committee.

From the outset, too, the management committee saw that staff administering the Family Fund would need frequent guidance on new issues of principle presented by the applications they received, and on the eligibility of families not decisively within the guidelines agreed with the Department. Only thus could a 'case law' develop which would make possible rapid day to day decisions. To meet this need a panel was appointed, able to meet as required in the Trust office in York from which the Family Fund was administered. The panel consisted of two members of the management committee, one of whom served as chairman, a consultant paediatrician drawn from outside the management committee, and the Trust Director. To this panel, which met at the same time each week, the staff brought applications which raised questions of eligibility or of the type or scale of the grants that should be made. It came to be known as the York Panel. Early in the administration of the fund, the panel was the Trust's main instrument in defining principles to guide the staff in identifying the forms of help appropriate to needs that many families had in common; in applying the guidelines to particular groups of children and in considering new types of care. Requests for transport and telephones came frequently to the panel; the use of treatment, or of educational facilities, outside the national provision were examples of issues on which the York Panel reached decisions of principle later confirmed by the management committee.

The third body appointed by the management committee came rather later and as a result of experience. The consultant paediatrician on the management committee was the source of reference on the difficult questions of definition to which the term 'very seriously congenitally handicapped' inevitably gave rise. He worked closely with a colleague who served on the York Panel. They found that a number of medical questions

arose on which they would be helped by wider discussion with professional colleagues. The management committee responded to this need by inviting three consultants from different areas of the country to join with the two already helping in the work of the Family Fund, to form a medical advisory committee. Its convenor was the paediatrician from the management committee; most of the work was done by the circulation of papers, though meetings were not excluded. The committee's recommendations were made to the management committee.

It would be invidious to attempt to set in any order of importance the contribution made by the different persons and organisations who co-operated with the Trust in building up the Family Fund. But some of the most critical advice came to the Trustees from Professor Ross Mitchell, Professor of Child Health at the University of Dundee, who from the outset served on the management committee and was chairman of the medical advisory committee. He and his colleagues not only devised workable definitions relating the term 'very severely handicapped' to the wide variety of congenital conditions with which the Trustees had to deal, but made these usable by the lay men and women who represented the Family Fund to the individual family, and provided the reports on which the Trustees' decisions were based. The fear that the Trust might be drawn into public controversy over its decisions had been one of the principal reasons for hesitation in taking on the task in the first place. Criticism of the Trustees' administration has, in fact, been negligible. The reasons for this are complex and are examined in Jonathan Bradshaw's evaluation of the Fund. But there is no doubt about the debt which the Trustees owe to Professor Ross Mitchell and his colleagues for the remarkable combination of professional competence and human compassion which informed the advice they gave to the Trustees, and for the day to day guidance which was always available to the staff of the Family Fund.

The building of a sufficiently flexible administration for the Family Fund raised questions of a different kind. First, there was its cost. The Trustees decided from the outset that the greatest possible use should be made of their existing administration, and for this they would make no charge. Thus, the Director was responsible to the Trustees for the administration of the Fund. The Trust's Finance Officer controlled the receipt of money, its temporary investment, payments to families, and all other outgoings, and incorporated these transactions into the ordinary accounts of the Trust. Second, the Trust had assumed responsibility for the Fund for three years only, and the work might well have come to an end by that time. It seemed likely that once the Fund was opened, and publicity given to the help that was available, the number of applications, and therefore the weight of administration, would rise very rapidly; it also seemed reasonable to assume that at some stage the number of new applications would fall and would settle at a level determined by the number of births of very severely handicapped children, by applications from some who had not at first applied to the Fund, but whose circumstances changed so that an application became necessary, and by a diminishing number who had not previously been reached by the publicity given to the existence of the Fund. Figure 8 shows the number of applications

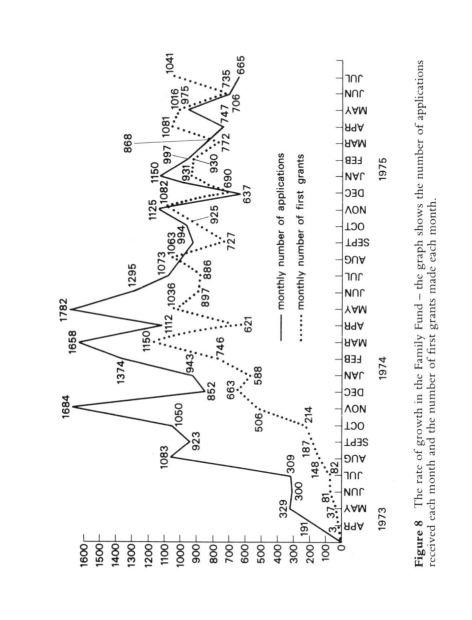

Figure 8 The rate of growth in the Family Fund – the graph shows the number of applications received each month and the number of first grants made each month.

received each month from April 1973, when the Fund opened, until July 1975, and the number of first grants made in each month. It indicates that the assumptions on which the Trustees planned their arrangements were broadly speaking well founded. As will be seen later, the extension of the Trust's responsibility for the Fund beyond three years gradually changed the nature of the task, in that the larger part of the resources were allocated to families which had already received help and were making further requests.

There have been two matters of controversy about the nature and scale of the administration of the Family Fund, on which Trustees have had to assert their view against a good deal of opposition. The first related to the role of professional social work in the administration of the Family Fund. Elsewhere in this book an account is given of the contribution which the Trustees have made to the development of the profession of social work. It has been second only to housing in the scale of Trust resources devoted to fellowships, training, and research. The Chairman of the Trust, Lord Seebohm, was Chairman of the committee which examined local authority personal social services and recommended the establishment of the social services departments, which were brought into being by legislation soon after the publication of the report. The Trust could, therefore, hardly be said to be in any way prejudiced against social work and those who practice it. Great pressure was brought to bear on the Trustees to accept the view that decisions on grants from the Family Fund should be made exclusively by trained social workers. The Trustees interpreted their task differently. They expected to identify quickly the stress within a family caring for a very severely handicapped child that could be reduced by some immediate aid beyond the family's own resources. Their involvement with the family would then cease, unless a second and different application needed to be made at a later stage. If the family required continuing support, whether from a professional social worker or any other trained staff, this was matter for the statutory services: it was no part of the business of the Trust to offer a continuing and parallel professional service. Nor were they directly in the business of supplementing a too low income. The key to the administration of the Fund, as the Trustees saw it, was the preparation of a report by a man or woman actually visiting the home. That person should have experience in visiting families of every kind and be able to assess what, in material terms, would be of the greatest help, in the particular circumstances, to the parents whose responsibilities included a very severely handicapped child. Their object was therefore to recruit social workers, health visitors, and other experienced people who would be ready at short notice to visit a family whose name had been brought to the attention of the Family Fund, and provide a report which would be so framed that, for the most part, an immediate decision on the action to be taken could be made by a small staff at the Trust headquarters, supported and advised by the consultative machinery just described, through which experience and professional advice – whether medical or social – was available. The person in charge of this operation immediately under the Trust's Director, might be a member of any profession or of none, but would primarily be capable of running a complex organisation,

subject to violent fluctuations in demand, with the maximum of efficiency and the minimum of cost. The critics of this view argued that a professionally qualified social worker alone was competent to visit a family and assess the need; the report coming from the social worker should then be examined by experienced social workers at the Trust headquarters; the administration within the Trust organisation should, therefore, be in professional hands. The Trust could not accept this view. The Director and his staff in other fields of Trust activity were accustomed to receive reports from a number of professions including architects, doctors, engineers, actuaries and accountants, and they expected these to be in terms which would enable a competent administrator to identify the issues and make relevant recommendations to Trustees. Indeed, it is difficult to see how the Trust could operate otherwise. The Trustees were therefore obliged to resist what might not unfairly be called professional politics; but they attached great importance to the professional competence of those who visited families who sought the help of the Fund, and to the contribution made by social workers as well as by the medical profession to the speedy and efficient decision-making organisation that evolved at the Trust headquarters.

The second controversial problem related to the scale on which the Family Fund should operate. The Trustees were advised that the total number of families in the United Kingdom likely to come within the criteria agreed by the government, was rather less than 100,000. There were, in the view of Trustees, three factors which limited the proportion of this 100,000 families who, at any one time, were likely to be in touch with the Family Fund. First, few applications were received for help in respect of children under the age of two years. This was for the obvious reason that the care of a tiny child is much the same whether handicapped or not. But there are important exceptions. Similarly, fewer applications were received in respect of older children. Some families seemed likely as a result of experience to have learnt how best to relieve the problems with which they were faced; for others, however, the difficulties clearly increased as the child grew older, though effective intervention by the Family Fund became more difficult as well. Third, and perhaps most important, the Family Fund had to take account of the social and economic circumstances of the family. By and large the kinds of help which, in the light of experience, it gave, were means of mobility; help with the problems of washing and drying clothes and bedding; the replacement of clothes and shoes, worn out more quickly than seemed to be allowed for in the statutory allowances; holidays for families who perhaps for years had not known a break from the continuing burden of the care of a very severely handicapped child. These things were accepted as part of the ordinary way of life, even by families of quite modest means. It was therefore to be expected that few applications would be received from more well to do families, though when these applications were received, they were likely to require more substantial expenditure which, though justified by the Trustees' criteria, was beyond the reasonable resources of the family. The number of applications which had to be rejected because the social and economic circumstances of the family seemed not to justify

help from the Fund was negligible; this indicated that its purpose and limitations had been successfully explained and were accepted. For these three reasons it seemed to the Trustees unlikely that more than one half or two-thirds of the number of families having at one time the care of a very severely handicapped child would find that they wished to apply to the Family Fund.

In the early days the Trustees employed professional consultants to use every available means to make known that the Family Fund existed, and was anxious to be in touch with families which it could help. As time passed, the effectiveness of mass publicity of this kind diminished. Indeed, a stage was reached when it stimulated applications from a large number of families most of whom proved to be outside the limits set for the Fund in the original agreement between Trust and government. A good deal of frustration and disappointment was thus generated. On the other hand, careful and continuous publicity directed through the medical services, the Supplementary Benefits Commission, the authorities for attendance allowances and such groups, proved to be most effective in ensuring that, as soon as a family became responsible for a very severely handicapped child, the help available from the Family Fund was brought to its notice and an application encouraged if there was a need that the Fund was likely to be able to meet. The Trustees, therefore, accepted that after a period applications would be likely to reach a plateau, made up of the three groups identified earlier, and did not feel greatly troubled when they were told that a proportion of families, known to have the care of a very severely handicapped child, had still not made any application to the Family Fund. The matter was of some importance because it affected the relationships between the Trust and the government. As will be explained later, the Trustees were asked at the end of the three years, to continue the administration of the Fund for a further period. They agreed to do this on a number of conditions, one of which was that the government would advance, at the beginning of the year, whatever sum the Trustees estimated would be required to enable them to continue to administer the Family Fund for the next following year, within the criteria and guidelines previously approved. The government, even in times of the greatest financial stress, continued to honour that obligation. It was, however, publicly stated by some who criticised the Family Fund, that publicity was being restricted in order that expenditure from year to year could be kept within the amount made available by the Department of Health and Social Security. In fact, the calculation began with the Trustees' own estimate of what was required, and not with a fixed sum which the government was prepared to provide.

The Family Fund opened for business in April 1973, but was available at the outset only to families having the care of very severely handicapped children between the ages of eleven and sixteen. This was to enable the organisation to be built up and to reduce the possibility of its being overwhelmed at the outset; the restriction also served to give some preference to families who might cease to be eligible because the child attained the age of sixteen. In August 1973 this restriction was removed and the Fund was open to all families having the care of severely handicapped

children of any age up to sixteen. The solid line on the chart (Figure 8) shows the sharp rise in the monthly rate of applications from that month. The rate at which grants were made is shown by the dotted line on the same graph, which follows a rather different pattern. Until May 1974, the number of applications received substantially exceeded the number of first grants made. As a result, the number of applications outstanding rose sharply throughout the period from April 1973 until June 1974. It is of some interest to observe the three sharp peaks in the rate of applications shown by the solid line already referred to. Each of these can be identified with a particular phase of the intensive publicity campaign launched and maintained during the early years of the Fund. The graph also indicates how short-lived in raising the number of applications was a burst of publicity through the media and in other ways. The steady growth in the rate of applications came from the consistent interpretation of the Fund to intermediaries, mainly in the health and social services. A record was kept as part of the research project, of the way in which each applicant first heard of the Fund, and this confirmed the conviction which grew within the Trust administration that professional and other workers in the health and social services were the most effective channel of communication to families eligible for help. The rate at which applications were dealt with, shown by the dotted line, was affected by another consideration. It was necessary at the outset, to seek the advice, in respect of each application, of the Director of Social Services for the area in which the family lived. The application was then usually referred to a social worker who visited the family and completed a report which was sent direct to the Trust. In acting in this way, the local authority social worker was representing the interests of the Family Fund and this was explained in the preliminary letter to the family. Local authorities were, however, very pressed indeed with their own affairs; the Trust was greatly indebted for the help received from Directors of Social Services in the early months but it was important to make a separate provision as quickly as possible. Thus over the first fifteen months, as already explained, a network of social workers and other trained staff was established throughout the country who were willing to give part-time service to the Fund and who could, by occasional seminars, sometimes in York and sometimes elsewhere, be kept in much more direct touch with the policies of the Trust and with the ways in which the Fund was developing. Directors of Social Service were still advised of every application and invited to comment on it; once a decision was reached the Director was informed. This network of part-time workers was largely completed during the latter part of 1974 from which time the rate of applications and the rate at which first grants were made moved together, and the number of applications outstanding, which rose to a peak of over 7,000, fell to a hundred or so; this figure was consistent with the time needed to visit the family and reach a decision on the help to be offered. The third change which enabled the Family Fund to keep abreast of the rate of applications was the modification in the procedure for reaching decisions at the Trust's headquarters. As the quality and consistency of reports from visiting social workers improved and issues of principle and practice were resolved through the consultative machinery, decisions

about most applications were made and implemented without further enquiry and delay.

In its later days, the administration of the Family Fund has been immensely helped by the introduction of improved equipment under the advice, particularly, of the technical staff of Rowntree Mackintosh Limited. The growing accumulation of files on individual applications not only demanded ever more space, but meant that the time taken in relating a telephone enquiry, or a letter, to the relevant file was itself more and more wasteful. The administration was changed out of recognition when all these files were put on microfilm and the microfilms themselves stored in cabinets in an electrically operated container, which at the touch of a button produced the particular tray containing the case record that was needed. At first, the microfilms were made by the staff of Rowntree

Table 16.1   *Types of items requested and type of items given to families helped by the Family Fund*

Item	Number Requested	% of families	Number Given	% of families
Vehicle	3,955	17.2	4,789	20.4
Fares	626	2.7	1,621	6.0
Driving lessons	702	3.0	2,643	9.7
Car hire	59	0.3	766	3.1
Vehicle repairs	100	0.4	346	1.4
Petrol/car maintenance	637	2.8	3,544	13.5
Transport general	378	1.6	1,138	4.8
Clothing	2,532	11.0	5,043	19.0
Bedding/beds	2,137	9.3	4,260	17.5
Holidays for child	200	0.9	256	1.0
Holidays for parents/others	71	0.3	338	1.4
Holidays for both	1,672	7.3	3,572	13.6
Washing-machines	4,470	19.4	8,491	36.6
Spin/tumbler-dryers	2,156	9.4	4,661	20.1
Furniture/carpets	711	3.1	1,443	6.0
Wheelchairs/pushchairs	551	2.4	428	1.8
Other aids	800	3.5	569	2.4
Alterations to house	1,254	5.4	733	3.1
Plumbing	162	0.7	324	1.4
Home help	80	0.3	60	0.2
Child minder	74	0.3	90	0.4
Debts	239	1.0	554	2.3
Telephones	1,585	6.9	1,951	7.7
Recreation for child	1,169	5.1	1,869	7.3
Other	3,140	13.6	3,781	14.7
Not specified	2,898	—	—	—
Total items requested	32,358	Total items		
Total families	23,032	specified		29,460
		Total families		
		specifying item		20,134

Mackintosh; later apparatus was installed in the offices of the Family Fund, and operated by members of its own staff. The flow of correspondence was enormous; to implement a decision on one application sometimes involved several letters. For a time the need was met by a system of standard letters, to which additions could be made, giving the details

Table 16.2   *Handicapping condition of applications to the Family Fund.*
(The figures relate to applications received from April 1973 to April 1976).

Handicapping condition	Number	% total
Cancers, malignant tumours	127	0.4
Benign, unspecified tumours	47	0.2
Diabetes	40	0.1
Other endocrine, nutritional, metabolic or allergic diseases	161	0.5
Haemophilia	161	0.5
Other blood diseases	99	0.3
Mental illness (autism)	1,234	4.0
Mental subnormality	9,972	32.3
Polio	14	—
Cerebral haemorrhage	37	0.1
Multiple sclerosis	5	—
Cerebral palsy (spastic)	5,215	16.9
Paraplegia/hemiplegia	154	0.5
Epilepsy/convulsions	933	3.0
Head injury	71	0.2
Other CNS	585	1.9
Heart diseases	635	2.1
Bronchitis	7	—
Asthma	60	0.2
Other lung diseases (cystic fibrosis)	326	1.1
Diseases and defects of digestive system	99	0.3
Renal disease	146	0.5
Diseases and defects of bladder	104	0.3
Diseases of the eye/partial blindness	313	1.0
Deafness	1,445	4.7
Other ear disorders	20	0.1
Blindness	517	1.7
Disease of the skin	45	0.1
Rheumatoid arthritis	61	0.2
Arthogryphosis	75	0.2
Muscular dystrophy	865	2.8
Sprains, fractures, etc.	44	0.1
Other diseases of the bone	493	1.6
Amputations	54	0.2
Spina bifida, hydrocephalus	5,566	18.1
Other congenital abnormalities	889	2.9
Burns	3	—
Ill-defined conditions	206	0.7
Total	30,828	100

relevant to the particular application. The introduction of a word processor not only reduced the quantity of routine clerical work, but raised the quality of the communication sent to families, and to those who advised them.

An analysis of the work of the Family Fund and the help that has been given is not within the scope of a report on the work of the Trust. It will, however, be of interest to readers to see Tables 16.1 and 16.2 which are included in this report by permission of Jonathan Bradshaw, and of the publishers of *The Family Fund*. They show, in respect of the first 30,000 children on whose behalf an application was made to the Family Fund, the principal handicap from which each child suffered and the type of help requested and given.

Prospects for the Fund

The Trustees agreed at the outset to administer the Family Fund for a period of three years. That period came to an end in March 1976. The Trustees were then asked if they would continue for a further period, since it had not been practicable during the three years for the government to introduce general changes in the provision for families with handicapped children that would have rendered unnecessary the work of the Family Fund. A mobility allowance had been introduced, which greatly reduced the demands on the Family Fund for help with problems of transport. Otherwise, the requests being received were much the same as those in the early days of the Fund. The Trustees gave long and anxious consideration to this request. They felt strongly that the administration of the Family Fund should not become a part of the permanent work of the Trust. Not only was it unrelated to the purpose for which the Trust was founded, but the Fund itself was designed to meet short-term needs, and to relieve immediate problems, whilst the general pattern of services to such families was being examined. The Trustees, therefore, agreed to continue to administer the Family Fund until the end of 1978. If no decision had by then been made by the government on the ways in which the service provided by the Family Fund was to be replaced, then the Trustees would bring the fund to an end in December 1978. If such a decision had been made, and help was needed to cover a transitional period, then the Trustees would continue beyond the end of 1978 in order to help in the introduction of any new services and provisions that the government might have decided to introduce. However, other factors intervened. Well before the end of 1978, the Secretary of State for Health and Social Services told the Trustees that financial circumstances were such that the government could not contemplate any substantial additions to the social services, and they therefore hoped that the Trustees would continue the service for families having the care of a very severely handicapped child that they had provided so successfully since 1973. The Trustees were placed in a difficult position. The seriousness of the government's financial problems was not in question; it would have been a serious matter for the Trust after five years to withdraw facilities which had brought untold

relief to more than 50,000 most needy families. The Trustees, therefore, agreed to continue to administer the Family Fund without a defined limit of time. It was assumed that the Trustees' estimate of the amount of money required in any given year would continue to be accepted; that the guidelines within which the Trust operated would remain unchanged, save by agreement of the Trust, and that there would be a regular review to see if any part of the help which the Trust was providing with government funds could be absorbed into the general services. The concluding chapter in the history of the Family Fund has therefore yet to be written.

That chapter will certainly show how critical were the implications of decisions made for reasons of expediency to extend the operation of the fund by stages from three years to a time without limit. In those years the number of new applications had fallen, for the reasons given earlier, to the level expected by the Trust. But in the absence of any provision within the social services to absorb the work the Fund initiated, repeated applications from those who had already been helped were inevitable. Washing machines and driers wear out, clothes and shoes need renewal, and another holiday break for a family under strain is urgent. So most of the resources of the Fund are given to those who have already received help, its cash requirements become more difficult to estimate with any precision; as time goes on the Fund must cease to be a short-term innovation to identify and meet needs, thereafter to be the responsibility of social services shaped by its experience. It must become a service parallel to those provided by statutory authorities and competing for resources which are unlikely to be adequate to a demand to which a limit can no longer be set.

What, from the point of view of the Trust, has been the outcome at the end of five years of an operation probably unique in the history of foundations? First, the impact on the lives of more than 50,000 families has been greater than anybody associated with the Trust thought possible at the outset. Work with the handicapped had not, after all, been within their experience, and the primitive conditions in which some parents wrestled with the problem of a grotesquely handicapped child, brought surprise and shock. But unexpected too, was the realisation of how unsophisticated and straightforward was the help necessary to relieve a substantial part of the physical stress and with it, very often, the severity of the emotional stress. Allowances to help with mobility are now a regular part of the provisions by the state for families of the kind the Trustees were seeking to help. At the outset, however, many families had been unable to go out of their home together for several years. Thus, by far the greatest demand on the Family Fund in its early years was for the purchase of second-hand vehicles. The problem of washing and drying clothes and bedding for a growing child who is doubly incontinent, and severely handicapped, is virtually insoluble in a small house, with inadequate heating and hot water. The gift of an automatic washing machine and dryer may so reduce the mother's burden as to raise the quality of family life especially when, as is often the case, there are other young children who create their own considerable quantity of laundry. Whatever misgivings Trustees may have had at the outset about accepting responsibility for the Family Fund, they valued the opportunity of offering help of this

simple kind to what are almost certainly amongst the most needy families in the community. New and novel ways of meeting the needs of handicapped children have seldom emerged; too low an income for facilities taken for granted by others is the problem the Trust has had to try to resolve. Secondly, the Fund has not brought the Trustees into public controversy in the way they feared. There have been a few highly articulate parents, whose needs were clearly outside the guidelines within which the Trustees had undertaken to operate, who have sought to gain the ear of Members of Parliament and Ministers, and even of the Crown, and have brought the Press to their aid. But the numbers could be counted on the fingers of one hand, and it is right to record that in no case have the Trustees had reason to depart from a decision as a result of outside pressure brought to bear on them.

Thirdly, the Family Fund has brought the Trustees and their staff into a quite new relationship with public authorities, both local and central. The use of public money in this way, and on this scale, has necessarily brought the Trustees' operation within the purview of the Public Accounts Committee of Parliament, and therefore of the Comptroller and Auditor General. They have appreciated and benefited from the visits of his representatives to their offices for two or three days at a time, and from the discussions which have taken place about administrative and financial procedures and the efficiency and the economy, as well as the effectiveness, with which public resources are used. Fourthly, the development and success of the research project has strengthened their already close relationship with the University of York, and has suggested new avenues of enquiry which will, without doubt, influence the programme of the Trust in the future. Indeed, perhaps the most satisfactory of all the decisions made rather quickly by the Trust at the outset, was to ask the University to monitor the work of the Fund; it has brought to a neglected area of social policy a highly competent group of researchers, and a unique body of data.

At the stage when this account is written, therefore, the Trustees have few regrets. But when a service of this kind is working so smoothly, incentives for government to develop new policies to bring the help within the framework of public administration are not strong. It is doubtful if new lessons of any significance will now be learnt from the operation of the Family Fund within guidelines established more than five years ago, so that the justification for an independently provided service is to that extent reduced. Decisions will become more rather than less difficult as time passes; it will be sad if the Trust were to be left in such uncertainty about government intentions for the Family Fund that the Trustees felt obliged to end their unsought responsibility for what are clearly public duties. Here may be experienced the political involvement they feared which almost deterred them from accepting the commission from Sir Keith Joseph in 1973.

Table 16.3 shows the amount of money distributed by the Family Fund in each year to December 1979; the amount received annually from the government; the interest earned on invested balances, and the administrative costs charged to the government. These costs, as previously explained, exclude any charge for the Trust's own staff and administration.

Table 16.3   *The Family Fund – receipts and payments*

Year	Received from DHSS £	Interest earned £	Grants to families £	Administrative costs £
1973	3,046,159	195,329	286,363	46,159
1974	164,348	263,728	2,677,344	164,348
1975	3,169,898	176,197	3,268,897	169,898
1976	2,700,000	80,826	2,083,807	170,395
1977	2,000,000	183,711	2,199,677	161,391
1978	2,200,000	116,087	2,655,150	179,367
1979	2,950,000	152,541	2,502,453	195,291
Total	16,230,405	1,168,419	15,673,691	1,086,849

Received £17,398,824   *Paid out* £16,760,540
Balance in hand at 31.12.79   = £638,284.

17   *The Trust and the City of York*

The Physical Environment

What part ought the Trust to play in physical, social, and educational developments within the city of York? A cathedral city, with a wealth of historical and architectural treasures, could clearly put to good use for its physical conservation and development all the resources which a trust on the scale of the Joseph Rowntree Memorial Trust could make available. It was in York that Seebohm Rowntree had conducted his studies of poverty which, with those of Booth, established a new tradition in empirical social research. Was there some way in which that association with York should be maintained? There was no shortage of initiatives in the development of voluntary and statutory social services which could profit from long-term support from independent funds. Did they have a special claim on Trust resources?

Two of the largest and most significant initiatives taken by the Trust in the city have already been described. In Chapter 9 an account is given of the Trust's work in housing action areas in the city, in the reconstruction of large houses in the Clifton area and the design of new buildings in the land which adjoined them, and in the construction of homes for the elderly. In Chapter 16 is recorded the creation of a research fellowship within the University of York to monitor the administration of the Family Fund and use the mass of information which it accumulated about families with handicapped children to identify their needs and how these might best be met. These arose directly from the Trust's continuing interests. There was almost unlimited scope, however, for the Trust to respond to proposals to support other developments in York simply because its Founder had his home there, its income for seventy years was drawn almost entirely from a business with its headquarters in York, and the Trust itself had its office within the city boundary.

Both the Trust Deed, and the Founder's Memorandum of Advice to his Trustees, made abundantly clear that the conservation and renewal of ancient buildings was no part of the purposes for which the Trust was established. Equally, Trustees were discouraged from spending any substantial part of the Trust's resources in making contributions to continuing services, whether voluntary or statutory. Throughout the history of the Trust, therefore, Trustees have, generally speaking, remained aloof from the changing pattern of voluntary service in York, and have judged proposals for expenditure in the area in which the Trust had its headquarters by the same criteria as were applied elsewhere.

In practice there have been exceptions, and some of them have been important. The Trust has taken three separate initiatives in the physical

development of the city; the considerable capital sums deployed in these projects have made an immediate impact on the physical environment of the city, and will continue to influence it over the years ahead. Then the Trust was concerned with the establishment of a University in York; subsequently it has influenced the pace and, in particular instances, the direction of its work. For the rest, exceptional grants which have been made from a sentimental attachment to York affairs have demonstrated the wisdom of the Founder's advice. A study of a considerable list of relatively small grants to a variety of organisations, almost all of which would not have been made outside the City, does not reveal any distinctive development which owes its origin or long term viability to Trust support. Indeed the participation in voluntary activity by a Trust with large resources, has sometimes reduced the rigour of the questioning which ought to take place before ventures dependent on voluntary funds are initiated.

The Riverside Garden, Plate 18, had its origin in events which were no direct concern of the Trust. In 1950 the Rowntree Company offered to the city of York an important riverside site opposite the Guildhall. On it had stood one of the earlier factories owned by the Company which, when the business was transferred to its present site, was used for warehouse accommodation and for receiving goods transported by water. Much of the site had been damaged during the air raids on York, and the Company decided to offer it to the city as a permanent open space, hoping that this might stimulate other improvements to the river banks, consistent with the commercial traffic which contributes to the city's life.

The Trust's part was to prepare a design for the use of this valuable site and meet the cost of implementing it. The plan was prepared by the Trust's Consultant Architect, Louis de Soissons, the construction work was carried out by a local firm, Messrs F. Shepherd and Son Limited, and the planting was the responsibility of Messrs John Waterer Sons and Crisp Limited, from a specification prepared by Mr Malcolm Sefton of Digswell.

At a ceremony in the Mansion House on 25 April 1959, the Lord Mayor on behalf of the city accepted the garden and undertook to maintain it in perpetuity as an open space for the citizens of York.

The illustrations show the unusual interest of the layout, the varied buttressings of the river wall, the details of the wrought-iron railing, and the walk of granite aggregate laid in bays between stone paving.

Mr de Soissons' design was itself a matter of some controversy. Some architects, no less distinguished, took the view that the passage of the River Ouse through the city of York was part of an urban scene, and a variety of buildings coming right up to the river was an important part of that scene. The character of the central part of the city, through which the river flowed, would be changed if gardens, with grass and flowers and trees, replaced the ancient stone and brickwork beneath which the river flowed. Arguments were also advanced in support of the use of this valuable site for a new building appropriate to a site opposite to the Guildhall, and providing for a pedestrian walk at an appropriate level beside the river. The gift of the site was, however, for the purpose of an

open space, and given this commission, Mr de Soissons decided that the garden should be primarily an architectural construction, incorporating trees and shrubs; but areas of mown grass and flowerbeds, for which others had pleaded, should be excluded. Now that the trees and shrubs have matured, and the brickwork and stone work have weathered, the merits of Mr de Soissons' solution to a difficult problem can be better judged.

In carrying out this proposal the Trustees secured two further incidental advantages for the city. In the middle of the old warehouse was a dwelling used in earlier days for a warehouse keeper. It was occupied at the time when the Rowntree Company made the gift, by a family which included an elderly man permanently bedridden. A right solution to the problems of the family had to be found, and this held up, for a matter of years, the implementation of Mr de Soissons' scheme. The family had lived in the immediate area for many years, and were unwilling to move to another part of York, though a number of attractive choices were offered. This decision was respected. The solution which ultimately emerged was an expensive one, but was a further contribution to the improvement of the riverside scene. A small house on the opposite side of the road became vacant and was found to be seriously dilapidated. It was purchased by the Trust, and extensively modernised. Into it the family was moved; the bedridden member now had an upstairs room, looking across the new garden to the river. He lived very happily there until the end of his days. Other adjoining property was later modernised, and now forms an attractive group of houses and shops, which might otherwise have been demolished. Plate 19 shows the result.

In accepting the gift of the new garden from the Company and the Trust, the local authority undertook to secure if possible a continuing riverside walk of which the garden would be a part. Thus, when a hotel was built on the adjoining site, the plan incorporated a walk-way continuous with the garden. Later, commercial premises bordering the river beyond the hotel were extended; as a condition of planning consent, the owners agreed to provide a pedestrian walk. The objective of a riverside walk, right through the city, was virtually achieved.

The Trust's second contribution to the environment of the city was the result of a proposal made by Mr J.B. Morrell, Chairman of one of the sister Trusts, whose initiative had been the greatest single factor in securing the establishment of a University near York. The work at the University of a landscape architect had attracted wide attention; Mr Morrell thought that his skills should be used to improve the appearance and amenity value of the River Ouse on its course through York. The Trust therefore commissioned the landscape architect to prepare a development plan, from Clifton in the north, to Fulford in the south, indicating how the different sites on either side of the river might be used, whether for amenities or for commerce, and what part new planting might play in what was essentially an urban scene. The architect's proposals, many of them controversial, have prompted developments which have changed the appearance of the riverside banks in the area covered by the survey. Some of the proposals have been implemented in the form in which they were made; others, including some which were technically impractical,

have stimulated authorities and agencies to consider different ways of meeting their requirements and fulfilling their statutory responsibilities. In retrospect, it is possible to see that the architect's skill lay in making proposals which were clearly right in themselves, even though his ideas on how they should be implemented proved to be beyond the resources of commercial and statutory bodies. But they represented a challenge, so that the architect's proposal became the object of policy although it might be achieved in different ways. Two examples from the report illustrate the point. Whether there will ever be a large lake on what are now the Ings, it is impossible to say. What has happened, however, is that the flood land essential to protect York from frequent inundation has been extended and controlled, so that the amenity value of the area can continue to be increased. There is not a ha-ha in place of the railing between the Museum Gardens and the Riverside Walk. But the importance of access has been recognised, whilst other open space which adjoins the river has been improved beyond recognition.

The Trust itself decided to make a contribution to the implementation of the plan – the third improvement to York's physical environment. When the River Ouse survey was presented as a display of charts and illustrations in the Guildhall, the Trustees announced that they would meet the costs of re-constructing the Riverside Walk between the two bridges in the centre of the city, in accordance with the architect's recommendations. Flag stones of Yorkshire stone were brought together, sometimes from demolished cottages in moorland areas, the architect's design for paving and planting were followed; the seats and waste bins he chose were used and were later introduced elsewhere. The new walk was opened by the Archbishop of York in 1967; a plaque records the name of the architect responsible for the design and for the River Ouse Survey from which the proposal came. It associates the Trust, the city of York, and the York Civic Trust through whose agency the Trust worked in sponsoring and, in part implementing the Survey. An impression of the new Riverside Walk is given in Plate 20.

The preservation and enrichment of the ancient city of York is not one of the objects of the Trust. But the Riverside Garden, the preparation of the survey plan for the river, and the construction of the Riverside Walk, have been notable contributions to the beauty of the city, and to its enjoyment by residents and visitors. They have also influenced other developments, over which the Trust itself had no control.

The University of York

The Trust corporately had no part in the series of initiatives which led ultimately to the establishment of a University of York in 1961. Individuals associated with the Trust served on the development and promotional committees which operated for a number of years before the establishment of a University became a real possibility. The Trust made some contribution to the cost of the summer schools in architectural studies, and subsequently to the Institute of Advanced Architectural Studies, designed,

with other comparable activities, to demonstrate the claims of York as a university centre. These were activities within the Trust's field of interest, and directly related to the work which it was established to support. With remarkable imagination and foresight, J. Bowes Morrell, the Chairman of the Joseph Rowntree Social Service Trust, purchased Heslington Hall when it came on to the market, because he was convinced that a university would be established in York, and that this was the most appropriate site for it. As such a decision was not in prospect, a problem was presented as to how the Hall should be used for what might prove to be an indefinite period. The Trust became involved in the planning of a number of flats which could use at least part of the accommodation in the Hall. As things turned out, none of these temporary arrangements was required. In 1959 the University Grants Committee indicated that an application for a University in York would be considered on its merits, with others which were expected. By 1960, the decision to establish a University of York had been made.

The Trustees thereupon made two decisions. They thought that as the university developed, it was likely to be receptive to proposals from the Trust for research and study in the fields of the Trust's current interests. There might thus develop a broad relationship with a York University, comparable to the partnership which the Trustees had at times established with other universities in relation to a defined field of study. The Trustees, therefore, thought it right to make a contribution to the general appeal which was being launched to help establish the university. Later they expected to discuss with the Vice-Chancellor and his colleagues, particular developments to which the Trust might give substantial support.

In consultation with the other two Rowntree Trusts, and with the Rowntree Company, the Trust contributed a capital sum, payable over ten years; these contributions taken together were a significant proportion of the total sum raised as the city's contribution towards the university foundation. In making a capital contribution, the Trustees made it clear that they would wish to join subsequently with the university authorities in promoting teaching and research in the social sciences, along the lines of the Trust's own interests. The first application of this policy arose from discussions with Lord James of Rusholme, the University's Vice-Chancellor, about the establishment of an Institute of Social and Economic Research. To make possible the establishment of this Institute early in the life of the university, the Trustees made a contribution towards its general expenditure over a period of five years, and reserved an additional sum, on which the Institute could draw at will, to finance two research projects, so that the Institute would have independent resources with which to start its work. Later it expected to attract resources from other organisations wishing to use the facilities that the Institute provided.

A second development within the university which was of interest to the Trustees, was the establishment of a Department of Social Administration and Social Work. The Trustees made a grant to the Department to enable it, early in its development, to establish a two year course leading to a higher degree. The grant was made on the understanding that provision

for the work would be included in the university estimates for the next quinquennium.

In later years, the Trustees sought the help of the university in two other substantial developments, which arose from its own interests, but which Trustees felt were likely to be a point of departure for wider studies appropriate to a university. They were concerned about the number of applications they received for grants towards local councils of social service and felt that the role of such bodies needed fresh examination. The Council of Social Service in York, which bore the name of York Community Council, was particularly in mind. Trustees in a personal capacity had been involved in the work of the Council for many years; they had given financial support when it had launched a new service – an adoption society, a family service unit, a marriage guidance council, a youth action group and so on. The Council itself received grants from local authorities and as new ventures led to independent, but affiliated, organisations, these too were publicly supported and made their own appeals. But the Trust found itself over a long period of years providing money for the Council's administration and sometimes sustaining the new ventures as well. The Trustees reached the conclusion that the study of community organisations should be promoted in its own right within a university even though the activities of the York Community Council might provide the focus for experimental field work.

In 1965 they opened discussions with the Vice-Chancellor of York University. Within the Department of Social Administration and Social Work a fellowship in Community Organisation was established to which Eric Butterworth was appointed. The Trust provided resources for the fellowship and later for the new structure for the Community Council which was based on his work. The fellowship led, when the period of Trust support ended after five years, to the creation of a readership as a permanent appointment within the Department. Eric Butterworth's work led to a professionally led Community Council which attracted and held an effective corps of volunteers and offered services which gained the co-operation and support of local authorities over a wide area.

The university similarly responded to a request from the Trust to establish a research fellowship to monitor the work of the Family Fund. The record of the work resulting from that fellowship is described in the account of the Family Fund in Chapter 16. Each of these research fellowships was related at the outset to work to which the Trust was committed, but opened up fields of teaching and research, the quality and impact of which has earned national, and in some instances, international recognition.

It has been a mark of the relationships established at the outset between the Trust and the university, that the Trust has not received a flow of requests for research and other grants. At different times over the years the Trust has contributed to expenditure in the university's Institute of Advanced Architectural Studies, related to new policies in urban renewal; it has supported studies in the field of chronic poverty; and it has helped with courses in the Institute of Social and Economic Research, designed to

prepare men and women from developing countries for leading posts in the field of economics and social policy. What has been common to this expenditure has been the coincidence between the development of the Trust's own interests and those of the university; there is every reason to believe that co-operation along these lines will continue over the years ahead.

The Lord Mayor's Flood Relief Fund

On the 28 December 1978 a coincidence of events affecting the River Ouse produced floods in and near York only marginally lower than the record floods of 1947. Moreover, the warning system virtually failed. There had been very heavy rain and the river was high. But in the upper reaches of the Ouse tributaries, the level had actually started to fall so that the danger point seemed to have past. Then something like a cloudburst occurred lower down in the Ouse catchment area, bringing enormous quantities of water quickly into the York plain and with none of the usual warnings. This rush of water occurred as an exceptionally high tide reached the Naburn Locks, over-running the weir and trapping the flood water.

Some 600 properties near the River Ouse and its contributory streams were affected by flood water, some to a depth of four feet. A large part of the personal possessions of many families was either lost or rendered useless.

On 6 January 1979 the Lord Mayor of York announced that he had established a Flood Relief Fund; four days later a meeting was called at the Mansion House to discuss the machinery for raising the money and allocating it.

At that first meeting an issue of principle was raised by the York Member of Parliament which was to have important repercussions later. He argued that a voluntary fund was unnecessary save as a supplement to a relief operation which should be funded from the rates and from government grant, and administered by officers of the local authority. For reasons which are not relevant to this account, his proposal was rejected by those representing the York District Council. A public relations and fund raising organisation was set up under the direction of an executive committee. To distribute the money, the meeting appointed a Grants Committee, to be chaired by the Director of the Joseph Rowntree Memorial Trust and serviced by the staff of the Trust. The Committee included the Honorary Treasurer to the Flood Relief Fund, the Chairman of the local Chamber of Trade, the Director of the York Community Council, the Organiser of the Women's Royal Voluntary Service, an official from the world of insurance, and a member of the District Council who was also Vice-Chairman of the Social Services Committee of the county authority. An official of the Supplementary Benefits Commission and of the local office of the Social Services Department attended as necessary. Meetings of the Grants Committee were attended not only by the Director of the Trust as Chairman, but by the Trust's Finance Officer, the Assistant Director responsible for the Family Fund, the Assistant Director in charge of the Trust's housing work and secretarial staff.

With the experience of the Family Fund as a guide, it seemed to the Trust that some clear guidelines should be adopted within which the Grants Committee could work. Seven criteria were established: the Executive Committee approved them in these terms:

a) The Fund is available for repair or replacement of furniture, household equipment, floor coverings and decorations damaged as a result of water in the house during the period since the 26 December 1978.

b) Payments cannot be made to compensate for the distress and anxiety resulting from the flood however grievous these may be.

c) No test of means will be made in administering the Fund; there are likely to be few applicants for whom the losses from the floods do not involve hardships.

d) The first responsibility for the cost of repairs and replacements rests on an insurance company where a policy exists. Some households will have policies which cover the structure and decorations; some policies will cover the contents of the house; some will cover both these needs; some will have policies that exclude damage from flood, storm, tempest; some will have no policy at all. The absence of a policy, however regrettable, will not disqualify a household from help from the Fund; on the other hand the Fund must not take over a liability which should be met by an insurance company.

e) Some households will be entitled to consideration for payments from statutory bodies. For example, those receiving supplementary benefits may be considered in such circumstances for Exceptional Needs Payments; Social Services Departments have certain powers. The Fund must not assume responsibility which should first be considered by local and central authorities.

f) Some households will have incurred expenses in moving, in finding temporary accommodation or in storing furniture, or in hiring portable heaters; these commitments are likely to qualify for help under e) above. In any event they have a lower priority in claims on the Fund and must be deferred until it is known how far the resources of the Fund will match the priority in a) above.

g) Repairs to the structure of a house will, for rented accommodation, be the responsibility of the landlord who would be expected to be covered by insurance; for an owner-occupied house such repairs will be the responsibility of the owner who again would be expected to be similarly insured. Where there is a mortgage on the property the building society or other lender would require this. Structural damage to property therefore is excluded though separate consideration will need to be given where there are exceptional circumstances.

The Trustees agreed that their staff should accept responsibility for making recommendations to the Grants Committee for allocations from the fund on one condition. This was that the Fund should be used only for

the repair or replacement of specific items of household furniture and equipment and personal possessions lost or destroyed by the flood waters. There was to be no distribution of cash. This was no academic point. At the outset there was some pressure to give immediate cash payments to householders known to have incurred loss, rather to boost morale than to meet any defined need. This would have led to unfairness between claimants and, more important, to public charges of inequity to which no convincing reply could be given. The acceptance of the condition to exclude cash grants meant that there was virtually no criticism throughout the operation of unfairness as between one applicant and another. The Trustees were anxious also at the possibility of political controversy that might prejudice their own work. The establishment of such guidelines at the outset had kept the Family Fund clear of public controversy and that experience was clearly relevant here.

The key to the procedure for arriving at recommendations to the grants committee for allocations from the fund was a visit by an experienced visitor (sometimes a social worker), whose task it was to complete a report giving a precise list of losses, with other relevant information about insurance, help from statutory bodies, and the height of flood water in the house. The Trust was able to draw for the most part on men and women in the York area who had experience of visiting homes on behalf of the Family Fund. It proved of great importance that the report, when completed, was signed by both the householder and the visitor. It thus formed an agreed basis for the help given, although it was open to the householder to ask to supplement the information at a later stage since many were still confused as a result of the shock of the floods.

Once the loss had been verified and accepted by the Grants Committee vouchers were issued to applicants authorising the purchase of floor coverings, up to an agreed price, from suppliers on an approved list who had offered the best terms to the fund. Applicants who had lost furniture or soft furnishings were asked to obtain estimates; a standard letter was sent which could be shown to suppliers. The estimate was placed before the grants committee; if approved, vouchers for the purchase were issued.

Electrical equipment – refrigerators, washing machines, and record players – presented a special problem. The Chamber of Trade arranged with a firm of electrical engineers to visit each home where loss or damage to this kind of equipment was reported. Immediate decisions were made; the grants committee received lists showing the cost of repairs or a proposal for replacement when necessary. The voucher system was then used to enable the applicant to proceed.

The Trust's Housing Officer took responsibility throughout for decoration, drying of homes and joinery work needed to the hundreds of warped doors. He based his action on the reports described earlier. He and a colleague visited some 250 homes; they usually made an immediate assessment and reached agreement with the resident on the help needed. A schedule was then prepared for formal approval by the Grants Committee. There were fears that the cost of redecoration would be very high. In fact all but a few residents when visited agreed to undertake the work with

neighbourly help if the cost of materials was met. The average cost was £50 to £60, against £200 when a firm had to be engaged.

The Grants Committee met at noon at the Trust's office each Friday during the operation. Staff prepared, in the course of Friday morning, a summary of recommendations taken from all reports received during the preceding four days, a list of estimates for furniture or other equipment received from households during the same period, a list of recommended payments for decorating material or, exceptionally, of estimates from decorating firms and a note of exceptional requests.

The meeting ended no later than 2 p.m. having made decisions on which immediate action could be taken in respect of all reports and estimates received up to the time of the meeting.

It was claimed that some homes had no heating because cash was no longer available for coin meters. Visitors therefore took a letter which invited an application for immediate help in cash with heating where a coin meter was in use or solid fuel was purchased. A number of such requests were received. A member of the Trust's staff went at once with £10 and a form of receipt. In fact there was no evidence of any such immediate need, and the time-consuming procedure was discontinued. Whilst it was in use thirty-three cash grants amounting to £350 were made.

Help with heating costs generally was, however, important. The managers of the Gas and Electricity Boards agreed to monitor meter readings in the flood areas, and to report the general level of consumption compared with the corresponding periods in the previous year. They also offered to visit and investigate any particular home where unusually high consumption was recorded. The Grants Committee then considered the order of help to be given to applicants to the Fund. In the outcome the Electricity Board recommended that payment by the Fund of fifteen per cent of the account for the relevant quarter for each house affected by the floods would be generous; the corresponding advice from the Gas Board was twenty per cent. Payment was made by a cheque direct to the authority or to the householder against a receipted account. In no circumstances was a cash grant made.

The Lord Mayor's advisers had thought that a quarter of a million pounds might be required to meet all the claims on the fund. The Trust's Housing Director, after a preliminary survey of the area, thought claims would amount to about half that figure. In the event, 426 applications were received and 408 households received help amounting to £73,569.61. There were two reasons why the need for help proved to be less than many expected. First the Trust sought the help of an experienced accountant who made meticulous inquiries about every application that showed that some kind of insurance policy was held. A network of relationships was built up with claims departments and assessors. Far more help was available from this source than had been expected. The Fund made grants to supplement payments from insurance companies where the terms of the policy required some deduction from the full replacement cost. Then the cost of redecoration was greatly reduced by the part played by the Trust's Housing Director in encouraging relatives and neighbours to take on the work if the materials were provided. The co-operation thus secured was

seen as a contribution to the relief fund and was worth many thousands of pounds.

Critics of the Fund argued that some families – especially the aged – might not see announcements in the local paper, or hear from their neighbours that help could be given. The most needy might miss the chance to apply to the fund. Once the rush of applications subsided, procedures were introduced to ensure that none lost the opportunity to receive help. From the electoral roll, and with the help of the city Environmental Health Officer, every house affected by flood water was identified. Two letters were sent and a personal visit made before the Fund's Executive Committee was told that no further claims would be received and all losses covered by the scheme had been met.

A further check that nobody was overlooked came from a different quarter. The York MP, who had opposed the setting up of the Fund and its administration by the Trust, wrote to all householders affected by the floods inviting comments on the Fund, and details of any complaints that the help given was inadequate to meet the loss sustained. He wrote also to the local paper giving notice that he intended to publish the results of this enquiry. Evidently a few complaints were received; they found their way through the District Council to the Trust office. One or two were found to be awaiting the outcome of an insurance claim; a very few, unhappily, were from those whom the careful procedure followed by the Grants Committee had identified as seeking to exploit the fund. A report on each complaint was sent to the MP; no further grants were found to be necessary as a result of his enquiries and the results of his survey were never published.

It was the experience of administering the Family Fund and the presence of a corps of experienced visitors that enabled the Trust to take on without notice this short but intensive operation. It was not welcome to the Trustees' staff. The Flood Relief Fund seemed to intrude into every Trust department and make demands that could be met only in the evenings and at weekends. The Trust was more than usually troubled about the possible impact on its standing in York and its relationships with Members of Parliament and local authorities. The areas affected by the floods were closely knit communities. Everybody knew what every other household had received. The scope for accusations of unfairness, unreasonable delay or insensitivity was endless. Donors to the fund as well as recipients of grants had to be satisfied that losses were fairly assessed and adequate recompense given. In the outcome the Trust received no criticism on these matters from the Lord Mayor, from those he had invited to be Trustees of his appeal fund nor from the general public of York. But the Trust was clearly identified, however unjustly, as an opponent of a strongly held political view that relief to the citizen in a time of emergency was primarily a responsibility of an elected authority drawing on resources provided by the whole community through its rates and taxes. In fact the Trust viewed its involvement with the Lord Mayor's Flood Relief Fund as it had its administration of the Family Fund. In the one, money came from private donations; in the other it was provided by the government. The source of the help was not the Trust's business. For both projects it was able to offer an effective service at the moment it was needed, and it was concerned to

relinquish, and not to retain, the responsibility it had with some reluctance accepted.

The York City Charities

During the period of municipal reform in the nineteenth century, some sixty separate educational, parochial and general charities had been brought together as the York Municipal Charities under a single body of Trustees. But the charities remained distinct; the Trustees had responsibility for seven almshouse trusts, each providing homes for elderly people, and all but one group in a state of dilapidation or wholly unsuited to the purposes which their pious founders had in mind several centuries earlier. No money was available to maintain or improve them even though other charities in the group distributed small pensions or grants at Christmas which took no account of present day provision of retirement pensions or supplementary benefits.

The Director of the Trust became involved as a Trustee of the Municipal Charities, whilst one of the Joseph Rowntree Memorial Trustees, William K. Sessions, had made a study of the ancient almshouses of York as part of the Nuffield survey entrusted to Seebohm Rowntree the findings of which were published under the title *Old People*. For nearly a decade, intermittent efforts were made to secure the support of the Charity Commissioners for a scheme of reform to bring the sixty charities into a single foundation able to direct its resources to meet current needs. The discussions were part of the wider movement for the reform of ancient charities which led Mr Attlee in 1950 to appoint Lord Nathan to be Chairman of a Committee on Charitable Trusts. William Sessions and the Trust's Director were invited to give evidence and, as part of their contribution to the committee's work, they drafted a scheme to bring into a single fund the resources of these sixty charities and to replace the series of doles on which much of the income was spent by more imaginative services for an elderly population now receiving pensions on a scale never before achieved.

Following the publication of Lord Nathan's report, in which the draft scheme for the York charities appeared as an appendix, the Charity Commissioners showed new interest in reform. They incorporated the substance of the proposals into a Parliamentary Scheme which became effective in 1956. All but one of the groups of almshouses were either sold or demolished; the resources from these sales secured additional land adjoining the most recently constructed almshouses and, with the aid of housing subsidies and the new foundation's own resources, the new homes described in Chapter 9 were built. Architectural, technical and administrative skill and experience came from the Joseph Rowntree Memorial Trust's staff. As the endowments sold to finance this building are replaced and other loans repaid, future Trustees of the York Municipal Charities will have new opportunities to respond to still changing conditions. It has been a profitable partnership of more than thirty years between the Trustees of a group of charities no longer relevant to current conditions and a much later foundation, itself promoting private legisla-

tion to authorise new tasks in accordance with its Founder's wishes. The relationships established by the Rowntree Trust with the Charity Commissioners in discussions over the affairs of the York City Charities between 1948 and 1956 contributed to the confidence which stood the Trustees in good stead during the difficult negotiations for the extension of their own powers described in Part I.

18 *Social Work Overseas*

Citizens Advice Bureaux and Councils of Social Service

A decision to allocate resources, or to withhold them, is an exercise of power. In the United Kingdom the scale of any one trust's operation is usually small in relation to the total resources available in the field in which it operates; this imposes a healthy limitation on the impact which a trust can make. Even so, in particular circumstances decisions by a body of trustees can be critical to the growth or decay of institutions whose influence on social policy may be important. In a developing country the decisions of an overseas trust may have more momentous implications. After their first tentative initiatives in the continent of Africa, the Trustees recorded in a report published in 1963 some of the questions on which they felt compelled to reflect. On what basis, and by what right, they asked themselves, should a body of people meeting in Britain decide to allocate money to this or that group, or to make possible this or that new development? For better or worse, such decisions might be important to the formation of social policy in situations of which Trustees had little direct knowledge and in which they could not be personally involved; their decisions might also have political implications impossible to foresee in situations of rapid change.

These considerations affect the way decisions are made but should not paralyse the will to give constructive help. The Joseph Rowntree Memorial Trustees have, in their work overseas, followed certain principles derived from their own past work in Britain.

First, they have ensured that representatives of the Trust should meet and come to know those whose work is being supported. The confidence which is sought in this way must be mutual; those using resources provided by the Trust should understand its work and outlook and feel able to be partners in it.

Secondly, within the limits imposed by their legal obligations as Trustees of a charitable trust, they have left the work they support to shape itself, and to be shaped, in accordance with the evolving pattern of a new and different society. Britain, from her own social history, has ideas and experience to offer; their practical application must be worked out through successes and failures in the communities to which this experience is offered.

Thirdly, the Trustees have usually helped by offering the services of people in whom they have confidence, who have the necessary training and experience, and who have been prepared to live and work for a period with those whose work the Trust is supporting.

Finally, the Trustees have supported appropriate organisations in

Britain as sources of continuing advice and help to newly-established groups overseas engaged in social work. They have had to seek ways of achieving this which are consistent with their own direct responsibility for the deployment of Trust funds.

Part I of this book records the powers given to the Trustees in 1954 to use resources outside the United Kingdom. They are able to seek reports and information on relevant work without geographical limit. Their powers to *promote* work outside the United Kingdom are limited in effect to the Commonwealth.

Over a period of twenty-five years, they have co-operated with voluntary organisations and with governments in Kenya and Uganda in East Africa; in Malawi, Zambia and Zimbabwe in Central Africa; and in Lesotho and Swaziland in Southern Africa. Some of these territories were known by different names at the time the Trustees began their operations, and in Central Africa the three territories were still part of a central federation.

The first initiative for work overseas came at the suggestion of one of the Trustees, whose business interests took him frequently to the countries of the Commonwealth. He observed that the pressures of rapid change on people unaccustomed to industrial and urban development, was not unlike those experienced by great numbers of families in the United Kingdom, in their adjustment to the social and economic changes brought by war. Advice centres, which later came to be known as Citizens Advice Bureaux, had played a crucial part in Britain in enabling families, often moved to strange places at short notice, to adapt to a new environment and unfamiliar and complex regulations. He thought that the possibility of developing a similar instrument adapted to local needs, ought at least to be explored. The way the Trustees went about this first proposal set a pattern for all their future developments overseas. They secured from the National Citizens Advice Bureau Committee in London the services of a senior and experienced officer willing to go to Northern and Southern Rhodesia, as they were then called, in order to discuss whether such a project would be helpful at all, what form it might take, and in what way the Trust could help. The immediate outcome of a first brief visit was not what the Trustees expected. They were asked to make available in the territory, the services of an experienced worker for a period of about six months. The hope of the voluntary workers and officials who presented this proposal, was that a network of advice centres should be established from the outset with government support, and training given in the territory for those who would be manning the bureaux. Moreover, it was hoped that a visit of this duration would allow discussions to proceed on a means of providing better co-ordination for the growing body of voluntary services, to which the new advisory service could from the outset be related. Again the Trustees looked to the National Council of Social Service, and its Citizens Advice Bureau subsidiary, to provide an experienced worker, who was willing to leave her work and home for a period of six months, to work with officials and voluntary organisations in the two territories.

Over the next few years, five men and women from established voluntary

organisations in Britain, went to different countries of Africa for periods lasting from three months to fifteen months, to advise voluntary organisations, and help to establish relationships with local authorities and governments which were likely to endure, even through radical constitutional change.

By 1969, steps to establish Councils of Social Service had been taken in six different territories. The Trustees thought that they had a responsibility to undertake some independent evaluation of the experience which had been gained, both to guide the Trustees in the decisions that they would have to make in the future, and also to offer their experience to others who might seek to extend to newly independent countries experience gained in the very different setting of the United Kingdom. They accordingly invited Wilfred H. Chinn, CMG, to undertake this evaluation. He was about to retire from his post as Adviser on Social Development to the Ministry of Overseas Development, having served in a similar capacity to the Secretary of State for the Colonies. He was familiar with the story of the social development of these countries under the colonial regime, and had some understanding of the political structure and social and economic aspirations of newly independent territories. This was a necessary background to any assessment of the relevance of the Trust's work. Wilfred Chinn was able to visit East and Central Africa from September to December 1969; his report to the Trustees was printed privately and made available to any who felt its contents might be useful to their work. The report included, as an appendix, a twenty-eight page report from Mr H.R. Poole, the consultant who had been involved in most of these developments, and who wrote a detailed account of the foundation of the Council of Social Service in Kenya. His paper is a comprehensive review of the negotiations with voluntary organisations and with government, and of the structure of the Council which emerged as a result. It concerned itself also with the relationships of the new body to tribal welfare societies and to the local co-ordinating groups of organisations which came to be known as Local Councils of Social Service. It is, in short, a case study of an initiative by a United Kingdom Trust to establish in an independent territory an organisation based on United Kingdom experience, but adapted to local needs, in consultation with indigenous voluntary organisations and with government.

The introductory paragraphs in Mr Chinn's report set the scene for the Trust's overseas venture, with a degree of understanding and sensitivity that makes them of continuing relevance to all who may be involved in the use of resources for the benefit of independent people of a different culture. Some paragraphs from Mr Chinn's introduction are, therefore, reproduced here as a background to an account of the work of the Trust overseas.

In former British colonial territories the provision of social services, such as they were, was, until the last war, left to voluntary societies, which, in effect, meant the Christian missions. The policy of the British Administration was to interfere as little as possible with African social structure and tribal tradition on the comfortable

assumption that their traditional social pattern had a built-in remedy for dealing with social problems. This was largely true so long as African society remained static and dependent on subsistence agriculture. It became progressively less true as contact with the West, and consequent economic development, resulted in the growth of towns and dependence on a money economy. It was not, however, until towards the end of the Second World War, and due in large measure to the disruption caused by it, that colonial governments officially recognised the presence of certain social problems and took somewhat hesitant steps to deal with them.

Colonial government thinking was (also) at this time influenced by the recommendations of the Beveridge Report and the subsequent acceptance by the state in Britain of responsibility for providing fundamental welfare services for all citizens. It began to be generally recognised that governments should take steps to ensure that adequate social services were available to everyone in need of such services. The operative phrase was 'take steps to ensure'. No colonial government was in a position to provide comprehensive social services, even if they knew, which was very doubtful, what services were needed.

As social problems grew more insistent and governments became more ready to accept a measure of responsibility for dealing with them, small subsidies were made from public funds to help to support selected, locally-based charities. The support was never adequate and was, at times, very selective, depending as it so often did, on the interests and magnanimity of certain senior members of the colonial government.

It was not until towards the end of the war that government accepted direct responsibility for administering welfare services. At that time, acting on advice from the Secretary of State for the Colonies, some governments set up departments of Social Welfare, and expatriate officers were appointed to administer very limited funds for often ill-defined services. There was little or no direct local involvement in welfare services; practically all voluntary charitable bodies were directed and staffed largely by European voluntary workers and local government welfare staff had to be recruited from a limited background and trained overseas or by expatriate trainers who themselves were unfamiliar with local conditions, traditions and customs, and had pre-conceived ideas about methods of social work. It was, therefore, not surprising that a pattern of western-type social work developed in most countries which tended to deal with problems as they arose, or as they were seen to be manageable, and the more fundamental problems resulting from rapid social and economic change were at first not recognised.

At the same time, and with increasing government support, voluntary societies extended their activities and increased in number. Attempts were made to include local participation in the administration of voluntary bodies and, in some countries to which reference will be made later, locally based organisations were set up. This was

particularly true of women's organisations which expanded rapidly to meet the demands of the spectacular change in the status of women.

With the growth of government welfare services came the need to consider the part which voluntary effort should play in such services. This became urgent as governments saw the need for stating their policy and aims in the social field. What were the voluntary bodies doing? To what extent were the services they gave essential or necessary to the government programme, and how competent were they to carry out those services? Were they competing with each other and/or government in the same field? In other words, was there waste of effort and overlapping of services, and to what extent should government do anything about it? The classic dilemma.

It must be remembered that while local people were playing an increasingly important part in the political life of their country and in its administration, voluntary social agencies were still largely dominated by expatriate individuals and their funds were largely provided from overseas. It was an extremely delicate situation particularly where missionary societies or branches of metropolitan societies were involved. Most of the voluntary bodies were well aware of the problem and steps were taken to deal with it. It was inevitable, granted the British background, that countries should look to Britain for a solution. As has been shown, this problem in Britain was tackled through the setting up of Councils of Social Service.

In African countries attempts at co-ordination of effort were first made through associations of bodies with roughly similar interests; for example, women's organisations and youth organisations. These attempts were only partially successful; they depended very largely on the interest and enthusiasm of single individuals and in the absence of accepted machinery, the influence of such bodies was marginal and their continued existence problematic. Governments tended to continue to deal direct with individual societies, and government subsidies, if any, and fund raising generally remained the prerogative of the society.

It must also be remembered that nearly all voluntary societies were either entirely run or dominated by expatriates whose motives might have been excellent but whose competence in the social field in Africa might leave much to be desired. Attitudes again sometimes aggravated the situation. A tendency to know what was best for the local people had constantly to be resisted, and an effort made to work *with* rather than *for* the African. This latter attitude was difficult to express as local people were not familiar with organised voluntary effort and the idea of providing voluntary services for individuals outside the extended family was foreign to custom and tradition. This difference in attitude and approach needs to be borne in mind when considering the functions of Councils of Social Service in Africa today.

As government welfare services developed and with the appointment of more and more trained social workers, the need for a better working relationship with voluntary bodies and concerned individ-

uals became apparent. For example, in the early 1950s the Kenya government established an Advisory Council on Social Affairs on which representatives of voluntary organisations predominated. This was an attempt to associate voluntary organisations with the activities of the government department responsible for social work and to obtain the collective advice of people engaged in a variety of social service activities. Similar bodies were set up in Uganda and Zambia which were even called Councils of Social Service. However, they were only partially successful due very largely to the fact that they were initiated and serviced by the department of government concerned, and were managed by Europeans. It became increasingly clear, however, to the professional government social workers that some permanent representative form of organisation of voluntary agencies was needed, and approaches were made to Britain for help and advice. In 1960 the Trust became actively interested in helping to set up Councils of Social Service in Uganda and Rhodesia, and in 1964, in Kenya.

So much, rather sketchily, for the historical background and certain common elements in the development of voluntary social services and government agencies.

The outcome of the two visits in 1950 by experienced staff from the Citizens Advice Bureau movement in the United Kingdom, was to establish in Southern Rhodesia, as it was then called, four bureaux; one in Salisbury, one in Bulawayo, and one in each of the two major townships in which most of the African population lived. The provision of central services for these bureaux, together with their impact on the work of many voluntary organisations, led almost at once to a proposal that there should be established an organisation like a Council of Social Service, to serve as a focus for this voluntary work, and to maintain continuing relationships with the appropriate government departments. The Trustees were again asked to provide experienced help in establishing a new body to serve these purposes. They turned again to the National Council of Social Service who recommended the appointment of Mr H.R. Poole, secretary of the Liverpool Council of Social Service. His committee agreed to release him for what seemed a novel enterprise. Thus began a relationship between Mr Poole and the Trust which continued for almost twenty years. From his base in Salisbury, he followed up on behalf of the Trust enquiries from Northern Rhodesia – later Zambia – and Nyasaland – later Malawi. Several years later he was again seconded to the Trust for services in Kenya. In 1976, he was appointed the second part-time Associate Director with the Trust and initiated the group of projects in the field of community organisation described in Part III.

In retrospect it would not be unfair to say that both those who sought the Trust's help in Rhodesia, and the Trustees themselves, might have reflected more carefully on the probable development of voluntary work in the territory; a study of the prospects for a Council of Social Service might then have preceded the establishment of a network of Citizens Advice Bureaux. Because the order of events was reversed, the Council of

Social Service, when it came to be established, found itself already with a major commitment to support a network of Citizens Advice Bureaux, and this effectively pre-empted any discussion of the order of priority for the tasks which fell to it under its charter. In other countries in Africa which established Councils of Social Service, the maintenance of a Citizens Advice Bureau did not usually rank high amongst the tasks to which these organisations felt that they should set their hand. For good or ill, the scale and number of activities initiated by the Rhodesia Council, was largely determined by its prior commitment to the Citizens Advice Bureaux.

The consultant sent by the Trustees remained in the territory for a year, and helped to bring into existence a broadly based Council of Social Service with the then Governor, Sir Humphrey Gibbs, as President, and a close working relationship with the relevant department of the Rhodesian government. There was established also a local Council of Social Service in Salisbury and one in Bulawayo, and a series of standing committees or conferences, concerned with women's affairs; with the welfare of children; with voluntary youth organisations; and with the care of the elderly. Some of these bodies were financed by the government, although serviced by the council. By 1970 the original grant from the government had not been increased; a discretionary covenant service established by the Council, had not grown in the way that was expected. More than two-thirds of the income of the Council in that year came from the Trustees of the Joseph Rowntree Memorial Trust. The Trustees for their part, expected, as did many political leaders, that the series of negotiations between the Rhodesia government and the British government, would lead to some political settlement in a relatively short time. In fact, the uncertainty continued until 1979, and throughout that period the Trustees continued to accept responsibility for the Council's work, in the hope that the progress which had been made and the experience gained, would remain available to the leaders of any new administration. In this decision, they were supported by Mr Chinn's comments on his visit to Rhodesia. He wrote:

> The Council has achieved a great deal in the last nine years, and its most important achievement is to be able to command the loyalty of the major voluntary organisations in the country. The managements of these bodies represent a considerable force of influential public opinion, and the Council provides a forum for such opinion, which might otherwise not find corporate expression in the present political climate. It may, therefore, be politic for the time being to let well alone on the assumption that government will come to depend more and more on the goodwill of the voluntary agencies through the co-ordinating machinery of the Council. Then would be the time to ask for an increased grant. There is no doubt about the value of the work which the Council is doing, and its progress particularly during this past six years of political change has been impressive. This is very largely due to the inspired, and dedicated leadership of the Director and the quality of the staff.

The Director of the Trust was visiting the country and was the guest of the Governor when the Unilateral Declaration of Independence was made. Forty-eight hours earlier a reception to mark his visit had brought political and social leaders – black and white – to Government House for the last time. Five years later, after the Lancaster House Conference, elections under the new constitution for Zimbabwe were held; early in 1981 the Trust's recently appointed Director went to Zimbabwe to fulfil the Trustees' commitment to engage in discussions with a new administration as soon as one was formed. Since his visit, the Council of Social Service has transformed itself to meet the new situation created by the formation of Mr Mugabe's government. Now it seems set for a new beginning with an African Director, a new name – Voluntary Organisation in Community Enterprise – a new programme and support from government and major voluntary organisations alike.

Many requests for financial support came to the Trust from the voluntary organisations trying to maintain their work in the same uncertainties that affected the Council of Social Service. The Trustees responded to only three. They maintained a close relationship with the college for adult education at Ranche House. The grants they made were directed to reducing the immense burdens falling on Kenneth and Lillian Mew on whose commitment and vigour this remarkable institution depended. They kept, over more than a decade, an interest in the work of Jairus Jiri; his first improvised training workshops for handicapped Africans were the foundation on which was built a training and sheltered workshop organisation renowned internationally. The timeliness of the Trust's help rather than its scale led to a close personal relationship with Jairus; the award to him of the MBE and an honorary doctorate must rank with the most deserved awards of those modest recognitions. What could be little more than a gesture of support was given to the voluntary effort by some women's groups to help overcome the difficulties of African children whose hopes for the future depended on success in examinations set by an overseas body, and written in a language which was not their mother tongue.

Between 1961 and 1963, the initiative taken in Southern Rhodesia prompted enquiries for comparable support in the neighbouring territory of Northern Rhodesia and Uganda. The Trust's consultant in Southern Rhodesia made several visits to the Northern Territory, in the course of his work in establishing the Southern Rhodesia Council for Social Service.

It was, however, a time of political change. The Federation which brought together Northern and Southern Rhodesia and Nyasaland was clearly about to break up. An initiative in Northern Rhodesia which seemed in any way to be related to an organisation established in Southern Rhodesia, was inevitably looked upon with suspicion. The Trustees were clear that all they could do was to assure those involved in these discussions that the Trust would be willing to give support over a period of years to any agreed proposals which might be developed, whether for Citizens Advice Bureaux, or for a more permanent structure for the Council of Social Service. In the meantime, a small grant was made so that a full-time warden could be appointed to a community centre in Lusaka, the membership

of which was equally divided between Europeans and Africans, and seemed thus to be offering an important service at a time of rapid social change. Because of the Trust's known interest in housing, an exchange of views also took place with African Ministers who were preparing to take office in Northern Rhodesia, including Mr Kenneth Kaunda who, within a short time, took charge of the government. There was no immediate outcome from these discussions. The Trust was later involved in two projects to help in the preparation of Africans for the new duties which independence brought to them. They met the cost of a course to train women to take over the role of personal secretary to ministers, a service which in the early days of independence had to be rendered by British women who had so served in the colonial regime. They also contributed half the cost of bringing ten Zambians to the University of York, some of whom were graduates in economics, and for whom the University provided a special course to strengthen the resources of Zambia in dealing with problems of national and economic planning. The initiative taken in discussion about housing with Mr Kaunda remained, in a sense, on the Trustees' agenda; it did not lead to practical action until some years later, when the Trust joined with the American Friends Service Committee in developing a housing co-operative in Kafue near the capital, and in the up-grading of areas occupied by squatters. This was one of a number of housing projects on the African continent, which emerged as a result of the Trustees' concern with Councils of Social Service; they are described in the next chapter.

The story of the Trust's involvement in Uganda had quite different beginnings. During her husband's governorship, Lady Cohen helped in the formation of a Uganda Youth Council. Its principal concern was to train leaders for the growing number of youth clubs; their membership included an increasing number of young Africans coming into the capital for work. Over a period of two years, the Trustees provided money so that an experienced youth organiser could go to Kampala and mount three types of training for youth leaders. The first course met the needs of leaders, and those who aspired to be leaders; it consisted of sixteen two-hour sessions with additional practical work. There was then a shorter course for older experienced leaders who had not had any opportunity for professional training; a third series of courses offered training in special activities in youth clubs. The number of those applying to attend the first course were so great that it had to be duplicated; students travelled to attend the evening sessions, sometimes in torrential rain, from places as distant as thirty-five miles from Kampala. Of the ninety-four who started the course, seventy-one finished it satisfactorily. The demand for training came from African, Indian and European youth leaders; a later series of courses attracted even larger numbers of applicants.

As a result of her experience with the Uganda Youth Council, Lady Cohen had also brought together many of the voluntary organisations in the country into a Uganda Council of Voluntary Social Service. It was an effective body for consultation, but had no staff with skill and experience to develop its work. Distances were too great for the Trust's consultant in Southern Rhodesia to extend his services to Uganda, so an experienced

Regional Officer of the National Council of Social Service in England accepted service for eighteen months in Kampala, as Secretary of the existing Council of Voluntary Social Service. During that time, he and his wife gave professional service to the council and explored the possibilities of establishing a Council of Social Service, able to employ its own professional and administrative staff. By 1965, a Council of Social Service had been constituted, with a Ugandan Secretary, to develop and extend the structure which the visiting consultant had introduced. There were now three standing conferences concerned with women's organisations, child care and the care of the physically handicapped. Five local committees had come into being, recognised by voluntary organisations and by the government, and known as joint welfare advisory committees. The administrative and secretarial work of these committees, was, with the approval of central government, undertaken by local probation and welfare officers, though the committees themselves continued as independent groups representing both voluntary and statutory services in the locality. At this point, the Trust provided an additional grant for one year so that a member of staff could be appointed, who would spend substantial periods of time with each of these local committees, in order to guide their work in its early stages, and to secure co-operation throughout the territory. Later the senior staff of the council were given opportunities to visit the United Kingdom to study the work of Councils of Social Service, and their relations with government and local authorities.

The early hopes for the stability of the Council were not realised. The very able African Secretary was, within a short time, offered a post with the United Nations. His place was difficult to fill. Political change brought different ministers and officials into the department which was most concerned with the affairs of the Council. Nonetheless, government support for the council's work continued; the proportion of its expenditure met by the Trust was reduced, whilst the relationship between the council and the Trust remained close. Even in the early days of President Amin, an Indian Treasurer was negotiating with the Trust and with the appropriate government department on financial support for the Council's work for a period of years ahead. On the return of the Director of the Trust from a visit concerned with these negotiations, it seemed prudent to consult the Foreign and Commonwealth Office before further funds were transmitted to Uganda. More dramatic events occurred almost immediately, and communication with Kampala ceased. The fate of those in Kampala who were responsible for the administration of the Council's affairs is unhappily not known.

In the adjoining territory of Kenya, there had been a Kenya Advisory Council on Social Affairs since the early 1950s. It brought together representatives of the larger voluntary organisations, and received from the government a small subsidy, whilst its secretarial needs were met by the department responsible for social welfare. In 1964 the Kenya government appointed an Adviser on Social Development from the United Kingdom, who submitted a paper on Social Welfare, which included proposals for a co-ordinating and consultative body representing the voluntary organisations. It was at this point that the Trust was asked if it would be willing to

give help; it was able once again to call on the services of Mr H.R. Poole, of the Liverpool Council of Social Service, who visited Kenya and undertook the negotiations which led to the establishment of the Kenya Council of Social Service. A full account of the formation of the Council is included as an appendix to Mr W.H. Chinn's report already referred to. The successful development of the Council's work in later years, was due largely to the skill with which the Council was established under an African director, with a predominantly African committee, whilst retaining the sympathy and support of those, mainly European, who had formerly served on the Advisory Council on Social Affairs. The Trust maintained its support for the general work of the Kenya council for a decade; it drew more of its resources from within the country, and received an increasing measure of support from the Kenya government.

When the regular grant came to an end, the Trustees agreed to meet the cost of two special projects. The Kenya council had been invited to serve as the regional office for the International Council on Social Welfare. It thus had a new task, when in 1974 the Seventeenth International Conference on Social Welfare met in the Kenyatta Conference Centre in Nairobi, and was opened by President Kenyatta. To enable the Kenya council to add to its staff in order to serve as the regional office for the International Council, and to organise the international conference, a grant was given for a period of three years. Support was also given for a period of three years for a research project into the role and potential of voluntary organisations in the development of rural welfare services in Kenya. The research was a joint responsibility of the Kenya National Council of Social Service, the Kenya government, and the University of Nairobi.

The Trust's involvement in the affairs of two other countries from which applications for support were received, has been more marginal. During his service for the Trust in Rhodesia, Mr Poole went, at the request of representatives of voluntary organisations, and with the approval of the Trust, to visit Malawi to advise on the possible establishment of a Council of Social Service. Those concerned with voluntary organisations, and officers in the government concerned with social welfare, were anxious that such an organisation should be established. At the political level, however, agreement was not reached and the Trust's representative returned to report that the broad measure of agreement necessary for the establishment of a Council of Social Service could not be achieved at that time. The need for some kind of consultative apparatus was, however, evidently recognised by the Malawi government, which itself established a Malawi Council of Social Service. This body consisted of five members nominated by the government; it is not representative of voluntary organisations, nor does the membership include a representative, as such, of government itself. However, the work of voluntary organisations in Malawi has continued to expand, and the Council is at least performing a useful function keeping alive the idea of co-operation between government and voluntary organisations in social welfare.

Swaziland was the only country to which a contribution was made for a Council of Social Service, but which has never been visited by a representative of the Trust, nor has there been any direct negotiations about the scale

PLATE 13 (a) and (b)   The Homestead, Seebohm Rowntree's home until his retirement from business, is now the headquarters of Rowntree Mackintosh Limited.

PLATE 14   The Fothergil site more than replaces in number the almshouses in York which were beyond repair.

PLATE 15 Dwellings designed for the Tuke Housing Association occupy the site of dilapidated storage buildings and garages along the boundary of the old Friends burial ground.

PLATE 16 (a) and (b) The Tuke Association has designed acceptable flats from property at the junction of Coppergate and Friargate, purchased from The Society of Friends, whose new Meeting House in Friargate is seen in the small picture.

PLATE 17 (a) and (b)   Clementhorpe is typical of many inner areas of provincial towns. The elevations to the street have considerable charm, much of which has been lost by the intrusion of motor traffic. Board Street is an example of the Trust's policy of radical re-construction, first applied at New Earswick, and now extended to a housing action area in the City of York.

PLATE 18   The Riverside Park opposite York's Guildhall was built by the Trust on a site given to the city by the Rowntree Company.

PLATE 19   The three storey house was modernised to replace a dwelling in the warehouse cleared for the construction of the Riverside Park, from which this picture was taken.

PLATE 20   Beyond York's Guildhall is the Riverside Walk, constructed at the expense of the Trust as a first outcome of the River Ouse survey.

or purpose of the Trust's support. In the late 1950s the government appointed an officer from the United Kingdom to establish a Social Welfare Service. He was anxious to make the best use of the contribution which voluntary organisations could offer, and he therefore proposed the establishment of the Council of Social Service. He approached the Trustees for their help. He assured the Trustees that the Swaziland government intended to make a regular annual contribution to the newly-formed Council, and the Trustees agreed to more than match the Swaziland government's contribution for a period of five years. In his report to the Trustees, Mr Chinn, who was able to visit Swaziland, describes the misunderstandings that arose because there were no direct negotiations with the government and with voluntary organisations. It later emerged that the Swaziland government made no contribution at all to the Council's expenses, and support came only from the Trust and from a number of voluntary organisations. Mr Chinn believed that the potential usefulness of the council was considerable. It had, at the time of his visit, a competent African chairman, and an energetic secretary, but was unable to engage in any effective programme without more resources than were provided by the constituent voluntary organisations. The Trust's last payment was made in 1969; no new initiative seems possible unless there is a new approach supported by the government, and carrying the commitment of some support from public funds.

Housing Overseas

A Housing Co-operative in Zimbabwe
The Southern Rhodesia Council of Social Service was formally registered on 14 April 1962. Late in 1961 the Director of the Trust visited Rhodesia, to join with the Trust's consultant in the final stage of the negotiations. New principles were being established, and a commitment to substantial expenditure over a period of years was involved. The arrangements for that visit included meetings in the African townships both with civil servants responsible for their administration, and with African community leaders. These discussions showed, if such a demonstration was necessary, that the quality of homes and neighbourhoods whether in Central Africa or elsewhere, is the key to any improvement in social conditions or in race relations. Evidence of the rising aspirations of African families lay in the comparison between houses then being built, and those thought adequate only a few years ago. In some areas there was commendable foresight and flexibility in designing homes which were capable of enlargement and adaptation for higher living standards.

As part of its housing research, the Trust had been studying the part that co-operative housing might play as a choice additional to renting and buying. The suggestion was made that the Trust might provide capital, so that a group of Africans could constitute a housing co-operative. The freehold of the land on which the houses were built would need to be vested in the co-operative, and responsibilities for management exercised by an elected committee. There was enthusiasm for this proposal by the

officials concerned with housing in the Department of African Affairs in Bulawayo; the support of Sir Humphrey Gibbs, the Governor, was immediately forthcoming. His authority for the vesting of freehold land in the co-operative was essential to the enterprise. A site was identified on which about forty dwellings with a small group of shops could be built, and the outlines of a constitution for a co-operative were agreed with government officials and with African community leaders who wished to see the project established. The critical part of the negotiations concerned the advance by the Trust of the capital cost of developing the site and the terms on which the members would re-pay the loan over a period of forty years. Within a few weeks the proposals were presented to the Trustees who immediately approved them.

There was some opposition in Rhodesia to the inclusion of a group of shops in the property to be owned by the co-operative. The Trustees attached importance to this, since the rent from the shops would provide the co-operative with an income beyond what would be available to them from the rents of the houses which they occupied. This income could be used by the members to provide facilities for children's activities and other community needs, without dependence on further contributions from the Trust, or grants from statutory authorities.

Building began in January 1963, and the families moved in before the end of that year. Problems arose over the initial down payment; an individual loan was made to a few members, which had to be repaid over a short period in addition to the ordinary mortgage payments. It was the responsibility of the elected committee to ensure that its members made their payments as they fell due, so that the co-operative could transmit to the Trust in equal half-yearly instalments, a payment of interest and capital sufficient to repay the advance within the forty year period. The Trustees owed a considerable debt to the Town Clerk at Bulawayo, who worked throughout with the members of the co-operative, and also to the solicitor of the National Federation of Housing Societies in Britain, who advised the Trustees on constitutional issues and on the formal contracts that had to be concluded.

It was an unusual venture; there was no precedent to indicate whether such an organisation was likely to be appropriate to the conditions of Central Africa, nor could it be foreseen whether an elected committee would be able to enforce what proved to be the stern discipline of regular payments from members of a co-operative unaccustomed to such a self-imposed obligation. It has to be recorded, however, that from the beginning of the Trust's association with the co-operative until the disposal of the Trust's interest in the mortgage some sixteen years later, the full amount of capital and interest was credited to the Trust without fail on the due date each half year. Even during the period of unilateral independence when the transmission of money became impossible, the due sum was credited to a bank in Rhodesia, and the Trust was able to nominate charitable organisations – primarily the Rhodesia Council of Social Service – to which the amounts standing to the credit of the Trust could be paid.

It was never the intention of the Trustees to recover the capital which they had advanced. The income generated by the houses and shops would

first cover the maintenance and improvement of the properties and then be used for social welfare organisations in Rhodesia concerned with the interests of African families. The project was brought to a completion, so far as the Trustees were concerned, more than fifteen years later, shortly before the negotiations which led to the transfer of power and the establishment of the new State of Zimbabwe. The Humanitas Trust had been founded in Bulawayo by a former Director of the Institute of Race Relations in Johannesburg, who in his later years made his home in Rhodesia. The Trust had wide powers in education and social welfare to advance the cause of Africans and their families. After somewhat complicated negotiations, the Trustees of the Humanitas Trust agreed to accept the interest in the mortgage, and to apply the monies paid to them to objects within their terms of Trust. There was an informal understanding that the two Trusts would confer from time to time about the uses to which the payments from the co-operative should be put. These consultations could not in any way limit the exercise by the Trustees of the Humanitas Trust of the discretion vested in them by their Trust Deed. The Rowntree Trustees were thus able to achieve their original purpose, postponed by the problems which UDI brought, of establishing a housing co-operative independent in its constitution, and owning the freehold of its properties, but contributing to other constructive developments in the country. The members of the co-operative gave their òrganisation the name of Mhlahlandhela Housing Co-operative; the word means 'the first of its kind'.

Whether in the new state of Zimbabwe the co-operative as a means of providing housing will be developed, is a question which lies in the future. What has been remarkable is the success with which the members of the co-operative have developed the site which they own, and the way in which the houses, skilfully planned to allow for enlargement and higher standards, now contrast sharply with the stark simplicity of the original buildings. One, and sometimes two cars are parked outside almost all the houses. There are now few uncovered floors, wall-to-wall carpets in some homes mark the rising prosperity of the owners. Kitchens and bathrooms are now equipped with modern fittings. The co-operative as a whole has a good income from the rents of the shops which the Trustees were determined to include in the scheme, whilst the founder members have an asset of considerable value, which they can sell to a buyer approved by the committee of the co-operative. The intention of the Trustees to make a provision for the emerging African middle class, has succeeded beyond what seemed possible at the time. It is a further mark of changing times that, even during the period of UDI, the members of the committee of the co-operative were able to entertain the Trust's representative in the leading hotel in Bulawayo, an establishment from which they would have been barred in the days when the negotiations were first opened.

This initiative led to a participation by the Trust in two housing projects in Zambia and later to the establishment of a housing co-operative in Lesotho, the independent republic constituted from the former territory of Basutoland. A brief account of these projects will complete this review of the Trustees' involvement in housing in the southern part of the African continent.

Self-build Houses for Squatters in Zambia

Building new houses is only part of the work which has to be undertaken to meet the needs of an increasingly mobile population in African territories. Zambia is part of the copper belt; its economy rests on mining and engineering, as well as agriculture, and the proportion of industrial activity in the total economy is probably higher than in other territories outside the Republic of South Africa. One of the consequences in Zambia is a substantial movement of the population from rural areas into Lusaka the capital, and into surrounding centres where industrial development is taking place. Extensive areas have been covered with improvised dwellings giving all the problems of a squatters zone, which in different forms is familiar throughout the Third World.

Representatives of the American Friends Service Committee, with experience of self-help housing in their own country, discussed with the Zambian government the possibility of a self-help housing development in the area of Kafue in which industry was growing. Indeed, it seemed that employment could be found for a number of those living in improvised dwellings if they had the security of a permanent home from which to meet the discipline of regular employment. The Trust's interest in housing, both in Zimbabwe and in earlier days in Zambia was known. The Trust was asked to meet a substantial part of the administrative expenses in launching a self-help housing scheme to which the main financial contributors were the government of Zambia and the municipality of Lusaka. The land and the services were provided by the government and the municipality, the administration and the technical skill were provided by the American Friends Service Committee, employing almost exclusively local people, whilst contrary to its general policy, the Trust's contribution took the form of hard cash without other involvement.

The principles on which the scheme was based were remarkably simple. A family wishing to secure a home need have no money, but demonstrated its commitment by accepting a discipline in construction, which ensured that those who embarked on the project would carry their work to completion.

Families were divided into groups of about ten. They were required to commit themselves to a minimum number of hours of labour a week. That labour had to be given by the members of the family; it could not be provided by employing others. The ten families had first to make, and stack ready for use, all the bricks required to complete the ten dwellings needed to provide each family with a home. Until all the bricks were made and their quality approved no work on the site could begin. This brick-making task was a heavy discipline requiring about three months concentrated work. A family who defaulted at this stage was replaced by another from the list of applicants. When the bricks were finished, technical advice was given to lay out the site and prepare the foundations. When, and only when, the foundation work for all the ten houses needed by the group was completed could the building of the walls begin and the construction carried up to roof level. Instruction was then given, and materials provided, for the construction of the roof. Thus it was always in the interests of the whole group to ensure that the work on all the ten houses went on at

the same speed; no advantage was to be gained by a great concentration of labour by one family on its own house; and there was constant pressure on any laggards to mend their pace.

The finance of the scheme showed equal ingenuity. The statutory authorities provided a float for the purchase of materials needed for the construction of the dwellings. This had to be repaid within two years of the completion of the house. As families required materials for the construction work, they were able to draw them from the store, the cost being charged to their float. If some members of a family were earning money, they might wish to pay for their materials, thus leaving the float untouched and available for extras beyond the basic dwelling. In the outcome, an estate was completed of which all those involved in the work could be proud; the loans were all repaid in less than the period set by the government. Having progressed so far, the community decided that it could continue to work together, and not only completed the housing site, but added a school for the children living on the estate with additional accommodation that the authorities could use for children living elsewhere in the same area. As in Zimbabwe the house plan had been so designed that families could later extend and improve their homes.

It was as a result of the success of this self-help scheme that the Zambian government asked the American Friends Service Committee if they would try to apply the same principles to the upgrading of the shacks in which very much larger numbers of families were living near the capital of Lusaka. This was a much more difficult project; the area was so extensive that it was not easy so to plan the work that some visual impact was made in any one place to serve as an example and a stimulus to effort elsewhere. But the benefit to a number of families was very great indeed, and the Trustees agreed to make a further financial contribution towards the expenses which the American Friends Service Committee were incurring.

A Housing Co-operative in Lesotho

As reports of these housing activities spread around Southern Africa an application was received from a university group in Lesotho who wished to begin a housing co-operative along the lines of the Bulawayo project in Zimbabwe, but incorporating some of the self-help ideas that had been successfully applied in Zambia. This was to be a direct Trust commitment, so that before decisions were made discussions were held in Maseru, the capital of Lesotho, both with the university group, and with the statutory authorities responsible for housing. The Trustees felt they should approach the matter rather differently from their first initiative in Zimbabwe. Lesotho was already an independent country, and the Trustees wished to avoid making a loan with interest and repayments passing to the credit of the Trust. Discussions with the group of co-operators and with government departments were complex. In the outcome the Trustees proposed that they should give a sum of money sufficient for the construction of the houses already planned by the first co-operative, and for a second project meeting the needs of a different community. The money was to be paid to the Lesotho government, which would hold it in trust and establish a revolving fund from which advances could be made to the

self-help groups already established; repayments over a relatively short period would finance schemes proposed by other similar groups. The Trustees also offered a grant to meet the cost of administering the fund in its first few years.

The Trustees kept in touch with the enterprise until the completion of the first group of houses. When the main part of the construction was finished a further loan was made to secure higher standards than those first contemplated. The Lesotho government agreed to undertake the administration of the revolving fund without payment of any additional grant by the Trustees. Time will show what demands may be made on this limited fund by other groups wishing to join together to meet their housing needs. In the long term it will be the impetus given to a wider movement for self-help housing in Lesotho that will be the Trust's main contribution; international funds to support the movement began to flow as the second project financed by the Trust's grant began to take shape.

Part V   *The Trust's Administration and Finance*

19 The Appointment and Service of Trustees

During his lifetime the Founder of the Trust had the sole right of appointing Trustees. On his death other arrangements came into operation; a distinction was then drawn between the Village (now Memorial) Trust and the two other Trusts founded at the same time. This was because the Village Trust, as the owner and administrator of housing estates, was permanent; the Founder expected the other Trusts to spend both capital and income within thirty-five years; longer term provisions for the appointment of Trustees was, therefore, less important.

For the permanent Trust, Joseph Rowntree made explicit provisions for the appointment of Trustees after his death. There are two matters of interest about them; first their consequences for the size of the Trust, and second the balance of power between the continuing Trustees and the outside body charged by the Founder with the duty to make appointments to fill alternate vacancies.

Clauses 6, 7 and 8 of the Deed of Foundation contain the provisions for the appointment of Trustees. Extracts from these clauses are reproduced in Appendix I; the appointments to which they have led are shown on page xix of the introductory section of the book. Clause 6 defines the circumstances which create a vacancy. Present day Trustees have imposed on themselves the additional rule that a Trustee shall retire no later than his or her seventy-fifth birthday. That self denying ordinance could, of course, be changed at any time; it has not been built in to the Deed of Foundation.

Clause 7 defines the power of appointment of Trustees during the Founder's lifetime; it is important because it had the incidental consequence of settling the total number of Trustees. The clause gives the Founder the sole right, first to fill vacancies occurring as a result of the provisions of clause 6, and second to make additional appointments. Joseph Rowntree made two additional appointments. With the six appointments made in the original Deed, a total of eight places on the Board of Trustees was thus created. So long as the Founder lived, or, after his death, four of the original Trustees survived, vacancies could continue to be filled. But this power ceased when the number of original Trustees was reduced to three. When that occurred in 1941 the number of Trustees remaining in office was six. Clause 8 then became operative. Two new appointments were to be made; this was done, and the number of Trustees was increased to eight. There was no power to increase it further. In a letter dated 26 April 1948, Seebohm Rowntree opened up with his brother Stephen, then Chairman of the Village Trust, the possibility of adding to

the number of Trustees because of the demands which the work of the Trust made on their time. 'I have been through the Trust Deed,' he wrote, 'and see no reference to any clause limiting the number of Trustees. If I am right in thinking this so. . .' He was not right; there is no such clause, but the effect of the clauses concerned with new appointments is as clear as if there were. Seebohm Rowntree was so advised, and he and his colleagues had to struggle on.

For the Village Trust, as the permanent Trust, clause 8 shows that the Founder nominated an outside body to make one of the two new appointments called for after his death and when the number of original Trustees fell to three, and to fill alternate vacancies subsequently. The other appointment and subsequent alternate vacancies were left to the continuing Trustees. He nominated two such bodies and left the continuing Trustees to decide on each occasion which one should act. The first was the London Yearly Meeting of the Society of Friends – the representative body of members of the Society in the United Kingdom; the second was the Yorkshire Quarterly Meeting of the same Society – the representative body of Friends in Yorkshire. The latter, following constitutional changes in the Society of Friends, is now called the Yorkshire General Meeting. Unless the Trustees decide between these two appointing bodies within three months of the occurrence of a vacancy, then the Yorkshire Meeting has power to proceed with the appointment. If the body chosen to make the appointment fails to act at its next session, or next but one, then the Charity Commissioners may nominate any public body to make the appointment. Strangely there are no time limits set for appointments by the continuing Trustees nor is any reserve power given to the Charity Commissioners to act in default. The first appointment under this procedure was made in 1943. The Trustees decided to ask the Yorkshire Quarterly Meeting to make the appointment. They asked the same body to fill alternate vacancies as they occurred until 1974. Then, because of the wider responsibilities falling on the Trust following the passage of the Joseph Rowntree Memorial Trust Act, they decided that their housing interests in Yorkshire were less relevant to the decision; for the first time in 1974 the London Yearly Meeting was invited to make an appointment to the Trust. The continuing Trustees did not make their new appointment until 1945.

Whether it was the London or Yorkshire body that was asked to make an appointment, there has on each occasion been direct consultation between the Trust and a committee of the appointing body about how best to complement the experience already available round the Trust table, and whether there are considerations of age or sex that should be weighed. But the choice of the person appointed rests with the appointing body.

There is one possible qualification. A carefully worded clause provides that any one Trustee (but not the Founder) can be removed from office by the unanimous resolution of all the other Trustees passed at a meeting specially called for that purpose. It is difficult in the light of experience to contemplate such a situation, but presumably the continuing Trustees could use this power to prevent the continuation in office of a Trustee

appointed by one or other of the outside appointing bodies whom they felt to be wholly unsuited for the duties falling on Trustees!

Some recent commentators have argued for a limit to the period of service of a Trustee as well as for a stated retirement age. The latter the Trustees, but the frequency of change, and the problem of finding men and been the lack of new life and thinking in a group of too long serving Trustees, but the frequency of change and the problem of finding men and women with experience to enable them to contribute adequately to a small body exercising wide and diverse responsibilities, and to give time not only to attend Trust meetings, but to be actively concerned in the work which the Trust supports.

The Trust's Administration

The character of the Trust has derived from the balance of responsibility exercised by Trustees and by the staff they employ.

The first Trustees were close relatives of the Founder, already sharing his concerns and his work. They were also Directors of the Rowntree Company of which he was the first Chairman. For the administrative and technical help they required in developing the work of the Village Trust they turned to the people they had already chosen as equipped to carry similar responsibilities in the Rowntree Company.

The directors of the Company, operating as Trustees, drew in consultants as needed. The work of the Trust, and its records, were distributed throughout the various departments at the cocoa works. The secretary to the Trust kept the minutes of meetings and prepared the accounts; more expert advice on accounts was available in the Company if required. The building department in the Company engaged and supervised the staff maintaining the houses the Trust built, whilst the distinguished architect whose work established the Trust's reputation in the housing field, was responsible directly to the Trustees and received his detailed brief from the Company's building department. Legal work fell to the Company's legal department, which as a result held the Trust's most important records. There were no Trust administrative staff paid as such; the one or two who gave most of their time to Trust affairs remained on the Company's pay roll and subscribed to its pension fund.

These arrangements worked well enough whilst first, Joseph Rowntree, then Seebohm Rowntree, was Chairman of the Company and of the Trust, and managed Trust affairs from within his personal office. Other Trustees were also Company Directors and similarly used their personal staffs. By 1946, when the Trust decided to move into new fields of work, the surviving original Trustees had long since retired from the Company. Within the Company's own organisation too, restructuring to deal with the growth of the business at home and overseas meant that the close knit, day-to-day involvement of cocoa works staff in the Trust's clerical, accounting, and building and maintenance work was no longer possible or managerially appropriate.

The legal department continued to give skilful service and the Company's solicitor acted for the Trust, but this was essentially a personal and a professional appointment.

As recorded earlier, the Trust in 1946 made a first appointment of a person to work with Trustees in developing their new ideas about their post war work. But there was no administrative structure into which he could fit. Seebohm Rowntree in 1948 wrote to his brother, then Chairman of the Trust, about the problem of an identity for the new arrival. 'I quite agree that we do want 'X' to exercise real authority, and I think he will do this without having any title. I believe that Henry Ford refused to give any man in his factory titles, and there is something to be said for that!' The outcome was that preparations for new work went on in isolation from the accounting and housing management work of the Trust. Left thus in limbo, and detached from the company departments that formerly nourished it, the administration ceased to develop. A Trust with an international reputation for progressive work in house design, and claiming leadership in the new fields into which it was moving, had, at its base, accounting methods, office administration and housing management, unchanged since the early years of the century.

When change came, it came quickly. The enforced move to a separate office outside the Company's headquarters meant the gradual assembly of the Trust's records in one place, thus providing the essential base for any coherent administration. A diversification of work at home and its extension overseas required more sophisticated accounting practices. Newly appointed Trustees came enthused by the potential for new development which they saw in a Trust with wide powers and growing resources. Later, a whole new enterprise came to the Trust with the responsibility for the Family Fund. The decision to diversify the Trust's endowment brought the need and opportunity for the exercise of skills in analysing investment opportunities and monitoring the outcome. By the end of the 1970s it would have been hard to find so small and compact an administration discharging so wide and sophisticated a programme of work. Its central principle was to meet increased demands by improved methods and more advanced technology rather than by an enlarged administration. The rewards have come in low administrative costs and high staff morale.

The Trust administers a thousand or so properties, and builds, converts and rehabilitates dwellings; it finances, from an income exceeding £1½ million a year, a hundred or more research projects within deliberately chosen fields of interest. It distributes over £4 million a year to individual families having the care of a very severely handicapped child, separately assessing each application; it manages an investment portfolio of some £25 million and, as the next chapter will show, monitors the outcome with a degree of sophistication to match that offered by any external fund manager. That there are eight Trustees to carry these responsibilities is, as the opening paragraph of this chapter shows, a coincidence. Those concerned with the administration of the Trust have come to regard it as an ideal number. There is a high degree of personal commitment to the Trust: very rarely is any Trustee absent from one of its meetings. Decisions which

shape the Trust's policy and programme are corporate decisions; individual Trustees are then separately involved with staff in their implementation. A small number of Trustees working in this way has implications for the calibre of staff they need to employ. Staff must reflect the attitude, interest and concerns of Trustees and thus bring proposals for corporate consideration that will give expression to them. This relationship is critical to the character of the Trust; it is neither a body of experts served by an executive staff, nor a lay committee advised by experts.

20   *The Trust's Income*

The Rowntree Investment

The Founder endowed the Joseph Rowntree Village Trust with land and buildings at New Earswick and a block of shares in the Rowntree Company – then a private, not a public company. He endowed the two other Trusts which he founded at the same time with separate blocks of shares in the same Company of which he was the first Chairman; in all, the shares so transferred gave the Trustees, subject to important qualifications, a controlling interest in the Company.

The qualifications were evidence of the Founder's wisdom. At the outset the Trustees of each of the three Trusts, and the Directors of the Rowntree Company, were virtually the same people. But this would not continue. The Company would have to appoint Directors to succeed the Founder and his immediate family; the Trusts each had powers after the death of the Founder to appoint new Trustees – and he made clear in his advice to Trustees that relationship to him was not to be held as relevant in considering new appointments; fitness for the office was what mattered. Joseph Rowntree had no wish to establish the Trusts as corporate shareholders able by a simple vote so to deploy their strength as to determine the policy the Directors should follow. He also saw that it might be wise in the interests of the Trusts for their Trustees to change their investments as time passed, though the Trust Deed provided that shares in the Rowntree Company should not be sold 'unless the Trustees shall consider a sale thereof to be necessary for the purpose, or in the interest of the Trust'. So the shares allocated to each Trust were, for voting purposes, divided equally between the Trustees, with any balance allocated to the Chairman. Each Trustee was entitled to cast his votes at any Annual or Special Meeting of the Company in any way he or she thought fit. The oft repeated statement that the 'Trusts control the Company' was true only if all Trustees of all three Trusts individually decided so to use their votes as to secure the passage of a particular resolution. As the Trustees together deployed only slightly more than fifty per cent of the total voting strength, one or two Trustees taking a line different from their colleagues, but in accord with other shareholders, could frustrate any proposal favoured by Trustees generally. When in 1897 Rowntrees became a public company, with some shares held outside the family and the Trusts, the possibilities of conflict inherent in these arrangements increased. On the one hand the Directors had a sense of security in the knowledge that no takeover or other attempt at control could succeed save with the agreement of virtually all the Trustees of the three Trusts; on the other hand, minority shareholders might feel that judgments other than commercial could

determine the response of the Trustee shareholders to the policy of the Directors.

During the period from 1954 to 1969 the Company continued to require funds for investment in business and it generated these from its own profits and by raising bank and other loans. No issues of equity were made and at a time when many companies were expanding rapidly by acquisition, the Rowntree Company growth was essentially internal.

The conservative dividend policy (dividend cover averaged 10.8 throughout the 1950s), and the limited market in shares because of the relatively small proportion changing hands, held down the Stock Exchange value of the shares and left the Company exposed to a bid which, paradoxically, the Trusts might find it difficult to resist in view of their legal obligations as Trustees.

Whatever unease might have existed, the issue was not brought into open discussion until the Trustees of the Village Trust – with a shareholding as large as the other two Trusts put together – sought as part of the extension of their powers by private legislation to enlarge their investment powers as a prudent provision against possible change. The authorities gladly agreed; indeed they pointed out to Trustees how large was now their endowment; its growth was a tribute to the enterprise of the Rowntree Company but, even so, some diversification of the investment portfolio should be considered. The investment powers incorporated into the Joseph Rowntree Memorial Trust Act preserved, unchanged, the Trust's powers to invest in the Rowntree Company or its successors; for any additional investment wide powers were given subject to a defined distribution between 'narrower range' and 'broader range' securities.

Two events of great moment in the history of the Company influenced both the scale and the timing of the changes made in the Trust's investment policy. In 1969 General Foods of America indicated an interest in acquiring the Company; the cash offer to shareholders was substantially above the current market price of the shares. The Trustees were faced with a predictable dilemma. They had been reminded by the Treasury Solicitors, in the discussions on their investment clause in the Joseph Rowntree Memorial Trust Act, that they were Trustees of a charitable Trust; any decisions they made in respect of shares they held as Trustees must be determined solely by the interests of the Trust. Their concern for a company or its employees must not deflect them from their duty to secure the Trust's best interests. On the other side there were pressures on them by reason of the common heritage shared by the Trusts and the Company, and from citizens of York who by a variety of means made it clear that they did not welcome the idea that the control of the Company, which was the City's largest employer, would lie in New York. Trustees also had to recognise that other shareholders saw a clear and immediate financial gain and there might well be resentment if Trustees, for reasons of their own, vetoed the offer.

Perhaps for the first time since the earliest days of the Trust, all Trustees of the three Trusts – some twenty-two persons – met on a Saturday morning to consider the offer and see how far there was a united view on the way Trustees should discharge the responsibilities which, by the

Founder's provision, rested on each of them individually. The Chairman of the Company, who in a personal capacity was a Trustee, made a brief statement and left the meeting. In the event, Trustees were unanimous in their decision. They included men of wide commercial experience and reputation, nationally and internationally. They were agreed that, notwithstanding the immediate cash advantage secured by the General Foods offer, the Trusts would gain financially in the longer term by the continuance of an independent Rowntree Company. It was a commercial judgment and it might have been wrong. In fact in less than a year the share price had risen substantially above the cash offer made by General Foods. Argument about the principles involved continued in the financial press, but no criticism could be made of the Trustees' judgment of where lay the interests of the Trusts for which they held personal responsibility.

The experience led the Memorial Trustees to consider at once the advice they had been given when discussing their investment clause with the authorities. They agreed to embark on a policy of gradual diversification of their endowments. The change in policy was not unwelcome to the Company. The Rowntree investment had led to a growth in the resources of the Trust beyond that of any other British foundation; the Trustees thought, therefore, that they should retain in the foreseeable future at least half of their endowment in Rowntree shares. For the remainder they should look to a spread between fixed interest securities – likely to increase resources for current use but not to lead to growth – and equity shares, selected with expert advice from outside the Trust, combined with the experience of the small group of Trustees appointed as an investment committee as required by their Act of Parliament.

There followed shortly a merger between the Rowntree Company and the Mackintosh Company to form Rowntree Mackintosh Limited. The Trustees, in common with the vast majority of shareholders, approved the merger. Their new investment policy had hardly begun to be implemented, however, when a blow fell which was the most serious internal crisis in the Company's history. It concerned the purchase of cocoa and resulted in a loss of £30m to the Company with, of course, a dramatic fall in the value of the Trustees' holding. The tragedy – for such it was – concerns this history only in so far as it influenced the Trust's investment policy or determined the scale of its operations.

It was widely said at the time that the 'cocoa crisis' had led to the Trust's decision to diversify its investments. This was not true. The decision to diversify had already been made and the new policy was already being implemented. The crisis confirmed the wisdom of the decision, but enforced a postponement of about a year in implementing it. Confidence in the future of the Company remained; the Trust's investment committee were clear that the share price, in relation to other securities which the Trust might wish to acquire, would recover in time and that diversification of the portfolio should therefore be postponed. Again the commercial judgment was right; a year later investment changes were resumed.

A changed Investment Portfolio

In 1954, when this account of the Trust's work opened, 99.94 per cent of the Trust's investment was in the shares of the Rowntree Company. In 1980 that proportion was 49.83 per cent. In the same year, 24.02 per cent of the portfolio was in other equity shares and 26.15 per cent in fixed interest securities. The objective which the Trustees had set themselves following the bid from General Foods had been achieved.

Table 20.1 shows in columns 4, 5 and 6 the stages of this diversification at five year intervals and then year by year from 1974. It also shows in column 1 the market value of the whole portfolio in each of those years and, in column 2, the percentage growth in value, taking 1954 as 100. In column 3 is the share index for the same years as measured by the De Zoete and Bevan Equity Index (the more usual Financial Times All Share Index was not introduced until 1962). Columns 7, 8 and 9 show the Trust's annual income from this portfolio, with the percentage increase from year to year, again taking 1954 as 100. For comparison, the movement of the retail price index, taking 1954 also at 100, is shown in the last column.

Figure 9 is easier to follow for the layman, and yet adds a degree of sophistication for the more technically minded. It includes the Financial Times All Share Index from 1962 when it was introduced; it shows separately the growth of the Trust's portfolio as a whole and that part of it which was invested in Rowntree shares; and the figures identify cumulative annual growth, that is investment income with capital appreciation (or depreciation) – an accurate measure of investment performance.

To maintain the real value of capital and income in recent years has been a principal preoccupation of those who advise charitable trusts on their investments. A few observations on the changes disclosed by the graph may therefore be welcomed by Foundation Trustees and those who advise them.

For the analysis on which this and the following section are based, and for the table and graph, the author is indebted to Mr R.S. Connelly, the Trust's Finance Officer from 1971–1981.

The graph shows that until 1970 the Trust's investments performed in line with the De Zoete and Bevan Index. The return during these sixteen years expressed as an annual figure was 9.59 per cent which compares with 3.73 per cent on the retail prices index leaving a real return of nearly 6 per cent a year.

After the abortive General Foods bid already described, the Rowntree Company's dividend policy changed; there was in consequence a sharp rise in the market value of its shares in 1971 and 1972. This is reflected in the abrupt rise in the Trust's investment performance over both the indices, identified by lines (a) and (b) on the graph. The year 1973 brought the cocoa crisis, described earlier, and then in 1974 the Trust's investments fell back with the share index in the collapse of that year. Thereafter, as the table and the graph show, the Trust began to diversify its portfolio; the graph shows the difference from that year in the performance of the Trust's portfolio as a whole compared with its Rowntree component. What is significant for the Trust's investment decisions during the period

Table 20.1 The Trust's investment and income 1954–80

	1 Investments at market value £	2 Indexed %	3 De Zoete and Bevan Index %	Proportion of J.R.M.T. Investments			7 Income £	8 Indexed %	9 Retail Price Index %
				4 Rowntree %	5 Other Equities %	6 Fixed Interest %			
1954	1789351	100	100	99.94	0.06	Nil	42499	100	100
1959	3510896	196.21	178.63	98.40	0.01	1.59	96421	226.88	116.18
1964	4916004	274.74	186.39	99.39	0.01	0.60	184936	435.15	135.76
1969	8228521	459.86	236.15	98.01	Nil	1.99	427711	1006.40	166.47
1974	2630741	147.02	96.28	89.29	1.33	9.38	394700	928.73	277.73
1975	11736971	655.93	234.67	77.15	10.36	12.49	479317	1127.83	346.83
1976	13829717	772.89	226.13	74.18	13.98	11.84	623717	1467.60	399.12
1977	24481105	1368.16	310.22	67.87	14.02	18.11	1026281	2414.84	447.54
1978	23543014	1315.73	319.76	66.05	14.17	19.78	1125862	2649.15	485.11
1979	20820271	1163.57	292.14	59.75	17.96	22.29	1571910	3698.70	568.76
1980	22637917	1265.15	361.76	49.83	24.02	26.15	1755701	4131.16	655.92

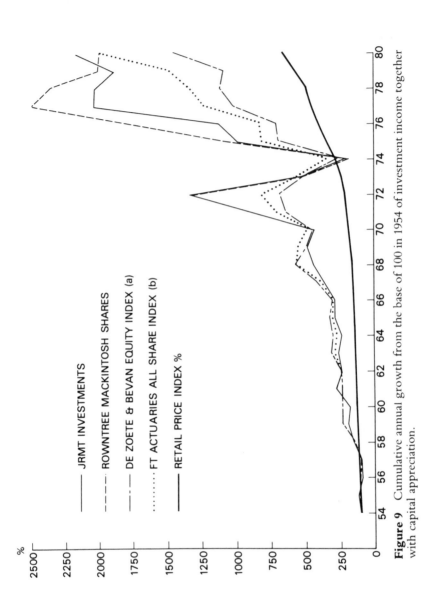

Figure 9 Cumulative annual growth from the base of 100 in 1954 of investment income together with capital appreciation.

%

2500
2250
2000
1750
1500
1250
1000
750
500
250
0

54 56 58 60 62 64 66 68 70 72 74 76 78 80

——— JRMT INVESTMENTS

– – – – ROWNTREE MACKINTOSH SHARES

–·–·– DE ZOETE & BEVAN EQUITY INDEX (a)

·········· FT ACTUARIES ALL SHARE INDEX (b)

━━━ RETAIL PRICE INDEX %

from 1975–1980 is that the Rowntree investment consistently outpaced the Financial Times All Share Index and this was the time when the transfer from Rowntree shares to a more varied portfolio was taking place. The advantage ceased in 1980 just as diversification ended. It will be explained in the next two pages how the Trustees have devised what may be called a 'trinitarian' structure of investment analysis and advice; if the time of the operation just described was to a large extent fortuitous, the pace was the result of skilful analysis at least to the extent of acting whilst the going is good! It was not easy to press ahead when the transactions involved the sale of large blocks of shares which were so outpacing the market.

The Making and Implementation of Investment Policy

The Joseph Rowntree Memorial Trust Act required the Trustees to appoint an investment committee on whose advice all investment decisions must be made. That provision was made because the Trust included in its membership Trustees with wide experience of finance and the management of investments. Four Trustees were appointed to the investment committee. They were served by the Trust's Finance Officer. His analysis of investment performance and proposals for purchases or sales were brought to the investment committee after consultation with the third partner in the enterprise, the Trust's broker. His concern with investment analysis was complemented by a particular interest and expertise in monitoring smaller companies – the sector of the market in which growth became more evident. Policy is settled by the investment committee; for example the portfolio includes a proportion of fixed interest securities with maturing dates spread over twenty-five years. This provides the flexibility necessary to meet claims on grants payable over a period of years, and, as on two occasions, to take up, and later dispose of rights issues to advantage.

Investment policy must take account of the fact that the high yield in recent years available from this part of the portfolio is obtained at the cost of nil growth to the endowment.

The Trustees' purpose was to balance equitably the needs of the present against those of posterity, and therefore to maintain the real value of current income and of the retained endowment. Table 20.2 shows the comparative figures at the beginning and end of the twenty-five years covered by this account.

Table 20.2   *Changes in the Trust's income and endowment over twenty-five years*

	Income	Retail Price Index	Endowment	F.T. All Share Index
1954	100	100	100	100
1980	4131	656	1265	499

Thus at an annual rate, income has increased by 15.39 per cent compared with 7.50 per cent by inflation, giving real annual growth at the rate of 7.89 per cent. The value of the endowment has almost doubled in real terms.

For nearly twenty of the twenty-five years covered by this record, the subject of investment never appeared on a Trust agenda. Virtually the whole endowment was in the shares of the Rowntree Company, transferred to the Trust by the Founder in 1904. For the last five years it became a principal commitment. The Trust was fortunate in having Trustees able both to control investment strategy and to establish from the analysis provided by their advisers an approved list from which actual purchases could be made in accordance with a timetable settled from day to day by their Finance Officer in consultation with the broker. The outcome of what by any standards has been a sizeable investment operation has been highly satisfactory; the future of the Trust depended on it. This was, and continues to be, the result of a complex interaction between experienced and expert Trustees, an administration which has developed skill in the measurement of performance, and the brokers, whose research resources provide the analysis from which discussion must start.

Conclusion

The twenty years from the mid-fifties to the mid-seventies was marked by rapid change in the conventions and values that informed personal, family and social life. They were marked, too, by an expansion in the activities of public authorities; the concept of a welfare society was more suited to the mood of the age than that of a welfare state. Every stage in human growth and development from conception until death, and every aspect of human experience – marriage, parenthood and bereavement – became matters of public concern, whilst public expenditure rose to meet the cost of the services it was thought should be provided.

Foundations concerned with social policy – and the Joseph Rowntree Memorial Trust was among the largest and most influential – responded strongly to this 'interventionist' philosophy and powerfully reinforced it. 'Foundations like Nuffield, Gulbenkian and the Rowntree Trusts', David Donnison has written of this period 'along with their counterparts overseas like Ford, were competing with each other to find innovative proposals for social research and social action to support. Although we prided ourselves on our independence', he writes of a research institution of which he was the head, 'we were in fact closely linked to the development of the public sector of the economy and the professions within it'. David Donnison might equally well have applied the comment to the Foundations to which, in part, he looked for support.

In the closing years of the period the economic climate in which the Trust operated had changed dramatically. The use of a rising income to show how to deploy increasing public resources to meet rising expectations, was a pattern of Foundation practice that had passed into history. An instinctive public awareness was growing – in no way dispelled by the rhetoric of politicians seeking power – that this was no temporary delay on the upward path, but a belated recognition of structural change inevitable from Britain's changed place in the world's economic and political scene.

The sudden turn of events faced Trustees and those who advised them with daunting questions. Instead of stimulating and responding to new expectations, on the assumption that public expenditure would then rise to meet the needs thus demonstrated, would the Trust have been wiser soberly to monitor the heady growth in social services – a course advocated and in measure implemented by some American foundations? Would the Trust have made a more abiding contribution to social policy if it had stuck to its last, and identified ways in which a new and different part could be taken in anticipating and meeting the changing need for homes? Housing conditions remain, after all these years, the greatest single cause of family and personal distress for which ever more costly palliatives are offered.

Did the Trust need a Private Act of Parliament at all? The Chief Charity Commissioner, when considering the case advanced by the Trustees for

the promotion of private legislation, put his finger accurately on the weak point in their argument. The Founder of the Trust, he reminded the Trustees, created three foundations. They were complementary. To each was given a field of activity, skilfully defined to take account of legal limitations, so that together they covered the whole field of his concern. He did not create, and clearly did not wish to create, three general purpose foundations developing separate and even conflicting policies, and collaborating only when their separate activities in a common field threatened to become embarrassing. The Chairman of the Joseph Rowntree Charitable Trust, which had powers adequate for all the new initiatives which the Village Trustees wished to launch, pressed a similar view. Even when it was clear that the Village Trustees were firmly set on their chosen course, he argued for a common approach to social research and experiment and was ready to accept a Village Trust appointee to guide the joint operations of the two Trusts.

It is difficult from the evidence to contest the view that the present day organisation of the three Trusts is very different from the Founder's intentions. Nor is it adequate as a justification of the policies which have led to this situation to quote the Founder's decision to leave future Trustees free to respond to the needs of changing times, which he made no claim to foresee. He was referring to the use of resources, not to the structure of the Trusts. Indeed the only reference he made to this latter topic was to hope that the restrictions imposed by law on the use of charitable funds would be relaxed so that the need for a separate noncharitable Trust would be reduced, allowing resources to be moved to the Charitable Trust with the widest powers for research and experiment, thus leaving the Village Trust to its own field of housing.

Part at least of the answer to these questions reveals the limitations within which a Trust operates. One of the most stimulating chapters of this record describes the change in the physical environment and the quality of life in a neglected part of York's inner area. Had the pioneer work which made those changes possible been carried through thirty years earlier, hundreds of attractive and low cost dwellings would have been saved and neighbourhoods to which families were devoted would have been renewed. They were, in fact, swept away by the bulldozer. Not much aesthetic or social satisfaction is aroused by the dwellings that have replaced them. For the Trust it must be said that it made great efforts to become involved in such work. Its case to the authorities for private legislation rested on the rejection by public authorities of its offered participation in a new approach to inner city deprivation. Perhaps it should have tried harder, and used its whole resources to demonstrate the revival of a deprived area as, in its early days, it demonstrated the creation of a new community at New Earswick. Such possibilities, which are but the fruits of hindsight, nonetheless merit reflection at a time when a Trust with much experience, substantial resources and, with due respect to others, uniquely dedicated membership and administration, faces the 'new occasions' about which its Founder wrote three-quarters of a century ago.

In practice the conclusion that housing was no longer the Trust's

primary commitment led to new ventures in social research and innovation which this book records. It has not excluded a later return to housing interests, likely to be of growing importance as the need for a wider choice in housing provision is recognised. In his monumental study (*English Philanthropy* 1660-1690, Harvard UP, 1964) Professor David Owen of John Winthrop House at Harvard University took special note of the radical changes made by the Trustees to equip the former Joseph Rowntree Village Trust for a different age.

'Among all of the assorted institutions and organisations that go to make up the British charitable world' he writes of the Joseph Rowntree Memorial Trust, 'none has shown a livelier awareness of "the new occasions" which "teach new duties", or a more imaginative understanding of the use of private philanthropy in semi-collectivist Britain.'

1960

Appendix 1   *Text of Clauses in the Deed of Foundation giving authority for the appointment of new or additional Trustees*

Clause 6   If any person appointed a Trustee of these presents shall die, or desire to be discharged from the trusts of these presents, and of such desire shall give notice in writing to the other Trustees or Trustee of these presents, or to the Secretary or Clerk of the Trustees, the office of Trustee previously held by such person shall be vacated, and a new Trustee shall be appointed as hereinafter provided in the place of such person.

Clause 7   The Founder during his life shall have the sole right of appointing a new Trustee of these presents in any such case as aforesaid, and shall be at liberty to appoint any person whom he may select to be such Trustee. The Founder shall also be at liberty at any time or times during his life by deed or writing to appoint any persons or person whom he may select to be Trustees or a Trustee of these presents, in addition to and to act in conjunction with the then existing Trustees or Trustee of these presents.

Clause 8   After the Founder's death the proper persons to appoint a new Trustee, or new Trustees of these presents, in any case mentioned in the sixth clause hereof shall be the surviving or continuing Trustees of these presents or a majority consisting of all but one of them, so long as the number of the original Trustees is not less than four; but for this purpose any retiring or refusing Trustee shall, if willing to act in the execution of this power, be considered a continuing Trustee. When the number of the original Trustees of these presents shall be reduced to three or less, two new trustees shall be appointed, one by the surviving or continuing Trustees or Trustee, and the other either by the London Yearly Meeting of the Society of Friends or by the Yorkshire Quarterly Meeting of the Society of Friends, as the surviving or continuing Trustees or Trustee shall determine. And thereafter the subsequent vacancies in the trusteeship of these presents shall be filled up alternately by the surviving or continuing Trustees or Trustee of these presents or a majority consisting of all but one of them, and by the said Yearly or Quarterly Meeting, as the surviving or continuing Trustees or a majority consisting of all but one of them may determine.

Appendix II   *Extracts from the report prepared by the Trust's Executive Officer following the first formal meeting on 6 November 1957, with the Charity Commission arranged on the instruction of the Trustees*

I summarised the changes through which the Village Trust was passing. They were:

a)   The income of the Trust had been increased in recent years beyond anything which the Founder could have foreseen.
b)   Housing had become the main responsibility of public authorities: any work by the Trust in the general field of housing was unlikely to be substantially different from that of local authorities and new towns corporations.

It followed from a) that if the Trust were to employ its income in the traditional way, it would have to purchase a substantial estate and engage in a building programme even greater than that which occupied the Trustees forty years ago. This seemed, for the reasons given in b) undesirable, and might well in any event be impracticable in view of all the restrictions on the purchase of large areas for housing development in competition with public authorities. . . .

The changing situation had already led the Trustees to undertake certain projects which were marginal to their main powers. The Assistant Commissioner and I went through together the clauses in the Trust Deed which illustrate the types of work in which the Trustees may engage; this showed that 'expenditure in acquiring reports and information' in clause 4(5) was the only activity of those listed in the Deed, which was called for increasing expenditure by the Trust. A situation was likely to arise, therefore, in which the greater part of the income of the Trust would be used in this way; moreover, the kind of reports and experiments which were engaging the interest of the Trust were only distantly related to the creation of the village communities. . . .

The Assistant Commissioner said that although the Trustees made no suggestion that their Trust had 'failed' he thought that the Commissioners were entitled to take a different view. The very large incursion into the housing field of other authorities might be said to have changed the situation so substantially that in this sense the Trust had 'failed'. He hoped, however, that it would not be necessary to seek a Private Act of Parliament to deal with the situation, especially at the present time. He referred to clause 29 of the Trust Deed, which appeared to give wide powers to the Trustees and the Charity Commission to amend the Deed, but said that this power was still linked with the main object of the Trust and was not, therefore, helpful in the present situation.

He thought that there was a way open to the Commissioners which might meet

the very real difficulty in which the Trustees were placed. He read section 16 of the Charitable Trust Act 1853, which authorises the Commissioners to prepare Schemes of Advice and Opinion. He said these were not often prepared, but they did enable the Commissioners virtually to widen the powers of a Trust and to free Trustees from any personal responsibility if questions should be raised. He suggested that such a Scheme should be prepared to cover a period of five years, and with a limit on the annual sum to be spent on these extended purposes. . . .

I told the Assistant Commissioner that I thought this proposal of a trial period of five years would commend itself to the Trustees. I told him of the series of consultations which the Trustees had arranged, and that these had suggested a variety of fields of action in which the Trustees were now feeling their way. It would be a pity just at this stage to be obliged to settle finally the area of work to be defined in a permanent alteration to the Deed. . . .

After discussion we agreed that if the Trustees decided to proceed in this way, their application for a Scheme of Advice and Opinion should be accompanied by an estimate, over a five year period, of income on the present basis, expenditure on maintenance and new housing work, and expenditure on ancillary projects traditional to the work of the Trust; this would then show the available balance which the Trustees would need to employ on the newer developments in their work. . . .

Appendix III *The First Draft of the objects clause presented by Counsel to the first conference with Trustees on 16 July 1958*

1. To undertake and carry on such charitable activities as are calculated to improve the living conditions or mode of life of the public or any section of the public in the United Kingdom or elsewhere and in particular (but without prejudice to the generality of the foregoing).

    a) to act as a Housing Trust and to provide and manage housing estates, residential accommodation or similar facilities for and for the households and dependants of persons of limited financial resources or persons who by reason of age or physical or mental infirmity or disablement are in need of care, attention or supervision and to provide or assist in the provision of educational facilities for the dependent children of all such persons.

    b) to provide and maintain or assist in the provision and maintenance of parks, open spaces, playing fields and similar amenities for the use of the public and particularly in neighbourhoods where the same are needed by reason of congested or otherwise unsatisfactory housing conditions or difficulties of access to open country.

    c) to use means as may be appropriate (including the provision of factories or offices) to provide or facilitate the provision of employment for persons living in any housing estate or neighbourhood (whether or not provided or administered by or in co-operation with or under the aegis of the Trust) where satisfactory housing accommodation is available.

2   For the purpose of discovering or attempting to discover how the resources of the Trust can most effectively be employed in attaining its objects and of providing other authorities and bodies having similar or cognate objects with information calculated to enable them to direct their activities into fruitful channels, to investigate, undertake research into and promote discussion of the causes, effects, prevention and amelioration of unsatisfactory living conditions, undesirable modes of life, social and industrial unrest and discontent, unsatisfactory family life and other social evils and to publish reports of such investigations, research and discussion.

3   To co-operate with, subscribe to and generally to assist financially or otherwise any body carrying on or intending to carry on any activity within the main objects of the Trust and to promote or assist in the promotion of any such body.

The Clause Defining the Trust's Housing Powers as Finally Approved by Parliament

4   Clauses 2 and 4 of the trust deed are hereby rescinded and, as from and after the passing of this Act, the trust deed shall have effect as if the following clause were substituted for the said clause 2:–
    '2. The objects of the said Trust are:–

(1)   To undertake and carry on such activities as are calculated to improve the living conditions, mode of life or physical, mental or moral well-being of the public or any section of the public in the United Kingdom or elsewhere in any parts of Her Majesty's dominions or the territories under Her protection and in particular (but without prejudice to the generality of the foregoing)–

   (a)   to provide, develop, construct and manage housing estates, houses or other residential accommodation or similar facilities for and for the families and dependants of persons who by reason of poverty, youth, age, infirmity or disablement are in need of such facilities or of care, attention, assistance or supervision and to provide or assist in the provision of educational facilities for, and for the dependants of, any such persons;

   (b)   to provide or maintain, or assist in providing or maintaining, for the use of the members of the public at large, and especially those members of the public who have need therefore by reason of their youth, age, infirmity or disablement, poverty or social or economic circumstances, in places where the same are needed by reason of congested or otherwise unsatisfactory housing conditions or difficulty of access to open country, or where the same are for other reasons calculated to improve the living conditions of the persons primarily intended to benefit therefrom, parks, open spaces, playing-fields and other facilities (including buildings), and to organise, or assist in organising, in connection therewith any activity for the purpose of recreation or other leisure-time occupation:

Provided that nothing in this paragraph shall authorise the undertaking or carrying on of any activity which is not in law charitable.

(2)   For the purpose of discovering, or attempting to discover, how the resources of the Trust can most effectively be employed in attaining all or any of its objects, or of providing other authorities and bodies in the United Kingdom or elsewhere having similar or cognate objects with information calculated to enable them to direct their activities into fruitful channels, to investigate, undertake research into and promote discussion of, and interchange of information with respect to, the causes, effects, prevention and amelioration of unsatisfactory living conditions, undesirable modes of life, ill-health (whether physical or mental), immorality, social or industrial unrest, disharmony or discontent, unsatisfactory family life or other social evils and to publish reports of, and disseminate information as to, the results of any such investigation, research, discussion or interchange of information.

(3)   To co-operate with, subscribe to and generally to assist, financially or otherwise, any person or body carrying on or intending to carry on any activity within the objects of the Trust and to promote or assist in the promotion of any such body.

(4)   Nothing in this clause shall authorise the Trustees to apply the funds of the Trust –

   (a)   in promoting, advocating or supporting or procuring any other person or body to promote, advocate or support any course of action of a political nature; or

   (b)   in supporting any object or in endeavouring to impose on, or procure to be observed by, any persons any regulation, restriction or condition which, if an object of the Trust, would make it a trade union.'

Appendix IV *Letter from the Board of Inland Revenue to the Trust's Parliamentary Agents concerning the Objects Clause in the Private Bill*

COPY

INLAND REVENUE,
Secretaries' Office (Taxes)
Somerset House, LONDON. W.C.2.

S.301 /18 /59

13th March, 1959

Gentlemen,

JOSEPH ROWNTREE MEMORIAL TRUST BILL

I am directed by the Board of Inland Revenue to say that their attention has been drawn to the above Bill, in particular to Clause 4.

The Board have given careful consideration to the proposed new objects of the Trust set out in that Clause and have come to the conclusion that, in the present state of the law, they cannot be regarded as charitable. In the first place the purpose expressed in the new paragraph 2 (1) (a) does not necessarily involve the relief of poverty and, following the decision in Re Sanders Will Trusts (1954) 1 Ch. 265, where the Court declined to infer any element of poverty, would not in the Board's view be charitable.

Paragraph 2 (1)(b) seems to admit of the provision of recreational facilities for a class of persons labouring under youth, age, infirmity, etc., who might be insufficient to constitute a sufficient section of the public. The requirement of 'public benefit' for recreational charities is specifically retained by the proviso to Section 1 of the Recreational Charities Act, 1958.

Paragraph 2 (1)(c) would permit the Trustees to engage in non-charitable commercial enterprises for the relief of unemployment among inhabitants of their properties, and its purpose could not therefore be regarded as charitable.

The Board have considered the effect of the words 'being charitable' in the new paragraph 2 (1) but they are advised that this expression does not suffice to cut down the detailed and specific description in paragraph 2 (1) (a), (b) and (c) of the main objects of the Trust, which purport to define in particular what the Trustees can do.

I have therefore to advise you that if the Bill is enacted in its present form it is the Board's view that the exemption from Income Tax at present enjoyed by the Trust would have to be withdrawn. This is presumably not the result intended by your clients. The Board suggest, therefore, that your clients be asked to consider re-drafting paragraphs 2 (1)(a), (b) and (c) so as to render the purpose they define

clearly charitable, and whether in place of the expression 'being charitable' there should be an over-riding limitation specifically limiting the objects of the Trust to purposes which are in law charitable.

I am, Gentlemen,
Your obedient Servant,
(sgd) A. TAGGART.

Messrs Sherwood & Co.

Appendix V Extracts from a note of a discussion with representatives of the Board of Inland Revenue, leading to a revision in the Trust's housing powers

The Board of Inland Revenue was represented by Mr W.A. Purdie, who is a Senior Principal Inspector in the office of the Chief Inspector of Taxes, and by Mr Watson, who is from the Charity (Claims) Department in Liverpool.

The Trust was represented by Mr H.W. Gamon and the Executive Officer.

Mr Purdie made it clear that the Bill and the powers which the Trustees were seeking were not a matter for his Department. He, however, felt some duty to draw the notice of the Trustees to what would be the results, so far as their claim for income tax rebate was concerned, if they did in fact obtain from Parliament powers which were not wholly charitable.

On the subject of the joint Opinion which the Trustees have received, Mr Purdie said that his Department looked upon Counsel with respect but not with veneration! Conflicting views about what was charitable were not uncommon, and his Department were bound by decisions of the Courts as they understood them, and could not regard the opinion of Counsel, however eminent, as in any way final.

On the main issue under discussion, i.e. whether or not the 'umbrella clause' served to limit the Trustees to what was charitable, Mr Purdie was quite clear that the Trustees would be jeopardising the future of the Trust if they were to rely on the present 'umbrella clause,' or the stronger version of it which Counsel had since proposed. Broadly, he thought the view would be that, where a clause gave certain powers which were mainly charitable, but also a possible 'fringe' which was not charitable, then the 'umbrella clause' was a right way of limiting the Trustees to the charitable part of the powers provided by such a clause. The 'umbrella clause' would not be effective however where a clause gave powers which were almost entirely non-charitable, and this he felt was the situation with some parts of the present objects clause.

We then came to clause 1(a) on the subject of housing which is the really difficult problem.

Mr Purdie made it quite clear that housing as such was no longer charitable. He objected to Counsel's addition to this clause in that the words used were taken from the Recreational Charities Act and were concerned only with activities covered by that Act. The provision of *housing* for people who needed it by reason of youth, age, infirmity or disablement was unlikely to be charitable. In his view, for example, the provision of special accommodation for millionaires with one leg would not be a charitable activity. His view was that the provision of housing under this clause should be limited to those who needed it by reason of poverty. In the light of recent court decisions, this was in his view the only way to secure beyond doubt the charitable status of the Trust.

Mr Gamon pressed strongly the view that the Trust already had these wider powers and that it would be a Gilbertian situation to secure a Private Bill but have more restricted powers than those enjoyed formerly. Mr Purdie said that as a

matter of policy they did not interfere with established trusts. They were, however, receiving many proposals these days for new charitable housing trusts with wide general powers and they were rejecting all of them. In reply to a direct question, he said that the Trust's present Deed would certainly not be acceptable as establishing a charitable trust if presented at the present time. Even if the form of words suggested by Mr McCombe had been used, i.e. adding powers to those already held, the Board would still have gone back to those powers and would have questioned them. . . .

This led to a frank discussion in which we tried to convey to Mr Purdie the very real dilemma of housing trusts. The Village Trustees, for example, had inherited a project which was a valid charitable activity at the outset, and for the administration of which they were still responsible. Plainly it was not possible to use these housing estates today for people who in any sense of the word could be described as in poverty. If the new powers were wide enough to embrace this activity, the Board would withdraw tax exemption not only on the housing activity (which was relatively unimportant for this purpose), but on the whole Trust income. If, on the other hand, the powers were limited to what was in law charitable, it must follow that the housing project would be *ultra vires*. This dilemma resulted from the changes in social conditions and was not of the Trustees' making. . . .

The purpose of the Trustees was to secure a valid charitable trust; New Earswick was not an object of expenditure of charitable funds (except for education etc. on which no question arose) but was a contribution to them, and we had no fear therefore of a review of the charitable status of this project so long as the Trust was safeguarded.

Mr Purdie wondered whether this did not present a possible solution. If the Trustees' estate had become a source of income, then the Inland Revenue were concerned with it only insofar as the income derived from the estate must be spent for charitable purposes. In other words, it became a form of investment. I told Mr Purdie that this presented an almost ideal solution from the Trustees' point of view and it had certainly not escaped their attention. . . . I said, however, that we were quite convinced that the Treasury Solicitor would not regard this form of investment as appropriate for charitable funds, and Mr Purdie agreed that this was likely to be the case. . . .

Returning to the draft clause, we asked Mr Purdie to have this quite acute dilemma in mind in considering the wording. We certainly wanted to safeguard the Trust's charitable status; but if, within this requirement, words as wide as possible could be used to define the Trust's housing powers, we might avoid drawing immediate attention to a situation which we felt must later be dealt with generally, bearing particularly in mind that so far as the Joseph Rowntree Village Trust is concerned, expenditure of its funds was not now at issue. Mr Purdie asked for a few hours to turn this over in his mind and he would then communicate with Mr Gamon on what would be appropriate wording for clause 1(a). . . .

29th April 1959.

Appendix VI *Publications recording the outcome of research and other grants made by the Trust since 1954*

The list contains only books published commercially or by a university or public authority. It does not include the many articles in the press or in journals, important though these often are in securing public attention for the policy implications of a particular project.

Housing Policy Since the War, David Donnison, Occasional Papers on Social Administration, 1960.

Housing Since the Rent Act, David Donnison, Christine Cockburn and T. Corlett, Occasional Papers on Social Administration, 1961.

Two to Five in High Rise Flats, Joan Maizels, Housing Centre Trust, 1961.

West Indian Migrants, R.B. Davison, Oxford University Press, 1962.

Housing in Transition, J.B. Cullingworth, Heinemann, 1963.

English Housing Trends, J.B. Cullingworth, Occasional Papers on Social Administration, 1965.

Private Landlords in England, John Greve, Occasional Paper on Social Administration, 1965.

Psycho-Social Aspects of Drug Taking, Howard League for Penal Reform, Pergamon Press, 1965.

God's People, M.J.C. Calley, Oxford University Press, 1965.

Regional Problems and Policies in the North-East of England, Papers on Regional Development, edited by Professor Thomas Wilson, Basil Blackwell, 1965.

The Teaching of Social Studies in British Universities, Kathleen Jones, G. Bell and Sons Ltd, 1965.

Housing, Taxation and Subsidies, Adela Adam Nevitt, Nelson, 1966.

The Rents of Council Houses, R.A. Parker, Occasional Papers on Social Administration, 1967.

Government of Housing, David Donnison, Penguin, 1967.

Racial Discrimination, Research Services Ltd, P.E.P., 1967.

Racial Discrimination in England, Daniel, Penguin, 1968.

The Development of a Housing Association, Unity Stack, Centre for Urban and Regional Studies, University Birmingham, Occasional Paper No. 1, 1968.

Adolescent Needs and the Transition from School to Work, Joan Maizels, Athlone Press, 1970.

Social Work in Scotland, The Scottish Council of Social Service or H.M.S.O., 1970.

Homes in High Rise Flats, Pearl Jephcott, Oliver & Boyd, 1971.

Moving Home, Clare Ungerson, Occasional Paper on Social Administration, 1971.

Housing Associations – Three Surveys, Kay M. Miller and Camilla J. Filkin, Edited by Dilys Page, Centre for Urban and Regional Studies, University of Birmingham, 1971.

Voluntary Housing in Scandinavia, John Greve, Centre for Urban and Regional Studies, University of Birmingham, Occasional Paper No. 21, 1971.

Residence and Student Life, Joan Brothers and Stephen Hatch, University of London Centre for the Study of Educational Policies, Tavistock Publications, 1971.

The Gift Relationship, Richard Titmuss, Allen & Unwin, 1971.

The Challenge of Outward Bound, Basil Fletcher, Heinemann, 1971.

A Question of Answers, W.P. Robinson and Susan Rockshaw, Routledge & Kegan Paul. 1972.

Local Radio and the Community, Centre for Mass Communications Research, Leicester University Press, 1973.

Criminal Homicide in Contemporary Britain – Some Selected Topics, Louis Blom-Cooper, Q.C., 1973.

Unattached Youth, Brian Lewis, Arthur Chisnall, and Auriol Hall, Blond & Briggs, 1974.

Housing and the Migration of Labour in England and Wales, James H. Johnson, John Salt and Peter A. Wood, Saxon House, 1974.

Mobility and Accessibility in the Outer Metropolitan Area, Hillman, Henderson and Whalley, P.E.P. 1974.

The Popular Press and Social Change, 1935–63, A.C.H. Smith and Others, University of Birmingham, 1974.

Adventure Playgrounds, An account by Jack Lambert as told to Jenny Pearson. Jonathan Cape and Penguin, 1974.

Bishophill, York: Appraisal and Renewal, George G. Pace, CVO, MA, FS, FRIBA. William Sessions Ltd, 1974.

Paper Voices, A.C.H. Smith, Chatto & Windus, 1975.

Gypsies and Government Policy in England, Barbara Adams, Judith Okely, David Morgan and David Smith, Heinemann Educational Books, 1975.

Tenants Participation in Housing Management – A Study of Four Schemes, Julia Craddock, Association of London Housing Estates, 1975.

The Family and the State – Considerations for Social Policy, R.M. Moroney, Longman, 1975.

Transport Realities and Planning Policy, Hillman, Henderson and Whalley; P.E.P., 1976.

Conservation and Traffic: A Case Study of York, Lichfield and Proudlove, Sessions Book Trust, 1976.

Voluntary Organisations Facing Change, John Lansley, Calouste Gulbenkian Foundation in association with the Joseph Rowntree Memorial Trust, 1976.

Widening Horizons of Child Health, Alfred White-Franklin, MTP Press Limited, 1976.

Mining and After – Social Change in County Durham, Martin Bulmer, Croom Helm, 1976.

Old People and the Social Services – A Study in Sunderland, Anthony M. Rees, University of Southampton, 1976.

Reforming the Welfare – The Politics of Change in the Personal Social Services, Phoebe Hall, Heinemann, 1976.

Degrees of Excellence – The Academic Achievement Game, Entwistle and Wilson, Hodder & Stoughton, 1977.

To Investigate and to Publish, J.A. Heady, Joseph Rowntree Memorial Trust, 1977.

The Future of Voluntary Organisations: Report of the Wolfenden Committee, Croom Helm, 1978.

Poverty in the UK – A Survey of Household Resources and Standards of Living, Peter Townsend, Penguin, 1979.

The Development of Housing in Scotland, Douglas Niven, Croom Helm, 1979.

Outside the State: Voluntary Organisations in Three English Towns, Stephen Hatch, Croom Helm, 1980.

The Family Fund: An Initiative in Social Policy, Jonathan Bradshaw, Routledge & Kegan Paul, 1980.

Impact of the Job Creation and Related Programmes, Hanby and Jackson, University of Stirling, 1980.

Evaluative Research in Social Care E. Matilda Goldberg and Naomi Connolly, Heinemann, 1981.

Sheltered Housing for the Elderly, Greve, Butler and Oldman, University of Leeds. 1981 (two volumes) A book based on these volumes is being published by Allen & Unwin in 1983.

Action for Care: A Review of Good Neighbour Schemes in England, Philip Abrams, Sheila Abrams, Robin Humphrey and Ray Snaith, Volunteer Centre, 1981.

Day Services for Adults – Somewhere To Go, Jan Carter. Allen & Unwin, 1981.

Undergraduate Attitudes to Employment, Geoffrey Brown, University of Lancaster, 1981.

Family Homes for the Handicapped, D.N. Martin, North Yorkshire County Council Social Services Department, 1981.

Workers' Co-Operative: Jobs and Dreams, Jenny Thornely, Heinemann, 1981.

Evaluating Social Care for the Elderly, E. Matilda Goldberg and Naomi Connolly, Heinemann, 1982.

Home Help in Coventry, Shena Latto, City of Coventry Social Services Dept, 1982.

Index